The Doctor Will See You Now

the junior doctor's back in hospital

Max Pemberton

HODDER

First published in Great Britain in 2011 by Hodder & Stoughton
An Hachette UK company

This paperback edition published in 2012

2

A CIP catalogue record for this title is available from the British Library

TPaperback ISBN 978 0 340 91995 8
eBook ISBN 978 1 848 94690 3

Typeset in MT Sabon by Hewer Text UK Ltd

Printed and bound by Clays Ltd, St Ives plc

Hodder & ~~~~~~~~~~~ papers that are natural, renewable
and recycl~~~~~~~~~~~ from wood grown in sustainable
forests. T~~~~~~~~~~~ esses are expected to
conform t~ the environmental regulations of the country of origin

To my grandparents, Chicken Wings and Pop, who have always been so supportive (and never complained that I call them ridiculous names).

Contents

I
Welcome Back

'CARDIAC ARREST! CARDIAC ARREST!' screeched the voice.

I let out a yawn, sat back in the armchair and stretched my legs out in front of me. I sipped the hot tea, gingerly. I wonder if there's a biscuit going? It began to dawn on me though that everyone in the doctors' mess was looking at me. I smiled back at them, nervously.

'Are you going to answer that?' asked Ruby, who was sitting next to me and looking at me with a disconcerting air of expectancy. She nodded towards my hand. I followed her gaze down and my eyes rested on the little black box that was nestled in my palm. We both stared at the pager.

'CARDIAC ARREST! CARDIAC ARREST!' it screeched once more, followed, this time, by a series of high-pitched bleeps. I looked up, startled.

'Oh, that's meant for me?' I said, my eyes widening in shock.

'Well, you're the one who is holding it,' said Ruby sardonically, 'and you are on call so, yes, it's meant for you.' This was all grossly unfair. It was my first day in the job and I'd only been at work for a few minutes and already people felt at liberty to have an emergency? I'd only just been handed the cardiac arrest pager by the night doctor and hadn't in my wildest dreams thought it would actually go off. Surely it's just civilised for people to hold off an emergency until I've had a cup of tea and a bowl of Coco Pops?

'Oh,' added Ruby, 'and it's convention here in hospitals when someone's heart has stopped that a doctor runs to the scene. Annoying, I know.' Did I detect a smidgen of sarcasm in her voice there? It then occurred to me that someone, somewhere, was likely to be dying and I quickly came to my senses. This was an emergency. I hastily stood up, put my cup of tea down and ran out of the doctor's mess on to the path outside, turning left towards the main hospital wards. Ruby had followed me outside.

'Where are you going you moron?' she shouted after me and beckoned me in the other direction. The pager went off again. She ran up to me and grabbed me by the shirt. 'You've got to take the shortcut to the wards, round the back of A&E,' she said as she pulled me in the opposite direction to the one I'd set off in. I had no idea where I was going or if I'd even know what to do when I got there. This was like being a junior doctor on my first day all over again.

For the past year I had been working in an outreach project for homeless people and people addicted to drugs and had grown accustomed to life outside of hospitals. Within twenty-four hours I had gone from hanging about on street corners, wearing jeans and a T-shirt and bribing patients with burgers so I could check their blood pressure, to being a proper, tie-wearing, stethoscope-waving medic. It had also been a year away from the menace of pagers. This respite had allowed me to forget the feeling of rising panic and anxiety each time one went off and I was required to run towards some unfolding tragedy with little knowledge of what I would find when I got there. It was true that I had learnt a lot over the past year, and not just where in the city was best to score some decent-priced crack (although if things were to get really bad, this knowledge may well come in handy). I'd come across some fascinating characters and they'd taught me a lot about life on the streets. I'd learnt about the nature of poverty and its inexorable link with disease and ill health. And of course, I'd learnt a lot of medicine, too. But what I'd lost, what had faded away without my even knowing it, was the practicalities of being a hospital doctor: where to pick up the pager, where handover takes place, where the blood forms were and even, it would seem, the shortcut to the wards. This, as much as clinical acumen, makes you a proficient doctor and in this moment I realised how much I'd lost. At least I had Ruby with me. She, and my other flatmate Flora, had spent the last year working in hospital, so they were by now old hands at running around pretending to know what's going on.

'Which ward are we going to?' shouted Ruby as we

belted through the A&E department and towards the wards.

'Erm,' I said, hesitating as I fumbled with the pager to see where it was telling me to go. The little display window was blank.

'Press the button a few times and the ward will come up,' panted Ruby. But before I had time she'd taken the pager from me and done it herself. I felt a slight prick of embarrassment. She wasn't on call and wasn't supposed to be with me and I here was I, not even able to work the blasted pager. 'Ward 4,' she said, and we ran up the stairs, two at a time, not bothering to wait for the lift. We arrived on the ward and looked around for signs of an emergency. Nothing. We couldn't see anyone and had begun to suspect it was a false alarm when we heard a cry. A nurse, covered in blood, hurtled out of a side room. Seeing us, she ran in our direction.

'I think he's dead,' she said desperately, and pointed back to the side room where she had just come from. Ruby and I rushed in. The first thing I noticed as I entered the room was the smell of blood. The scene that met me was like nothing I had ever seen. It was truly horrific. There were large pools of viscous, bright red blood all over the floor. An anaesthetist dressed in surgical scrubs, red with blood, was towering over a man on a bed. The anaesthetist glanced up at us and wiped some blood from his face.

'You from the crash team?' he asked. I stepped forward to introduce myself but Ruby had already grabbed an apron and pushed past. She rolled up her sleeves and took a needle from the side table, utterly unfazed by the scene into which she had just walked. 'Ruptured oesophageal varices,' said the anaesthetist, distractedly, as he worked on the prostrate man. These are swollen, dilated veins in the gullet that are liable to rupture, causing a massive haemorrhage. They are caused by liver disease, usually cirrhosis, which means that blood finds it increasingly difficult to pass through the liver and so pressure builds up, causing the veins to swell. To compound the problem, the liver is involved in regulating the clotting of the blood so when it's diseased, the normal clotting mechanisms fail and the only hope to stop bleeding is to put pressure on the bleeding vessels deep down in the gullet.

The anaesthetist was trying to insert something into the man's throat and as he did, the man jerked back and his head turned towards me. Ruby instinctively moved to the side. He opened his mouth and torrents of blood shot out and splattered against the wall. His head lolled to the side as more blood spewed out and cascaded on to the floor, spraying me as it did. I stood, paralysed by the horrendous scene for a brief moment.

'Max!' said Ruby sharply, and I jolted back. I rolled up my sleeves and took a step towards the bed, knowing I was stepping in a pool of blood as I did so. 'He'll need a wide-bore cannula in both arms. You get this one, I'll get the other,' Ruby said as she took the lead and handed me a needle in a packet. It was the width of a pipe cleaner and only reserved for use when someone is losing large quantities of blood, which need to be replaced quickly. I'd actually never inserted one this wide before, but the slight stickiness of blood under foot told me that now was not the time to mention this. Ruby began shouting orders to the nurses, who hurriedly returned with bags of blood and equipment. I looked down at my hands and to my shame realised they were shaking. He had lost so much blood his arm was cold and pale as I took hold of it to try to locate a vein. I tightened the tourniquet around his arm, but could still see no veins. I decided to stick the needle in where I thought a vein should be, but before I could even open the packet, he stopped breathing. We tried to resuscitate him but it was futile. The three of us stood around the bed, panting, covered from head to toe in blood, the dead man lying in front of us. My hands were still shaking.

'Welcome back,' Ruby said.

Ruby and I stood round while the anaesthetist filled out the necessary forms. I could feel dried blood in the webbing of my fingers, and decided to wash my hands yet again. As I did, I thought about how I had just witnessed the traumatic, horrific ending of someone's life and yet I didn't even know his name.

'What does it matter?' replied the anaesthetist when I asked him after washing my hands. I didn't know how to answer. Maybe it didn't matter, but it seemed so strange having just witnessed the most monumental moment in someone's life, to have held his arm as his life ebbed away yet not even know who he was. The anaesthetist got up and left and Ruby and I stood quietly. Two cleaners arrived with buckets and mops to clean up the room while a nurse telephoned his family. Ruby flicked through the notes.

'He was alcoholic,' she said bluntly, 'that explains it. You don't often see someone empty their entire blood volume out of their mouth like that. What a mess.' What a mess indeed, I thought, remembering the look on the man's face as he had turned and vomited blood all over the floor. We walked off down the corridor in silence for a few moments. 'Simon,' said Ruby, turning to me.

'What?' I asked.

'Simon. That was the man's name. I just saw it in his notes. You wanted to know.'

I smiled. 'Thanks,' I replied, and we walked off towards the doctor's mess to change.

I hadn't thought to bring a clean change of clothes so I had to change into surgical scrubs, which at least made me feel a bit more medical, and then made my way towards my new ward. The ward I was attached to was a medical ward with geriatrics – or 'care of older people' as we're now supposed to call it. I'd chosen this job because the consultant, Dr Webber, was a specialist in dementia but also covered general medicine, meaning I'd get experience in both and would even get to cover the dementia outpatient clinics. I was keen to take a job where I would be able to get more experience in dealing with physical health problems before further specialising in mental health. My experience working for the Phoenix Project had taught me that caring for someone's mental health often involved being proficient in caring for their physical health, too. In some ways, one of the downfalls of modern medicine is the way it is compartmentalised. Of course, it makes sense that people specialise and become experts in one area. But the downside, especially with regard to mental health, is that it cleaves off the mind from the rest of the body. Things become either 'medical' or 'psychiatric', when in reality there is a complex interaction between the two and things aren't as simple as that. Once someone is in the mental health system it's easy for their physical health needs to be neglected. This is particularly relevant to older people. For me, this job was an opportunity to hone my clinical skills in general medicine as well as learn about the mental health problems of older people.

'Hello darling,' someone shouted out as I walked on the ward. I looked over and a lady was getting up from a chair in the lounge and making her way towards me in the corridor. She stopped before she got to me, however, and turned to a member of staff who was handing out cups of tea. 'Oh, isn't it a nice surprise, my son has come to see me.'

I looked round but there was no one behind me. The woman handing out cups of tea looked up and smiled and gestured to ask if I wanted a cup. I shook my head.

'Come and give your old mum a kiss then,' said the woman as she approached. Now, it had been a while since I last saw my mum, but even so, I was fairly sure that it hadn't been so long that she was now in her eighties. 'You naughty boy for not coming to visit your old mum sooner,' she scolded, and began tugging at my surgical scrubs. I went to move away but before I knew it she lurched forward to kiss me. As I pulled my head away she missed my cheek – meaning I got a full, wet smacker on the lips. There were definite top notes of porridge in that kiss. I stood stunned for a brief moment. Had I just been sexually assaulted by an OAP, I wondered to myself. Then she began crying. 'I do everything for you and this is how you repay me,' she started sobbing. I looked into the lounge where the other patients were sitting. Oh great, this looks good. Less than an hour into the job and one person has died and I've reduced another one to tears. Excellent start.

'No no, don't cry,' I said as I tentatively put my arm round her shoulder. She began to try to pull me towards her but I managed to resist. For several minutes I stood on the ward in this odd embrace, craning my neck away from her puckered lips, until a nurse finally rescued me.

'Valerie, you leave the nice young man alone and come back and finish your cup of tea,' she said as she ushered her away. 'I've told you before about kissing strange men,' she said. I slightly resented being called strange this early on in my job. I mean they hadn't even heard about my party trick with a milk bottle yet. I watched as the nurse led Valerie back to her chair and she resumed watching television, transfixed by Phillip

Schofield. Ah, I thought to myself, conclusive evidence that she must be mad.

'I'm Marsha,' said the nurse, walking back towards me with her hand outstretched. 'You must be the new doctor?'

I nodded.

'Sorry about that, Valerie has dementia and she's a bit disinhibited at times. It's been made worse by a urinary tract infection, that's why she was admitted. She's no idea of what the year is or how old she is, and any young man she see she assumes must be her son.' She gestured for me to follow. 'I'll show you round the ward if you want.'

'Does her son visit?' I asked.

'Oh no, he's been dead for years. She doesn't remember that of course, so in a way, it's a blessing. Through here is the sluice.'

The sluice did not need a formal introduction as I could smell it long before I could see it.

'It does get a bit whiffy at times on the ward,' said Marsha seeing my reaction, 'but you get used to it.'

'That's something to look forward to,' I muttered under my breath.

Marsha led me through to the bays where the patient's beds were. There were four beds to a bay, and along the corridor on the other side were single rooms.

'MRSA,' she said with exaggerated mouthing motion as though there was some social prohibition on saying the word out loud.

She led me through to the little office I was to call

home for the next twelve months. It was very narrow and uncomfortably full of furniture. I counted three desks and five swivel chairs. I went to sit down on one.

'No, not that one, it's broken,' warned Marsha, as my buttocks hovered above it. I moved to another one. 'No, that one's broken too. In fact, I think that only that one is OK,' she said, pointing to the one with a large brown stain on the seat that I'd deliberately been avoiding. 'It's tea,' said Marsha encouragingly, gesturing towards the stain. I love the NHS.

I spent the rest of the morning meeting my patients, taking blood and dealing with a list of jobs that had been left for me by the former incumbent of my post. Twice Mrs Crook – the incompetent administrator who I remembered from my first year in this hospital – paged me by accident on the cardiac arrest bleep.

'Oh, I'm always doing that!' she said, giggling, after I had run full throttle to her office and stood there panting and sweating. 'Silly me, I wanted to page the catering manager.' I was quite tempted to ensure there was a life-threatening emergency taking place in her office if she decided to make it a hat trick.

I also had the joys of the usual induction lectures on fires and infection control and so on with some of the other new juniors. Ruby and Flora didn't have to attend, as they'd been in continuous employment with the hospital since we all began our junior doctor year, so I was forced to endure them on my own without anyone to roll my eyes at.

By lunchtime, I'd decided I'd had enough of hospitals. I never thought I'd say this, but give me a crackhead with a knife and tuberculosis over a lecture on health and safety in the workplace any day. I went back to the ward to collect my jacket and dump the pieces of paper I'd had thrust at me at the induction into the drawer of one of the desks, where there were several other identical piles of paper languishing from doctors over the years who had done exactly the same.

'Dr Webber will be around later, he'll want to meet you and say hello, I'm sure,' said Marsha, popping her head round the door. She was short and had a large, pudding bowl face with a mop of dark hair that looked like it had been dropped from a great height onto the top of her head. She had the sort of smile that made you want to tell her your troubles and the sort of body that made you want to avoid her sitting on you. I finished up my work and left the ward, but not before Valerie attempted to accost me, still under the misapprehension that I was her son.

'Take me with you,' she said as I hurried towards the main door of the ward. 'They're keeping me prisoner.'

I hesitated for a moment as I reached the main door.

'You're my son, you've got to help me,' she called after me but I couldn't bring myself to turn around, not knowing what I'd say to her. Surely it was wrong to collude with her and pretend to be her son, even if it did give her a moment's pleasure? But then, telling her I wasn't would only cause confusion and upset in an already addled mind. I turned round, deciding that this was likely to be just one of many tricky situations I'd be faced with over the next year, and now was as good a time as any to learn to deal with them. Valerie, however, had lost all interest in me and instead was preoccupied with helping Marsha feed the goldfish in the aquarium in the corridor.

'That one has got a pretty tail,' I heard her say as I slipped out of the door.

I made my way to the canteen. It was exactly as I'd remembered it from when I'd been here a year ago. The decor, the layout and the staff were all exactly the same. Judging from the dried, frazzled, inedible food they were serving, it seemed perfectly possible that the food was also the same. The man behind the counter serving the food was sweaty and had a large angry boil on his forehead that seemed to be menacingly close to bursting at any moment and gave a level of excitement and tension that you wouldn't expect when watching someone spoon out lasagne onto a plate. I seemed to remember the same boil from last time. It was hardly a great advertisement for the food, or indeed the hospital. Couldn't a community-spirited dermatologist have taken him aside behind the refrigerators and given it a quick lance with a plastic fork?

As I stood, deciding if I was more likely to get botulism from the couscous or the carrot soup, someone suddenly flung their arms round me.

'Look who it is, Mark!' shouted Lewis as he tried to rugby tackle me to the floor. This was more successful than he had thought, firstly, because he actually did play rugby and secondly, because I didn't. I lost my balance and clattered into a pile of trays. The man with the boil glared and his boil looked even redder than usual. 'Oh thank God you're back here, someone to save us from this place,' said Lewis, still jumping around. 'We've all missed you so much.' It was nice to get such a warm welcome, even if it did come with a minor concussion. 'You remember Max, don't you Mark?' said Lewis, turning to Dr Palache.

I still couldn't get used to calling him by his first name. Dr Palache was the radiologist who had, in our first year, helped us all so much. Although at first he'd seemed scary and distant, over the year he had warmed to us juniors and provided impromptu counselling behind the back of A&E over a cigarette or three. Of course, he'd warmed to one of our group even more than the others and he and Lewis were still living together in apparent domestic bliss. I hadn't seen Lewis for a few months, so we caught up over lunch and Dr Palache joined us. They sat across the table from me and I began to feel as though this were actually an interview for a job I wasn't sure I'd applied for – or that I particularly wanted.

'So do you have firm career plans?' began Lewis, but before I could even answer he continued, 'Where do you think you'll be in five years' time? I hope you're planning on taking your membership exams soon and are thinking about getting some publications out this year.'

Oh my God, he's officially nagging me. He's actually become my mother, I thought to myself. 'I'm just getting some more experience of hospital medicine and then I'm going back off into psychiatry. It's all planned. Sort of,' I said.

Lewis frowned, unconvinced. 'You've got to be focused, Max, hospital life is cut-throat, don't you forget that.'

'I'm going to become an old age psychiatrist, Lewis, not a pirate on the high seas.'

Lewis wasn't listening. 'I've still got one more year here and then I'm off into nice leafy suburbia to be a GP with nice old ladies and all the Quality Street I can eat,' he said, gloating.

Dr Palache shook his head, 'We've talked about this before – you'll get bored too quickly. You don't want to be looking at bunions and sore throats all day long, you're too smart for that. You want to become a consultant, do some academic work.'

'Don't tell me what I want, Mark. I'm very focused on becoming a GP. I want to become president of the Royal College of General Practitioners, you know that.'

They then had a minor domestic argument that also managed to bring in Lewis forgetting to pick the car up from the garage and Dr Palache never putting the CDs back in their cases. You know what I said earlier about domestic bliss? Scrub that.

At least it gave me time to eat while their banter continued in the background. Soon though, the conversation turned to the hospital gossip. Lewis had always been a master at extracting information from people, and now that he had unrestricted access to the upper echelons of the hospital hierarchy in the form of Dr Palache, he knew everything.

'You know about Trudy, Mr Butterworth's secretary?'

I nodded, remembering that Lewis had told me some time ago that they were now an item. Trudy had been an absolute lifeline to me in that first year, thanks to her endless supply of cakes and tea. She had expertly managed Mr Butterworth for years as his secretary and it was good to think she was now doing this on a personal level too. He certainly did need someone to manage him. Although he was a consultant surgeon and therefore thought himself to be God – and he had certainly managed to strike the fear of God into me when I worked for him – according to Lewis she ruled him with an iron fist. No doubt clutching a slice of Battenberg.

'Well, have you heard that she's now said if he doesn't propose before Christmas, she's ending it with him? Between you and me, he's asked Mark to help pick out an engagement ring but she doesn't know that yet,' he said in a conspiratorial whisper. 'And there's a new secretary, started this week, who's covering your ward. I don't know what her name is but apparently the three Marys don't like her.'

I laughed to myself when I remembered the three Marys. These had been the secretaries who did all my typing in the first year, all called Mary and who teased me mercilessly.

Just then a dark shadow came over the table. Small children wept and the lush undergrowth outside withered. Ok, maybe I made some of that up, but somebody was looming over the table and as I looked up, I immediately recognised it as Housewives' Favourite. My skin crawled. He totally ignored me. This was the man with whom Ruby had had an affair and who, it later transpired, was married and expecting a child.

'I've got a carcinoma in situ booked in for three. Wondered if you'd have a quick look at the scans,' he said with a flick of his head. Dr Palache nodded and made to stand up.

'You remember Max, don't you?' said Lewis, turning to Housewives' Favourite.

'No,' he said without even looking at me, which I took to mean, yes, he did remember me.

I made my way back to the ward and was met by a flustered looking Marsha.

'He's here,' she said frantically.

'Who?' I asked, bemused.

'Him,' she said, keeping her head stock-still and gesturing somewhere behind her with her eyes. I looked behind her and noticed a small, stocky, bald man. He smiled at me. My eyes then rested on someone else sitting down in the nursing office, scowling at him with tears in her eyes. 'He's not in a good mood,' said Marsha in a stage whisper, 'just made one of the social workers cry,' she added.

'I'm Dr Webber and you must be Max?' said the

man, moving forward towards me. Something happened to his face. I think it was a smile, but it wasn't very convincing. It may have been wind. 'Here's your timetable and here's my mobile number,' he said, thrusting a piece of paper into the hand I had outstretched to shake his. 'Call me if there are any problems,' he continued, and with that, he left.

'Was that it? Was that Dr Webber? I thought you said he'd want to meet me and say hello?' I said, turning back to Marsha after he'd left the ward.

'Well, he did meet you and he did say hello,' she replied. Technically this was true, but it certainly wasn't the welcome I had been expecting. 'Really, you don't want much more from him, not when he's in one of his moods,' said Marsha with a nod, 'he'd just make you cry.'

'You mean I'm going to have to work for someone like that for the next year?' I said, my heart sinking.

Marsha nodded and handed me a box of tissues. 'You'll need a good few boxes of these if you're going to work on this ward,' she said with a chuckle and walked off.

'Put the kettle on,' I heard Ruby shout as I walked through the door of our flat. I went into the kitchen to find her sitting at the circular kitchen table within arm's reach of the kettle.

'Are you joking?' I said, then remembered that she had helped me earlier when I'd been holding the crash bleep and would help when I needed it again, which I inevitably would. I had already learnt this much about medicine for certain: your success was not based on how much you knew or even what ground-breaking research you had undertaken or novel treatments you had discovered but on who you kept on your side. Biscuits, tea, coffee, cake, sandwiches, chocolates combined with a few kind words: this was the junior doctor's currency in the nuanced system of bartering that went on in hospitals. A thoughtful cup of coffee for the harassed receptionist meant your patients were squeezed on to the outpatient lists; allow a nurse to push in front of you in the queue for lunch and they'd do a cannula for you that afternoon; notice a secretary's new hairdo and she'd put someone else on call over the bank holiday. Although Ruby was a dear friend, she knew this system too and friendship, when it came to the economics of the hospital bartering system, was not a factor. I filled the kettle dutifully.

'How was your first day?' I asked. Ruby was continuing to work in trauma and orthopaedics – bone surgery – but was now working for Mr Griffiths, a very famous and eminent surgeon. She had been keen to make a good impression on her first day so had spent most of the previous night swatting up on surgical technique although, it transpired, this had been pointless as he had been in a meeting all day and she had been forced to do a ward round and fracture clinic on her own.

'I saw twenty-eight patients in clinic today,' she said with a sigh as she sipped her tea, 'it was like being in a war zone, except with no prospect of me being invalided home.'

Just then, Flora, our other flatmate, flew through the front door. 'You won't believe it,' she said, stopping to catch her breath.

'Yes, I know, I saw the rota,' replied Ruby, shaking her head, 'what a nightmare, you've got to be so careful.'

'What?' I asked. 'What's going on?'

'Housewives' Favourite,' answered Ruby, shaking her head once more in disgust and lighting a cigarette, 'Flora's working for him.'

'Do not sleep with him,' Ruby and I chorused together.

'Oh please, you two, give me some credit. I'm not stupid. That man makes me feel sick,' said Flora, as she sat down heavily in the chair. 'And it gets worse,' she continued, as I poured her a cup of tea. 'I have to go back there in a bit – he expects me to clerk in all his stupid private patients that come in at 7 o'clock.' She paused for a moment to take stock and light a cigarette. 'Oh God, I hate that man,' she said with a loud whine and turned to Ruby, 'you're so lucky you're working with Mr Griffiths. It's not fair, I want a good consultant like yours.' She sipped her tea, sulking.

Of course, it would be several months before any of us realised – to our absolute horror – how wrong Flora was.

2
History Lesson

'You're the new secretary?' I asked incredulously, looking round the room. This can't be right. 'But you're . . .'
I hesitated for a moment. The three Marys sat on the
other side of the room, each with their arms folded,
their heads slightly to one side, smirking as they
watched the scene unfold. 'You're . . .' I still wasn't
sure what to say. I screwed up my face. 'How can I put
this . . . you're a boy.' He raised an eyebrow though
still didn't look up.

'Yeah,' he said, chewing gum loudly, 'you can get
male secretaries you know.'

'Yes, I know that, but I mean, you're actually a boy.
As in, a child.' I knew things were bad in the economy,
but had we really resorted to child labour in the NHS?
What next, trained toddlers performing laparotomies?

'I'm eighteen,' he mumbled with disinterest.
Although his lack of eye contact was annoying, it was
eclipsed by the fact that he was conducting the whole
conversation with the earphones from his iPod in.

'Can you hear me?' I said.

Silence.

I waved my hand in front of his face to get his attention. He still didn't look up.

'Yeah I can hear you, I ain't deaf,' he grunted. Oh. My. God. This boy was possibly the most frustrating person I had ever met.

'Right, well, Craig, it was, erm, nice to meet you,' I lied.

Craig mumbled something again.

'Sorry, what was that?' I asked.

He repeated the mumble.

No, still not getting that. Someone was going to have to explain to him that he might have to exert some energy and actually use the relevant parts of his mouth to speak. He reached into a drawer in his desk and produced a disk.

Another mumble.

I'd given up trying to understand him. I looked at the disk he had handed me – a DVD with all my induction material on it – something else to furnish the inside of my desk drawer. As thrilling as it was to be listening to someone who had yet to start shaving, I had places to go and people to see. I walked towards the door.

'Before you go, we wanted to say how much we've missed you,' said Mary 1.

'Ah, that's nice,' I replied.

'Yes, we *wanted* to say how much we missed you, but we didn't miss you,' interjected Mary 2.

Mary 3 burst out laughing and was joined by the others. I knew they had practised that before they saw me.

* * *

Back on the ward, Dr Webber was waiting for me. He was doing a ward round later, but before that, he informed me with a gentle sigh, he had a treat for me. Now for most people a treat might involve a large glass of wine and a box of Milk Tray, maybe a meal out – who knows, even a trip to Thorpe Park. In medicine, a treat means being able to escape the confines of the hospital and venture into The Real World for a few hours. My treat manifested itself in the form of Miss Rosen, an eighty-nine-year-old lady who had the early symptoms of Alzheimer's disease. As her memory had begun to fail, her GP had become concerned about her ability to manage at home and had asked Dr Webber to assess her. Dr Webber had already seen her at home several times and arranged for her to be allocated a social worker, but now some awkward questions had begun to surface. He was making another home visit today and, since I had been a good boy, I got to accompany him.

We rang the doorbell and waited. And waited.

'Are you sure she's in there?' I asked.

'Patience,' replied Dr Webber. Eventually I could hear shuffling footsteps from the other side of the door and a jangle of keys.

'Who is it?' came a high, thin voice.

Dr Webber knelt down and as he did, the letterbox was pulled open. He began to pass his hospital badge through the letterbox and a small bony hand snatched it and retreated. The letterbox snapped shut behind it. Another long pause. Then finally the door opened.

Miss Rosen was small and frail; a generic, standard, run-of-the-mill old lady. Grey hair, wrinkles, you know the sort. She led us through the hallway and up a flight of stairs to the sitting room. Like its owner, the house and décor were old, but when she closed the front door it was peaceful and calm and the fact that there were no fitted carpets or that the faded floral wallpaper was peeling and stained didn't seem to matter.

'You two gentlemen go in front, I'm rather slow on the stairs these days,' she said, and waited on the half landing for us to overtake her.

Dr Webber and I went into the sitting room. It was full of old dark furniture and trinkets on every available surface. There was a high-backed chair with a small table next to it on which were piles of letters, a magnifying glass and some old photographs in tarnished silver frames. I couldn't see a television but there was a large, old radio sitting in the fireplace. At the far end of the room were two tall casement windows. The curtains were partially drawn and the thick, grey nets let in little light, but through the gloom I could see paintings hanging on the walls.

'Look,' said Dr Webber, pointing to a painting, and I squinted at it in the available light.

'What is it?' I asked.

'Just look, I'll tell you later,' and motioned at the other paintings before Miss Rosen shuffled into the room.

Miss Rosen clattered about in the kitchen off the sitting room for several minutes before re-emerging.

'I can't find the tea bags,' she said, puzzled, then asked if she'd offered us tea. Dr Webber declined. So much for a treat, I thought.

'We'll be here until next Tuesday if she makes us tea,' he said under his breath when he saw my disappointment. 'So,' he began, as Miss Rosen took a seat in the high-backed chair while he sat on the sofa and I perched precariously on a stool near the fireplace. It was strange watching him talk to Miss Rosen. He was like a different person; he was utterly in his element. He seemed to go through a metamorphosis – his mannerisms, the way he spoke, his tone; everything about him changed. He even seemed to physically alter. He visibly relaxed and appeared more animated and agile. This wasn't the same miserable, remote misanthrope I'd heard about or seen on the ward. This man was passionate and charismatic. It was mesmerising to watch the transformation. He teased Miss Rosen gently, made her laugh, coaxed things out of her, put her at her ease. As I watched him talk to her, I found myself starting to warm to him. Miss Rosen's short-term memory was clearly quite impaired. Dr Webber asked her a series of questions – known as a 'mini-mental state exam', which is a standard, basic way of assessing someone's memory and cognitive function – and it became apparent she didn't even know what year it was, let alone the day of the week.

'Oh, you know, it's, erm, oh, you tell him,' she said, looking at me when Dr Webber asked the date.

'Oh, he doesn't know anything, that's why he's here,

he's just learning,' joked Dr Webber and gave me a wink. She seemed flustered and frustrated and Dr Webber gently changed the subject. 'Miss Rosen has lived here for many years, haven't you?' said Dr Webber, encouragingly. 'Tell Dr Pemberton about how you came to settle in England.'

Miss Rosen's face brightened. She looked at me with a slight smile and opened her hands as though opening a book, her palms facing upwards.

'My family fled the pogroms in Russia in 1922. I was only a baby. In the dead of night they collected everything they could carry that was of any value and left. My grandparents stayed and we never heard from them again. They perished.' She stopped for a few moments, remembering.

'You know about the pogroms?' asked Dr Webber while Miss Rosen was silent. I nodded. We'd covered this in GCSE history. A pogrom was an organised, violent persecution of a particular ethnic group, typically Jewish people, and ripples of them had occurred across Europe at the beginning of the twentieth century, building to a tidal wave of anti-Semitism. I remember learning about them at the time and thinking how distant and dry it was, but here I was, speaking to someone who actually remembered them. Suddenly it wasn't history; it was her story.

'We went first to Romania and settled in Oradea,' she continued, 'but just a few years later there were pogroms there also. My father was an art dealer so we picked up the paintings and fled once more. We went to Germany, he set up his business there, and then the Nazis came and nowhere was safe. We fled across Europe. My father had many friends and contacts and in each place we stopped he would buy and sell pictures.' She took one of the photographs from the side table, leant across and handed it to me. 'That's my father,' she said as I looked at the stern man in a suit staring back at me. 'Eventually we settled in England, started our new lives here and this became my home.'

'And he was an art dealer here also?' I asked.

'Oh yes, he was well known in the art world. Many of his friends were artists and he kept selling their art when we settled here. Some of them became very successful, you know. At the time, it was modern paintings, but now they are old I suppose.'

'You knew Picasso, didn't you?' said Dr Webber encouraging her to continue.

'Oh, that man, I remember him. He and my father were good friends for many years. I remember as a girl playing under the table when he visited and seeing his shoes. Blue they were, real blue. Such a funny man. Who wears blue shoes to visit someone?' She shook her head at the memory. 'On my eighteenth birthday he gave me that painting,' she said, and pointed to a picture on the wall. I turned round and caught Dr Webber's eye as I did so.

'Get up and look at it,' said Dr Webber, 'the next time you see it, it will be on the news and being sold at some auction house.'

I got up and looked at the painting.

'And what about the other paintings?' I asked.

'Ah, they all have a story. My father not only sold pictures, he loved them also. He was not a business-man always. He couldn't bear to part with the ones he fell in love with,' she laughed gently, 'and he fell in love with a lot of them.'

It seemed remarkable that a brain that couldn't remember who the prime minister was or where the tea bags were could remember so much history, down to the colour of someone's shoes eighty years ago.

'And did you ever work?' I asked, returning to my seat.

'I helped my father sometimes in his shop and I would help my mother run the house. I never married and when they died, there was just me. The house is too big for me now but it is so full of memories that I can never leave it.'

I sat, thinking quietly. This place, with her inside it, was one of the last remnants of a world that was nearly gone. It was a tiny, fragile thread, about to snap at any moment, linking us back to another time. There was a noise downstairs and I looked at Dr Webber in surprise. Someone had come in and was walking about.

'Is that you, Paula?' Miss Rosen called out.

Footsteps on the stairs and then a plump, pale woman in her early forties appeared at the doorway. She looked at Dr Webber and me with suspicion but said nothing to us.

'Alright, Esther, yeah I got your bits for you. I'll put the change on the side,' she said, and walked into the room and through to the kitchen, putting the bag down loudly on the table. 'Well I can see you got company so I'll come back later with your tea, alright?'

Miss Rosen nodded. 'Thank you dear, so kind,' and Paula walked out, pointedly ignoring the two of us. We heard her close the door and Dr Webber got up to leave.

'Well it's been lovely to see you again,' he said, giving her a cheeky grin.

'Oh, you can come back any time,' she said, struggling to her feet.

'We'll see ourselves out,' insisted Dr Webber.

'And you come back to visit too, young man,' she said.

'Thank you, I'd like that,' I replied. When we got outside Dr Webber suggested we have a coffee and talk over the case. Seeing the way he'd been with Miss Rosen, I'd started to like him. And he paid for the coffee, which helped.

'There's an issue with Miss Rosen about that woman – Paula – who came in,' he explained as he stirred his coffee. 'She lives in a flat next door and is her carer of sorts; makes her dinner and visits her each day.'

'Oh,' I said, surprised, 'that's nice, isn't it? I thought she seemed a bit off with us though.'

'Well she's become very defensive since social services have become involved. Miss Rosen is very vulnerable and that woman's motivations aren't clear.'

'Is Miss Rosen wealthy, is that what you mean?' I asked.

'The house alone is probably worth several million. All the others on the street have been converted to flats but hers is still a five-storey house. But it's the paintings that will be worth the serious money,' he explained. 'She owns paintings from some of the major artists of the twentieth century. She has no one in her life; no family to leave anything to. In the room we were sitting were millions of pounds worth of art hanging on the walls. She has no idea, but her social worker is worried that her neighbour does.'

I sat and drank my coffee in silence. It made me feel sick that someone might use someone else like that, particularly someone as sweet and gentle as Miss Rosen.

'Things like this are rarely straightforward, though,' said Dr Webber, breaking the silence as though he knew what I had been thinking. 'She speaks highly of Paula,' he said thoughtfully. 'If the promise of a few paintings means Miss Rosen isn't lonely and she's looked after, is it so bad?'

'But it can't be right,' I said, indignantly. 'It's financial abuse.'

'You can call it that, I suppose,' said Dr Webber. He paused, and something in his face changed. 'I'm a few years off retirement. Sometimes I think about what it will be like when I'm in my eighties. I'm divorced, I don't have children. One day it might be me sitting on my own and I think that if I had a few paintings that meant someone came and visited me, that wouldn't be such a bad thing.' I knew he had told me something acutely personal but I didn't know what to say. He glanced at me briefly and I looked away, busying myself with finishing my coffee before standing up, ready to go back to the ward.

Dr Webber and I did go back to see Miss Rosen several times and in the end it was decided that Miss Rosen had the capacity to make decisions about her care and the arrangement with Paula should be allowed to continue for as long as was possible. It meant that Miss Rosen could stay in her home with someone she liked looking after her, rather than having an assortment of carers from social services traipsing in and out or suffering the upheaval and indignity of moving into a home.

A few years later, I picked up a discarded newspaper from the seat opposite me on a train. I absentmindedly turned the pages until suddenly, there in front of me, was Miss Rosen's Picasso. It had just been sold at auction. I read the report: unknown to the art world; never been catalogued; an outstanding example of his work, and so on. I read with excitement and remembered my visit to Miss Rosen. Then it suddenly occurred to me: Miss Rosen must be dead. It didn't say who had sold the painting.

I leant forward and looked at Mary 1's computer screen.

'Are you on Facebook? How did you get on? I thought the hospital banned that.'

'He downloaded something from the Internet,' said Mary 1, pointing to Craig.

'He's done it for all of us,' added Mary 2.

Mary 3 was unusually quiet and was still staring at her screen.

'My sister's just had a pasty,' she said, out of the blue. We all looked at her, bewildered. 'She's just done a status update,' Mary 3 explained. Craig sat, chewing gum, oblivious to the mayhem he had helped create by circumventing the hospital's security software. He was typing dictation, which he listened to through an earpiece in his left ear, and I stood and stared in disbelief as I realised he was doing so while still listening to his iPod through one earphone in his right ear. I could only imagine what it must be like in his brain, having to process the steady monotonous drawl of an outpatient letter dictated by Dr Webber against a soundtrack of full volume drum and bass.

'If you want to get on Facebook, just let me know, yeah?' he mumbled without looking up from his typing. 'It's well easy to get round the hospital security, it's a joke.'

'Erm, thanks,' I said, slightly perplexed as to how it was humanly possible to simultaneously listen to an iPod and dictation, type and listen to conversations going on around you.

I went next door to see Trudy. She was on the phone but saw me hovering by the door and beckoned me to sit down. I looked round the room while I waited for her to finish her conversation and was amused to notice a photograph on top of the filing cabinet of her and Mr Butterworth. They were possibly the oddest couple I could have imagined; her, bubbly, cheeky and irreverent; him, dry, dusty and withdrawn.

'Well surely he wouldn't try that again?' she said as she handed me a piece of Swiss roll. 'God knows what it is about him, never seen it myself,' she continued, then paused. 'I know!' she screeched suddenly. 'It's certainly not that, I've seen it, and really it's not much to write home about,' she said. I tried to make it look as though I wasn't listening to her conversation, despite sitting directly opposite her. 'Well, I'll ask him, he's sitting in front of me. I must go,' she said, and put the phone down.

'Ask me what?' I said, a little embarrassed at her candidness.

'Well,' she began, leaning forward conspiratorially, 'you know I'm not one for idle gossip,' she said. I laughed, then realised she actually meant this seriously. I straightened up in my seat.

'Erm, right.'

'Well, your friend, you know, the little one who's working in surgery?'

'Flora, you mean?' I asked. 'She's working for Housewives' Favourite.'

'That's her. I happen to have it on good authority – well, from Petra in the canteen who heard it from Douglas in waste management that, how can I put this delicately?' I wasn't convinced that Trudy was capable of putting anything delicately, 'You know, that they're at it.'

'At what?' I asked.

'It,' said Trudy, gurning slightly and rocking back and forth in her chair to emphasise what she meant.

'What, Flora and Housewives' Favourite are sleeping together? Already? She's only been working for him for a few days, that's a bit quick, isn't it?' I scoffed.

'Well apparently he's been giving her the eye for some time, and now he's her boss, you know what he's like. And Douglas said he saw them round the back of the bins this morning.'

'No, this is rubbish, she wouldn't do that and just because they've been seen smoking together doesn't mean they're having an affair, it's ridiculous.' Trudy didn't seem convinced.

'We'll see,' she said in a menacing tone, then pushed a large piece of Swiss roll into her mouth.

I went to the ward and was met by Marsha.

'We've had pathology on the phone, they need to speak to you.'

Pathology is a strange place, populated by even stranger people. After all, who in their right mind would get job satisfaction from looking at people's body fluids? They spend all day every day putting samples in machines for analysis or looking down microscopes at bits of things that have been coughed up, cut out or scraped off someone. It's all the revolting bits of medicine without any prospect of a Thank You card and box of Celebrations. The other thing about Pathology is that, regardless of when you call them, they can take anywhere from a lifetime to an epoch to answer the phone.

I phoned, and after waiting for so long plate tectonics could have actually moved me near enough to the lab to talk directly to them, they answered the phone.

'Oh yeah, we've got a result for you on an HIV test you requested for Adel Mokaba, date of birth 25th of July, 1975.'

I looked down my list of patients and saw her name. She'd been admitted a week ago, before I'd started work, with difficulties breathing, weight loss and malaise. She was a refugee from the Democratic Republic of the Congo, having fled the war there and come to the UK five years ago. She worked as a cleaner in a local office block.

'It's positive for the HIV antibody,' said the voice abruptly at the other end of the phone. 'You'll need to inform the patient and repeat the test for clarification,' he continued, then hung up.

The result was not a surprise. Investigations when she had first been admitted had shown that she had aspergillosis, a severe disease caused by fungus growing in her respiratory system. In essence, she had bread mould growing on her lungs. Mould spores are present everywhere but in healthy people the immune system prevents them from ever causing a problem. In people with a compromised immune system, however, spores that are inhaled are not destroyed, and instead begin to grow in the warm, damp environment of the lungs. I stood up and walked over to the bed where she was lying. I drew the curtains around her and sat down on the chair next to her.

'Do you remember the blood test we did a few days ago for HIV?' I asked.

Adel looked at me and smiled, 'Yes doctor.'

'Well, the results have come back and they show that you have been infected with HIV.' I waited for a response.

'Thank you, doctor, for telling me,' she said quietly. We talked briefly about what the diagnosis meant, and that we would refer her to the HIV doctors for specialist input.

'How would I have got this though, doctor?' she said, still smiling gently. 'I have only ever had sex with my husband.'

In that moment, I suddenly realised the wider implications of what I had told her. She had never been in a hospital before, had never received blood products while in the Congo, had never injected drugs, so most likely, her husband had given it to her. I felt nauseous.

'Well, your husband will have to be tested as well,' I explained, trying to avoid directly answering her question. 'We'll arrange everything with the HIV doctors.' Adel kept smiling but I could tell that she understood what I was thinking.

'I think he will be very sad at what has happened,' she said delicately. 'I thought things would be so much better when we came here and started our new life, but maybe that was not God's plan.'

She, just like Miss Rosen, had come here to start a

new life, I thought. It made me profoundly sad to think that people's lives were perpetually affected by other people's hateful actions, and yet still people held on to little shards of hope that somehow, somewhere, things would be all right; that there would be a sanctuary for them. And I'd had to ruin that for her by telling her she had HIV. Not the new life she'd hoped for.

We all met in the Doctor's Arms, the pub across the road from the hospital. It was actually called the Carpenter's Arms, but I'd never seen a carpenter in there, and given its close proximity to the hospital, many years ago the nurses had renamed it and it had stuck. They clearly enjoyed the joke that, after a busy shift, they'd fall into the Doctor's Arms. Though some nurses I know are happy to fall into anyone's arms, regardless of medical qualifications.

Ruby and I sat in the corner while Supriya and Lewis ordered the drinks. I could see the broad-shouldered Lewis towering over the petite Supriya as they jostled with nurses and physiotherapists for the attention of the barman. The supremely sensible Supriya didn't drink, of course. She was still avidly focused on pursuing her dream – but most rational people's nightmare – of becoming a part-time clinician and part-time academic and lecturer, specialising in the kidneys. She had already sat one of her membership exams – the examinations all juniors have to sit for membership to the relevant Royal College, which was needed to become a consultant – and was studying for the next, a whole six months before she was due to sit it. To the casual observer, her dedication was admirable. For those who had to work with her, it was sickening.

'Right, I've got an hour and then I have to go back to revise endocrinology,' she said, as she returned from the bar carrying some of the drinks.

Lewis stood behind her and raised his eyes to heaven although we all knew he was just as bad as her when it came to being focused on his career. He, too, was revising for his membership exams although pretended that he wasn't. He was one of the people at medical school who would stand outside the examination hall bemoaning the fact that he hadn't done a jot of revision and then miraculously ace the exam. We all knew he was a secret swot, but he was otherwise so personable we let him indulge in his delusion that he wasn't. After some time Flora arrived, looking flustered.

'You ok?' I asked, pushing a gin and tonic in her direction. 'How come you're late?' She mumbled some excuse but was busy texting.

Conversation soon turned to the new junior doctors who had started on the wards. It was strange to think that we were no longer the one-celled organisms in the evolutionary chain of medical careers, no longer quite the lowest of the low in the hospital pecking order. As we had now been doctors for two whole years (two down, only thirty-eight to go!) there was now a whole stratum of junior doctors below us. Since we had begun that first year, though, the training of junior doctors had undergone quite a lot of change. EU legislation known as the European Working Time Directive had been passed, decreeing that junior doctors were now unable to work more than forty-eight hours a week averaged over a twenty-six-week period.

On the face of it, that seems like a very sensible thing. No one wants to return to the Bad Old Days when people were working 800 hours a week. It wasn't good for the doctors and it certainly wasn't good for the patients. But the prescriptive legislation and the way it was implemented by trusts has had profound and cataclysmic effects on the way that doctors now work.

In order to comply with the legislation without directly employing more doctors, the hospitals have had to draw up rotas of Byzantine complexity to ensure that all the junior doctors' working hours comply. The knock-on effect of this has been a funda-mental change in the way that hospital medicine now operates. Prior to the new legislation – when my friends and I started work – junior doctors were attached to a team, typically composed of a newly qualified doctor, or 'junior house officer', a 'senior house officer', a registrar and a consultant. This 'firm', as it was called, was a tried and tested way of deliver-ing patient care. I'm not saying it was perfect – after all, my surgical firm in my first job was composed of: Daniel, who so hated life in hospital he left to work in the city; Sadsack, a morose failed vet; and Mr Butterworth, an autistic misanthrope. It felt like being adopted by the Addams Family but even so, when it came to knowing what was going on, who was doing it and when, it worked. It's often the juniors who are most involved in a patient's care and under this system, the junior doctors knew the patients and the patients knew them. It was a well-oiled machine with an inbuilt support structure for the junior members. The roles and responsibilities were clear and there was a strong sense of belonging, which ensured that juniors would follow their patient from the moment they were admitted, or seen in clinic, to the point of discharge.

But all this was wiped away with the swish of a politician's gold-nibbed fountain pen. The elaborate and abstruse rotas that have replaced the usual 'on call' system for doctors in their first year on the wards has meant that juniors are no longer attached to a particular consultant or team – rather, they float between teams, providing cover. Both the patient and the doctor become casualties in this. Junior staff are expected simply to do jobs handed over to them with no understanding of why or how their actions affect the well-being of the patient. There is no appreciation of cause and effect and no true ownership of the work done. Junior doctors have become fleeting, transient figures in the overall care of a patient, who often sees none of them more than once. This results in a diminished experience of healthcare, leaving patients confused, isolated and scared at the lack of continuity. They have to explain the same problem to each doctor they see, investigations are not followed up, things slip through the net. It's not safe. Apparently, it's 'progress'.

To add insult to injury, the hours haven't really changed. Certainly there are fewer, but in some specialties in particular, the hours are still punishing. Ruby, for example, who is in surgery, still routinely works hours after she's supposedly finished and probably averages about sixty hours a week. All that's happened is that because we're officially working less, we get paid less. The hours we work are supposed to be monitored on 'diary cards', which are forms – just what a hospital needs more of – that are completed by the doctor every few months, giving a snapshot of their working pattern, and are then scrutinised to ensure that they are not working more than they should. It requires total, absolute compliance, and if it is found that one doctor has worked just half an hour over the stipulated time, the entire rota is deemed to have 'breached', with severe financial penalties for the trust attached. So there is an implicit – and sometimes explicit – pressure put on the junior doctors by management or senior doctors to be 'creative' on their monitoring forms. We all know that if we tell the truth, the trust will be fined, its debts will increase, redundancies will follow or services will be reduced, and this will only make the situation worse and further affect patient care.

'I don't know how they manage now,' said Lewis whilst opening a packet of nuts, which Ruby quickly delved into. 'The Foundation Year doctors get so little support, it's nothing like good enough.'

Since our first year, there had also been a

'rebranding' exercise and we'd all got new titles. The most junior doctors – the house officers in the first and second years – had been rebranded 'Foundation Year doctors', and those juniors above them, which now included all of us, got the snazzy title of 'specialty doctor'.

'I feel sorry for them,' Lewis continued, 'they have no continuity. They need the continuity of being with one team and the firm hand of one consultant.'

'Well, you certainly had the firm hand of one consultant in your first year,' said Supriya, referring to Dr Palache, and she smiled cattily at Lewis who stuck his fingers up at her.

'Come on children, behave,' interjected Ruby. Flora remained silent but continued to look towards the door expectantly.

Ruby shot me a glance then turned to Flora. 'You expecting someone?' she asked casually.

Flora looked flustered. 'Oh, um, no, just waiting for my medical students. I said they should join us, thought it would be good for them, team building and all that.'

'What about Housewives' Favourite?' asked Ruby, and I glared at her from across the table. I knew she was trying to provoke Flora but this really wasn't the time or place. Lewis was like a bloodhound when it came to gossip and he just needed the slightest whiff that something might be going on and it would be all over the hospital before you could say 'verbal diarrhoea'.

'What about him?' replied Flora, defensively.

'Just wondering if he was coming too, you know, team building and all that.' I glared once more at Ruby and she backed down. Flora didn't say anything but shrugged a reply. There was a brief, awkward silence.

'So what's Mr Griffiths like, then?' I asked Ruby.

Her face lit up. 'Oh, he's amazing. I mean, he's quite intimidating and he expects everything done yesterday, but it's such a great opportunity working for him. He's doing pioneering surgery, it's really incredible. And I assisted in removing someone's leg this afternoon.'

'That's not medicine, that's butchery,' said Lewis in a slightly supercilious tone.

'Talking of getting legless, anyone else want a drink?' asked Flora as she got up to go to the bar.

The evening shift in A&E had ended and the nurses had come in for a drink. The place quickly became crowded. Ruby and I went out for a cigarette and by the time we returned, some of them had joined the table so we stood by the bar. I told Ruby about what Trudy had told me.

'Well if Flora is getting mixed up with him, she'll be sorry. I know from bitter experience.' I nodded, and thought about how I'd tried to warn Ruby about him in our first year but she had refused to listen.

'I think maybe we shouldn't talk about it to her though, it will only antagonise her.'

'I know, you're right, I just cannot believe she'd be so stupid, especially after she saw what I went through.' It was getting late and as we finished our drink, we looked round for Flora. She was nowhere to be seen.

'She's probably gone home in a mood with you for bringing up Housewives' Favourite in front of everyone,' I said to Ruby. We walked home alone, the darkness stretching out ahead of us. When we got home, though, Flora wasn't there.

3
Hard Times

'Sex,' said Mr Gillespie, and shrugged. A look of horror came across my face. That wasn't the answer I was expecting. I cleared my throat and looked around the clinic room for the 'dirty old man' panic button. There wasn't one. Damn the NHS and their cost-cutting exercises.

'Right,' I said slowly, 'so what has, erm, sex got to do with this?' I could feel myself going red as I realised that it appeared I was about to embark on a conversation with an O.A.P. about S.E.X.

I was seeing Mr Gillespie in the outpatient clinic because he'd had a stroke and had been referred by his GP for follow-up, but while I had been talking to him, it had become clear that he was also very low in mood.

'You wanted to know what's making me depressed,' continued Mr Gillespie, 'and if I'm honest, doctor, it's sex. I've not really talked to anyone about this, because, well, it's embarrassing.'

He wasn't wrong there. It's one of those topics that just isn't talked about openly in polite society. Certainly not when you meet someone for the first time, unless you like them very much indeed.

Doctors aren't immune from social etiquette and while we're sanctioned to enquire about the most intimate bodily processes, sex is still a topic that tends to be shied away from in the consulting room. Outside of the sexual health clinic, it's something that, if at all possible, is best avoided like the clap. It seems a little too intrusive, a little too personal and it isn't easy to drop into conversation with a patient without sounding out of place. This is made worse by the fact that once it becomes obvious that the topic should be raised, there is the inevitable stuttering, gazing at the shoes and going scarlet from the doctor. Using euphemisms is rarely effective and inevitably ensures the consultation descends into a script for *Carry On Doctor*. Some of the embarrassment stems from the fear of being misconstrued as a pervert, but often it's never discussed because doctors don't think about it as a legitimate area of enquiry. It's the realm of magazines and late night Channel 4 television programmes. It's not a 'medical' area. The patient's embarrassment, combined with that of the doctor, ensures that it rarely raises its head as a topic of conversation.

The problems start at medical school. Certainly we dissected the male and female sexual organs in anatomy classes – although if the truth be told, it was mainly the girls that dissected the penis and testicles, while the boys watched with pained expressions, squirming about while their eyes watered. We were taught about sexual diseases, and spent alarming afternoons in the library gaping at revolting pictures in textbooks, which made several people take vows of celibacy. But people as sexual beings and the actual mechanics of sex – the way that things can go wrong and things that can be done to put them right – were not discussed. I got what I know about Viagra from Richard and Judy.

'I just can't do it any more. At least, not like I used to,' he continued. I squirmed in my seat. It just didn't seem right to be talking to someone of another generation about the birds and the bees. This was all horribly reminiscent of 'the talk' with my parents when I was a teenager. I had a sudden flashback as I sat trying to compose myself in front of Mr Gillespie.

'And when mummy and daddy really love each other . . .' I remembered my mum saying, as she blinked at me with a fixed smile.

'Yeah, I know,' I interrupted quickly, dreading where this conversation was inevitably leading. I looked at my parents sitting opposite me on the sofa. My dad had an air of contained panic, which was giving him a strange expression as though he were constipated. My mum was holding a booklet.

'Sometimes they give each other a special kind of cuddle,' she persevered, swallowing hard as she continued with her speech, her voice faltering slightly.

'Yeah, thanks, really,' I interrupted again, wondering who out of the three of us was the most red by this point.

'And sometimes then what happens is that daddy's . . .' her voice faltered.

'OK OK OK, thanks, that's enough,' I screamed.

'. . . pe—' she began to say.

'Enough!' I screamed back.

'Basically, what your mother and I want to talk to you about is,' began my father. He was doing so well up until this point, and in fact I was now rather enjoying watching them trying to avoid using any even remotely naughty words, 'conjugal relations,' said my father after a lengthy pause in which he was clearly trying to find as obscure a word as possible.

'Making love,' my mother butted in, presumably fearing that conjugal relations sounded too much like something to do with international politics and I'd grow up with an unhealthy interest in the United Nations.

'I know, it's fine, I know all about it,' I said, attempting to defuse the situation.

'Any questions, it's in this booklet,' said my dad as he swiped it from my mum and pushed it in my hand. 'Let's go get a takeaway,' he continued, which was dad-speak for 'discussion over'.

To give my parents their due, throughout my childhood they did try to talk to me openly about sex. As a teacher, my mum knew only too well about the smutty misinformation that was abound in the playground, but it didn't make it any easier for them. Every sex-based discussion was a buttock-clenchingly embarrassing event for all concerned. But of course children aren't stupid. I'd already heard it all before from my best friend James, who in turn had heard it from his sister, who'd heard it from her friend, who apparently had overheard her mother explaining the birds and the bees to her father. Sure, it was a while before I realised that, in fact, fellatio wasn't a type of coffee that you drank before having sex, but by the time I needed to know what went where and how, I'd figured out the basics with help from *This Morning* phone-ins. No parent likes to think that their teenager is having sex, but conversely, no self-respecting teenager likes to think that their parents are, either. But sitting in front of Mr Gillespie, this was the first time it had ever occurred to me that my grandparents might be at it as well.

It's true that if the sexuality of any group of people is inevitably ignored, it's that of older people. There seems to be a feeling that, come a mythical, unspecified age, you're deemed 'old', and therefore aren't having sex anymore. You're making jam and listening to *The Archers* on the radio, instead.

'I thought you were a widower, though?' I asked, looking through Mr Gillespie's notes, which were sitting on the desk.

'Well, it's been five years since my wife died,' he explained. 'A year or so ago I did an adult education course, just to get out of the house, and it all started from there.'

'You did an adult education course in sex?' I said, aghast.

'No,' he said with a laugh. 'I did a course at the local college in computers, and then I bought myself one. I registered with a few dating sites and started seeing some ladies.'

By now my initial embarrassment had subsided and I was fascinated. Apparently, the dating scene for older people was thriving.

'But dating isn't like it was when I was a youngster,' he said, wide-eyed. 'All they want now is nooky.' This was all a revelation to me. 'Some of them even expect it on the first date. I mean, when I was a teenager we'd be lucky to cop a feel after months of dating. Now, they're in your pants before you're even halfway through your prawn cocktail.'

'Maybe you're meeting the wrong kind of ladies?' I ventured. 'I'm sure there are plenty of women out there who want companionship and to take things slowly.' He looked at me, horrified.

'What? Are you joking? I want to have sex. I'm an old man, time is not on my side, I don't want to take things slowly. I just can't do it.'

'Well, there are other ways of satisfying someone,' I said tentatively, disbelieving that I was about to start giving sex tips to a septuagenarian.

'I know about that, son,' he said, rolling his eyes, 'but it makes me feel down that I can't, well, get it up. It's like I'm not a proper man.'

'I know, it must be very hard,' I said, and immediately realised this was an unfortunate word. 'Difficult, it must be very difficult,' I corrected myself, but not before Mr Gillespie gave a knowing smile.

'There's one woman, doctor, Mavis. She's wonderful, I really like her. She's been very patient with me already but I know that if I don't deliver soon, she'll move on. It's really getting me down.'

It was clear that this was very important to him, probably more so than managing his diabetes, or his stroke. Why shouldn't he get help for his sexual problems, just like a younger person would, if that's what he wants? He deserved to have as active a sex life as possible. I explained that given the complexity of his medical problems, any one of them – or indeed all of them – could be contributing to the problem and that really, a specialist should see him. We agreed to refer him to the urologists for an assessment. He smiled a wide smile and stood up to shake my hand.

'Thanks so much, doctor. I'll admit to being a bit embarrassed.' He looked down, briefly, lost for words. 'I mean, you're quite young to be talking to me about sex.'

'It's fine,' I said, smiling to myself.

I left the outpatient clinic and went to the administration block. Trudy and the three Marys had already left, but Craig was sitting at his desk. He was wearing his usual uniform of a baggy, untucked and unironed white shirt with the top two buttons undone, and a tie, loosely tied in a knot that sat, askew, halfway down his chest.

'Hello, you're here late,' I said, as I put the dictation tape on his desk.

He didn't look up or remove his earphones, but grunted, 'Yeah, I wanted to get this work finished. I hate leaving stuff till the next day.'

In the few weeks I'd been working in this job, two

things had become apparent about Craig. Firstly, while they were clearly delighted that he could help them bypass the hospital computer security so they could shop on eBay all day, in general, the three Marys despised him. This was related to the second observation: he was actually really good at his job.

OK, he had the interpersonal skills of a colostomy bag, but he was a teenager, so this was to be expected. It was obvious that his poor eye contact and articulation was just because he was very shy, and over time he'd shown that he was not only competent, but excellent at his job. He was efficient and organised to a degree that put me to shame. He planned ahead and ensured that notes and relevant scan results were waiting for collection on outpatient clinic days, letters were sent promptly and without mistakes, and GPs were contacted to ensure that any management plans had been seen and initiated, and he rearranged the office filing system to make it more efficient. He was even steadily making his way through the medical records of patients once they were discharged from the ward, and ensuring that everything was filed in the right order. Trudy was similar in this respect, and certainly without her über-organisational skills in my first year of work, I'd have drowned under a sea of paperwork within weeks. But she had years of experience and Craig had started only a month before I had. He was temping, and traditionally temps did as little work as humanly possible while not getting fired. Most of them didn't actually do the job they were paid for, let alone ones they weren't.

'You have any plans?' I asked. 'For your career, I mean. You're not going to temp forever, are you?'

For the first time, he looked at me full in the face and removed both his earphones. 'No, I ain't doing this for the rest of my life, you mental? This is just my gap year and I need to earn some money, don't I?'

'You know what you're going to study?' I asked.

He shrugged. 'Well, I wanna be a doctor, but I don't know, it's well competitive, innit, and it's a well long course so it's gonna be expensive.'

I was certainly not expecting him to say that he wanted to study medicine.

'No one from my family's been to uni so they ain't that keen for me to go. They think it would be better for me to get a job and start earning proper wages like, but I ain't that keen, I wanna study. My dad's a plasterer and I don't wanna do that, just ain't my thing.'

'What grades did you get at A-level? You know you need good grades, don't you?'

'Yeah, I know that, I ain't daft. I got all As. I done maths, biology, chemistry and sociology.'

I stood, open-mouthed. He was not your usual temp. Or your usual prospective medical student.

'Well, good luck. If you want any help with your application, let me know,' I said.

'Cheers mate, sound,' he replied. Then put his earphones back in.

*   *   *

I made my way back up to the ward to collect my things and finish up.

'How was outpatients?' asked Marsha, who was wearing gloves and pushing a commode.

'Oh, erm, interesting,' I said, as I sat down to fill out some blood forms for the morning. There was a brief silence. 'Do you ever think about old people having sex?' I asked.

Marsha looked at me with a mixture of bewilderment and exasperation. 'I barely have time to think about me having sex, let alone other people, old or otherwise,' she said, and carried on towards the sluice.

I arrived home in the evening sunlight. Flora and Ruby were still at work, so I was alone in the flat. It was wonderfully peaceful and I decided to make the most of it. I sat down at the kitchen table, put my feet up on a chair, turned on Radio 4 and had some home-made jam on toast to unwind.

Several days later, Dr Webber gave me another 'treat'. This time, I was allowed out all on my own, although I was not excited about the prospect of visiting a nursing home. I had bad memories of those places.

The large wooden door swung open and a tall, wiry woman in uniform greeted me. She was holding a cloth in one hand and looked at me, blankly.

'Hello, I'm Max, I'm a doctor, I'm here to see Mrs Broadhurst? I got a referral from her GP?'

'I'm the domestic,' she said, 'but wait here and I'll get someone.'

I stepped inside and stood waiting in the hallway. From where I was standing, I could see into a large dining room with three rows of long tables. It was already set for lunch, although it was only 10 o'clock in the morning. On the other side of the hallway there was another room, and through the doorway I could see a row of armchairs around the perimeter and several elderly people dotted around, sitting in them. On the other side of the room a large, flat screen television blared out mid-morning pap, although no one appeared to be watching it. One woman looked up and smiled at me.

'Are you here to see me?' she asked expectantly.

'No, I don't think so,' I replied, and her face fell in disappointment. 'Sorry,' I added, but she'd already put her head back down on her chest.

I turned round and saw the matron making her way down the stairs, holding a pile of blankets in her arms. She smiled at me, showing a row of perfect white teeth.

'Well, thank you for coming, doctor,' she said as she reached the bottom of the stairs, 'so kind of you. Can we get you a cup of tea? I'm sure Claire can rustle up a piece of cake for you, too, I know you busy doctors don't get time to eat properly.' She laughed a throaty laugh and ushered me into her office while she abandoned the blankets on a nearby side table.

Her office was surprisingly sparse and tidy. Along the far wall were shelves with lever arch files in neat rows and, below them, several filing cabinets. I sat at her desk, which was empty except for a photograph of a young girl, a pot of pens and an ink blotter. She put a lever arch file in front of me.

'Her room is the far room at the end of the corridor on the second floor. Anything else you need, I'll be upstairs finishing off making the beds. Just shout.'

She closed the door behind her and I looked down at the file. I turned to the clinical notes section and read some of the entries.

Mrs Broadhurst had dementia. This is really an umbrella term for a number of conditions that cause problems with memory and thinking and understanding. Alzheimer's is one type, but the type that Mrs Broadhurst had was 'vascular dementia'. This is caused by small parts of the brain involved in memory and cognition dying off due to problems with blood flow to the brain, usually as the result of a stroke. It's different from Alzheimer's in that, rather than a steady progression, the sufferer has a stepwise deterioration, with symptoms remaining at a constant level for some time and then suddenly deteriorating further as the brain experiences another episode of injury.

She had been in the nursing home for the past four years, but recently her behaviour had become increasingly difficult to manage and she was aggressive towards staff. According to what the nurses had written, however, for the past week things seemed to have improved. The entries in the clinical notes were brief, but they all stated that there were no problems and that she was sleeping well. I was relieved, although a little puzzled. It seemed odd that things should improve so dramatically.

I flicked through the notes and saw little in the way of biographical information, except that her husband had died fifteen years ago and her son lived in America. There was a contact for a niece that lived in Scotland, but apart from that, nothing else about who she was. I closed the file and left the office.

I walked out into the hallway and thought back to the first time I'd been in a nursing home. It seemed strange to think that because of the experiences I'd had then, I was standing here now. I even remembered her name: Mrs Plemming. She had been crying out. That was how it all started.

'It's fine, just lock the door,' said Jackie, one of the health care assistants, in a clear attempt to terminate any further discussion on the matter.

'Erm, right, OK,' I replied, uneasily. 'I'm not sure we should do that, really.' Jackie stared at me with blank, glassy eyes with her head on one side and a slight snarl beginning on her lips.

'Just shut the door and lock it, otherwise you're going to have to be in and out of here all day. Pretend you can't hear her,' she replied, before picking up the barely touched breakfast tray and leaving me alone in the room with Mrs Plemming.

I knew what I was about to do was wrong. I knew that no one deserved to be locked in a room for hours on end, certainly not someone vulnerable, scared and alone. Mrs Plemming may have had dementia and her behaviour may have been difficult to manage at times, but this was a nursing home, for goodness sake, surely we had more humane ways of treating someone than this? Apparently not. I closed my eyes, screwed up my face and shut the door. And locked it. Despite my protests, for the rest of the summer, every morning, the same scene was repeated. It was standard practice to lock the disturbed or distressed residents in their rooms for hours on end while we washed and dressed the others or so the staff could have a quiet shift. Sometimes when we came to unlock the doors they had fallen on the floor. Often they were found to have been sitting in their own urine. This experience, when I was seventeen and working in a nursing home over a summer holiday, would stay with me and set the trajectory for my career. The idea had been to learn about practical healthcare before beginning medical school, but what I learnt was that older people are mistreated and their rights are ignored. A valuable lesson, perhaps, but one I'd have rather not had.

I walked up the stairs and down the corridor to Mrs Broadhurst's room. The door was open and inside she was lying in bed. I introduced myself but it became apparent that she was barely conscious. I tried talking to her, but nothing. I felt for a pulse and she was certainly alive, just sleeping. Or rather, sedated. She half opened her eyes as I stood up from her bedside, but closed them again. This wasn't right. She'd been given something, I thought to myself. I went back and found the matron who was in a room on the first floor, stripping a bed. She smiled at me.

'All done then? Doubt you could get much from her, but it was nice of you to come, it's appreciated.'

'What's she been given?' I asked, determined to get to the bottom of what was going on.

'Oh, just what she's been prescribed,' she said. We went to the clinic room and she handed me the prescription chart. As well as medication for high blood pressure and cholesterol, she had also been put on olanzapine, an antipsychotic.

'Who started that?' I asked.

'The GP,' she said breezily. 'We told him we couldn't manage her any more like she was, so he prescribed that and since then she's been as good as gold.'

I was still learning but this seemed to me profoundly wrong. She wasn't being cared for; she was being knocked out. I left the nursing home and returned to the hospital, determined to talk to Dr Webber about this as soon as I could.

I went to the doctors' mess to make a cup of tea and collect my thoughts. Lewis was sitting on a chair surrounded by notes for dictation.

He lowered the Dictaphone and looked at me. 'Have you heard?'

My heart sank. 'Look, I don't want to hear about Flora and Housewives' Favourite,' I said irritably.

Lewis looked at me, open-mouthed. 'What?' he said, and I suddenly realised that this was not what he had been talking about.

'Oh, nothing,' I said quickly, but it was already too late.

'You don't mean that they're sleeping together?' said Lewis. 'Who told you that? Oh, this is just too funny.'

'No.' I said sternly. 'Look, Lewis, please, just leave it. Don't. I don't know what's going on, it's just rumours. We're her friends, we should be supporting her, not talking about her behind her back.' Just then Lewis gestured to stop and I turned round to see Flora coming into the mess.

'What are you two gossiping about?' asked Flora, innocently.

Lewis was unflustered. 'Well, I was just telling Max about what I'd heard. Apparently, the hospital is planning to close down the A&E department.'

'What?' exclaimed Flora and I in unison.

'You cannot be serious,' scoffed Flora, 'that's ludicrous, they can't do that. Where will all the sick people go?'

'It's one of those daft management things, streamlining services or whatever they call it,' said Lewis, shaking his head.

I missed the rest of the discussion as at that point, my pager went off. It was A&E referring a patient who was having a heart attack.

That evening we all went out for dinner. Supriya had arranged it, as she was taking the evening off from revising. This was a rare occurrence, so none of us dared to decline. It was actually a welcome change from the strained exchanges that had been taking place at home. Flora had been acting strangely ever since her disappearance a few weeks ago from the Doctor's Arms. She'd not returned that night and when Ruby and I had gone into work the following day, we found her sitting coyly in the doctor's office, drinking tea with Lewis. Ruby immediately asked where she'd been, but Flora fobbed her off by saying she stayed round a friend's house.

'What friend?' asked Ruby, indignantly. 'We're your friends.'

'You're not my only friends,' Flora replied, tetchily.

'She stayed at mine,' interrupted Lewis with a shrug. 'God, if I'd known it was going to cause a problem I wouldn't have asked her to.'

'Well we were worried about you and your mobile was off,' said Ruby.

'Yeah, it ran out of battery. I said I'd stay with Lewis to keep him company while Mark is at a conference,' Flora said, tossing her hair aside.

It was all perfectly feasible but there was some odd, intangible thing that afterwards made me suspicious. Since then, Ruby and I had not seen much of her. Partly this was because we'd both been working, getting home late and catching up with other friends. But Flora's absence in the flat was noticeable. Usually even when we were all frantically busy, we'd run into each other on the stairs or the bathroom, or stumble across one another passed out around the kitchen table. But not Flora; not since that night. And tonight, as we sat in the restaurant, she seemed uneasy. She rarely looked at Ruby and seemed wary of opening up too much. She wouldn't drink anything and hardly ate her food, just pushed it around the plate with her fork. After the meal we all went back home and Lewis and Supriya joined us. We piled round the kitchen table and Lewis started droning on about some obscure case he'd seen that week. Lewis had a habit of doing this.

'Oh God, he's starting again. I knew you wouldn't be able to get through the night without at least one obscure medical reference. It's so boring!' said Ruby, pretending to bang her head on the table.

'It's actually very interesting,' began Lewis, as Ruby lit a cigarette.

'Someone open the wine, quick. If anyone's got any Rohypnol, I'll have some of that too,' she said, inhaling deeply.

Flora got up.

'Not for me,' she said, as I handed her a glass. 'Actually, I'm beat, I'm going to head to bed I think.'

'You OK?' I asked.

'Yeah, I'm fine, sorry. Just feel so tired, that's all. You have a good night.' And with that, she went upstairs.

4
Something Shocking

I stood at the head of the operating table, my hands shaking.

'Place the electrodes on the side of her head,' said the consultant standing next to me.

I hesitated. A nurse and the anaesthetist looked at me from across the room, expectantly. I looked down at the anaesthetised Mrs Thomas. She'd had depression for years, and despite being tried on numerous antidepressants, nothing had worked, and so it had been decided to give her ECT or, 'electroconvulsive therapy'.

ECT involves an electrical current being passed through the brain via two paddles placed on either side of the head, until the patient has a seizure. This has got to be one of the more controversial treatments available on the NHS. ECT has had bad press. It was used as a panacea in the 50s and 60s, and the legacy of this is difficult to erase. The circumstances under which it is done, now, are tightly controlled and techniques have dramatically improved. Undoubtedly it works for some people.

I'd put my name down on the weekly ECT list volun-
tarily, as it was something I would have to experience
if I wanted to train in mental health after I'd finished
this job. But when I was standing there, paddles in my
hand with a patient lying face up in front of me, I
didn't feel ready. I just felt confused and under pressure. Another nurse came into the room and looked
quizzically at the other one. I opened my mouth to
speak but no sound came out. How was I going to
articulate my unease in front of a room full of professionals for whom this was all in a day's work and who
just wanted to get this over and done with and go on
their tea break?

While things have moved on since the days of *One
Flew Over the Cuckoo's Nest*, obviously popular culture
had affected me and I felt uneasy about doing the treatment until I fully understood what it was I was doing.
How ECT works remains unclear, although there are
numerous theories. While controlled, it seems crude and
there is still much debate over it. It is not without risk,
and a patient's cognition and memory can be affected.

Given that it has provoked such criticism and gener-
ated such controversy in the past, I didn't feel I knew
enough about the procedure yet to do it myself. Mrs
Thomas was an inpatient and had consented to having
it done. She actually wanted it done. But then again,
this was someone who was on section – legally detained
in hospital under the Mental Health Act. Society didn't
even allow her the right to vote. Could I really be sure
she was making an informed decision about this?

It was all very complex and as the assembled team of doctors and nurses stood round me, waiting, I felt under immense pressure to do as I was told. The consultant stepped forward. He was a professor of neuropsychiatry who had lectured me at medical school. I wondered if there would be ramifications for my future career if I refused to do it. I just wanted to do the right thing, but at that moment, I had no idea what that was.

The medical profession has a clear hierarchy and much of being a junior doctor is about obedience and deference to those in a superior position to you. But what about when things become a matter of conscience? Can blindly following authority be justified? I stood, the ECT paddles in my hands, and thought back to a lecture we had been given at medical school about an experiment that was conducted in 1963 by a social psychologist at Yale University, Stanley Milgram.

The results of the now famous 'Milgram Experiment', published against the backdrop of the Nuremberg trials, were to prove very shocking even now. We had been taught about it at medical school to ensure we understood the role authority played in controlling behaviour.

In the experiment, Milgram had recruited a group of participants, each of whom were supposedly allocated either the title of 'learner' or 'teacher'. In fact, all the genuine volunteers were allocated the role of 'teacher', while actors, masquerading as volunteers, played the role of 'learner'. The teachers were told to ask a series of questions. When the learner, strapped into a chair, answered incorrectly, the teacher was instructed to administer to the learner an electric shock. Although the teachers weren't aware of this at the time, the learners did not actually receive the shock administered. For each question answered wrongly, the voltage of the shock was increased, with the voltage display showing switches ranging from 'slight shock' to 'danger: severe shock'. The last two switches showed 'XXX'. As the voltage was increased, the actor playing the learner role began shouting out and asking for it to stop, and many of the volunteers expressed concern about what was happening. At this point, the experimenter assured the volunteer that he or she took full responsibility and to continue with the experiment. No volunteers stopped before 300 volts, and sixty-five per cent continued to the maximum 450 volts. It showed that an alarming number of people will bow to authority and do what they are told, even if they think what they are doing is wrong.

My mum loved this experiment. She told me about it long before I was taught it at medical school. She used it to emphasise to my sister and me the importance of questioning things.

'Remember, you never have to do anything you don't want to,' she would say, although this never seemed to extend to the washing-up.

Surely I shouldn't do this if I didn't want to, regardless of the powerful position that the person standing next to me had?

'I . . .' I began, faltering slightly. 'I don't want to do it,' I said resolutely. I grimaced an apology. The consultant looked back at me with an air of bewilderment, took his hands out of his packets and moved closer to me. 'What do you mean?' he asked. The anaesthetist glared.

'Can we get on with it?' she huffed.

I tried to explain my unease, that I didn't feel ready to do such a procedure without understanding more about it.

'It's part of your training,' he said, 'you have to do it.'

'I just don't feel comfortable,' I repeated, as I put down the paddles and walked out of the door. My hands were still shaking. Where was my mum when I wanted her?

I made my way to the administration block to seek comfort and cake from Trudy. This never failed to help me clear my head. If I was lucky, I reasoned, she might even hold my pager for me for a bit. I went into her office and found her standing by the filing cabinet, making a cup of tea.

'Tea? Coffee?' she asked, gesturing with the kettle she was holding.

'Tea, please,' I said.

'What you been up to?' she asked, cheerily, as she busied herself with the teabags.

I explained about Mrs Thomas and the dilemma I had faced.

'Oh, don't let it worry you. I never do anything

people in this place tell me and look where it's got me – head of admin for the hospital. Not bad considering I've only got a GCE in needlework.' She paused for a moment before adding, 'Admittedly, it's probably down to the fact that over my time as a secretary I got to see lots of the internal memos, so I blackmailed most of the management into giving me what I want. But even so, I say that shows initiative.'

'Yes, and possibly an unprofessional disregard for confidentiality and the law.'

She produced a Battenberg from her bag and unwrapped it.

'Actually, that reminds me, do you know anything about this rumour that's going round about A&E being closed down?'

Trudy had just begun cutting a slice but stopped. She left the knife embedded in the cake and leant forward over her desk.

'Who told you about that?' she asked suspiciously.

'Lewis. People were talking about it in the doctor's mess. It's not true, is it?'

'Well,' began Trudy, sitting back. She put her hand around the knife handle once more and resumed drawing it heavily through the remainder of the cake. 'I'm not one to gossip.'

Really, I thought, the level of this woman's self-delusion knows no bounds. 'But, I do happen to know that the rumours are true.'

'What? Are you serious?'

'Oh yes, the trust's already in advanced discussions

with the health authorities. I've seen the emails and minutes from the meetings. It's all been kept very hush-hush, they don't want the public to know about it until the last minute.'

'But they're not allowed to do that, surely? Isn't there supposed to be some sort of public consultation, some opportunity to object or something?'

'Oh Max, for all your education, you are dense sometimes. Don't you know how these things work? They've made their minds up; it's a done deal. They'll do some half-hearted consultation exercise, they'll give no notice and not advertise it, do the whole thing on the quiet and by the time it's public knowledge it will all be far too late. They do it all the time. Wards get closed, services get cut back, what, you think they go round knocking on everyone's front door checking it's OK with them?'

Of course, she was right. It happens like that all the time. Just last year the day hospital suddenly lost an occupational therapist in a 'restructuring exercise', for her to be replaced with a vending machine and a poster saying 'Stay Healthy, Keep Active'. Several wards had been closed in the year I was away working in the community and on each occasion, by the time the staff had known what was happening, it was too late and objecting was futile.

'There's nothing you can do, Max,' said Trudy. 'Just don't get ill around here, that's my advice.'

I was sure there was something I could do, though, it was just that I didn't know what, exactly.

* * *

Mrs Doherty leant across to put her hand on her husband's knee as she quietly sobbed into her handkerchief. She patted his leg gently and he moved his hand over and took hold of hers and began to stroke it.

'Don't cry, love, it will be OK,' he said, smiling benignly.

She laughed as she dabbed her eyes. 'Oh, excuse me doctors, sorry, it's just me being silly,' she said while Dr Webber and I smiled and nodded at her. 'I'm just so happy. Thank you so much,' she said, and then turned to her husband. 'The nice doctors are going to prescribe you a special drug that will help you with your memory,' she explained.

He continued to smile benignly at us, evidently forgetting that we had just spent the past fifteen minutes discussing his memory problems.

Mr Doherty had recently been diagnosed with Alzheimer's disease and lived with his wife, who was his main carer. I had met with them last week in the outpatient clinic to review Mr Doherty. His wife had come with a printout from the Internet that her son had sent her, and she had wanted to ask about the possibility of my starting her husband on an acetylcholinesterase inhibitor.

My heart had immediately sunk.

These drugs work by inhibiting an enzyme that is present in the brain. This enzyme breaks down the neurotransmitter acetylcholine, which is important for the nerves in the brain to communicate with each other. Acetylcholine levels are reduced in Alzheimer's disease. By inhibiting the enzyme that breaks this chemical down, the levels in the brain are increased and this is thought to help delay the deterioration in memory and cognition that is seen in this type of dementia. The problem is that the tablets cost about £2.50 a day and NICE – the National Institute for Health and Clinical Excellence, a quango that advises on which treatments should be available on the NHS – have deemed them not 'cost-effective' enough to be prescribed in the beginning stages of Alzheimer's.

It's easy for NICE to make this assessment, slightly harder for me to have to relay this to Mrs Doherty, and understandably very difficult for her to accept it. She had clearly been pinning all her hopes on this medication. She was so bereft in the clinic when I'd seen her, I asked her to return the following week to be seen by Dr Webber, too, just to see if there was any way round this. It was, in part, a stalling tactic, but part of me also hoped he would disregard government guidelines and prescribe it anyway.

The issue, as Dr Webber explained to me before we went in to see Mrs Doherty and her husband, is that with this decision, NICE had moved away from merely assessing the clinical merits of a medication, and instead begun making arbitrary judgments on whether or not people are worth spending money on. It doesn't seem right that an unelected, unaccountable organisation makes this decision.

'The infuriating thing is that NICE have completely failed to understand how these drugs benefit the actual patients and their carers. They don't offer a cure, but no one ever said they did. However,' Dr Webber had explained, 'these drugs can save carers an hour in carer time a day, an important reduction in a heavy burden, which makes it more likely that patients will be able to stay at home longer – something that NICE failed to take into account. The cost of full-time care is more than £100 a day. When viewed like that, £2.50 seems quite a bargain.'

Mrs Doherty had begun our meeting by explaining that they would pay privately for the tablets. 'I know they're not the answer to all the problems and that he's going to get worse regardless, but I can't just sit by and do nothing. If they mean he can stay at home with me even for a few more months, then it's worth it.' She smiled gently at us and my heart ached.

She was right that they were not a panacea, but they did offer benefits to some people. NICE have acknowledged that while research has shown their clinical effectiveness, they insist the tablets are not cost effective.

'We don't have a lot of money, so I've made enquiries about releasing some of the equity in our house,' said Mr Doherty quietly.

'That won't be necessary,' said Dr Webber, wielding his pen and prescription pad. 'We're going to start your husband on them straight away.'

The look of relief on Mrs Doherty's face was overwhelming. And that's when she broke down in tears. She knew that the outlook was bleak for her husband. She knew that he was only going to get worse. But they had been married for forty years and she was desperate to care for him as long as possible. The medication offered her this hope. When faced with situations like that, is it any wonder that doctors working in dementia desperately try to find loopholes in order to ensure that their patients continue to get these drugs? They aren't doing this to waste NHS money; they are doing this because, with a duty of care to their patients, they cannot bring themselves to deny them a drug they know might help. The drugs are currently still allowed in 'moderate' Alzheimer's, despite the fact that the benefits are most noticeable, and indeed of most use to patients and their carers, in the early stages of the disease. So doctors, with a wink and a nudge, exaggerate the severity of impairment in order to keep within the rules and this is precisely what Dr Webber did.

'We'll just write down that he now has a moderate level of impairment. There, problem solved,' he said, as he handed over the prescription.

I was delighted for Mrs Doherty and her husband. But why had it come to doctors lying on forms in order to put the welfare of their patients first? She left the clinic with her husband holding on to a little bit of hope in the form of a piece of paper she was clutching.

I saw a few more patients on my own and after the clinic ended, I went to find Dr Webber to discuss my visit to the nursing home to see Mrs Broadhurst a few days previously.

'She was barely conscious,' I explained tentatively. 'It just doesn't seem like a humane solution to her behavioural problems.'

'It's not,' replied Dr Webber with a shrug. 'There are times when anti-psychotics can be of real use in managing patients with dementia, but mostly they're abused. They're used for the benefit of the staff, rather than the patients, and as doctors, we aren't employed to make the lives of nursing home staff easier.'

I felt relieved that Dr Webber agreed with me.

'There have been numerous reports in the newspapers about the problem, it's been discussed in Parliament, it's a real issue.'

'So what shall I do?' I asked.

Dr Webber sighed. 'Well, that is the question.'

I waited for him to elaborate but he didn't. 'I mean, the GP was wrong to do what he did, wasn't he?' I added.

'It's easy to say that the problem is with the prescription, and on the face of it, it is. It's being used as a chemical cosh, and that's wrong. Everyone happily joins in the chorus condemning their use. But when you explain what the answer is, everyone suddenly falls silent.'

'What?' I asked, bemused. 'What is the answer?'

Dr Webber moved some notes from the desk where he was standing and perched on the edge. 'Managing demented patients who are acutely disturbed,' he explained, 'requires considerable skill, patience and, above all, staffing levels. But it remains a Cinderella specialty, with services being cut, staff levels on elderly wards reduced, budgets for training frozen and access to specialist care limited.'

'But it's supposed to be a nursing home,' I said in disbelief.

'That means nothing. Staff in nursing homes usually have little or no training in dealing with this group of patients. The owners of these homes are focused on the profits, not the patients, and to get the sort of quality, highly trained staff that is needed would cost too much. There are some good quality nursing homes, but getting into them isn't easy.'

'But what do I do about Mrs Broadhurst? She's got no one, I can't just leave her there.'

'Well, I'd talk to Jeannie, one of the social workers about doing a further assessment, and think about getting her moved to somewhere they can manage her more appropriately without dosing her up to the eyeballs.'

I left Dr Webber dictating letters and walked back to the ward, feeling angry and frustrated. I understood what he was saying, that this was a wider, larger problem to do with allocation of resources, poor training of staff and a general disregard for this kind of patient, but that didn't make it any easier to condemn Mrs Broadhurst to a life of only half-consciousness. Yet despite being angry and frustrated, it was this kind of situation that I found myself attracted to, working with this patient group. Walking back to the ward, I suddenly got a fire in my belly and decided that if I achieved nothing else during this job, it would be to ensure Mrs Broadhurst had received the care she deserved.

When I tell people that I plan to specialise in mental health care for older people, they respond in one of two ways. Either they joke that they'll be needing my services – to which I reply that my first patient shall be my mum, who I shall take great pleasure in locking away (that was a joke, in case you're reading this, Mum, please don't disinherit me) – or they recoil in horror.

'Oh! How depressing! Why would you want to do that?' they ask in disbelief. Even Ruby turns her nose up in disgust, and this is from someone who hacks off people's limbs for a living.

People point to the fact that there is no cure for dementia, that it is unforgiving and relentlessly bleak and that it's a constant uphill battle because of poor funding and limited resources. This, perversely, is precisely why I want to do it. It enrages me that the most vulnerable group of people should be so disenfranchised. I was inspired to work in this field by a manager of a day hospital where I worked before applying to medical school. She treated each patient with dignity and respect and encouraged me to see each one as an individual. Unfortunately, she is in the minority. Often the hardest thing to battle against is not the disease itself, but the apathy and complacency it engenders in others. It's this attitude that's depressing, not the patients.

* * *

I returned home and as I walked through the door I could hear Flora and Lewis talking in the kitchen. I went through and sat down at the kitchen table and lit a cigarette.

'How was your day?' asked Lewis. I told him about what happened with Mrs Thomas and the ECT. His mouth fell open.

'You did what?' he gasped.

'I walked out,' I said.

'No, I don't mean that, I mean why did you ever volunteer in the first place? It's barbaric,' he replied in disgust.

'Well no, it's not like that at all,' I began, finding myself now in the odd position of defending ECT having refused to do it only ten hours earlier.

'They strap them down on the table, screaming. I've seen the films,' he said. I was surprised at Lewis. Usually he was very calm and clinical, but this was irrational. It wasn't like that at all.

The front door slammed and Ruby put her head round the corner, 'Oh, Lewis, nice to see you, have you come round to cook for us?'

'Certainly not, and judging from the washing-up piled in the sink, even if I had, I doubt there's a clean pan in the entire place.'

'That's Ruby's fault,' I said, not liking to be associated with the squalor she existed in. Hopefully he wouldn't go upstairs to my bedroom and see the piles of dirty plates on my desk.

Ruby sat down at the table and dropped her bag on the floor, pointedly.

'Right, Ruby, we were just talking about ECT. What do you think about it?' I was confident that Ruby would provide a sensible, rational analysis.

But before she could answer, Flora, who until now had been strangely silent, suddenly stood up and delivered a shock of her own.

'I'm pregnant,' she said, before sitting back down to stunned silence.

5

Team Member

'It looks like an aubergine, doctor,' said Mr Clements, his face contorted. Now, at this point, I had no idea what he was referring to but I reasoned that the only thing that should look like an aubergine is an aubergine, and it certainly doesn't take a medical degree to realise no part of the human body should ever look like one.

'Right, what exactly looks like an aubergine?' I asked, tentatively, as I pulled the cubicle curtain across. Mr Clements looked down and I followed his gaze to a blanket draped over his lap where there was a discernible bulge.

'Down there,' he said, embarrassed.

'You mean, your penis?' I asked. He gave a slow, pained nod. 'You mean it looks like that in size, or in colour?' I asked, in an attempt to prepare myself for what I was about to see.

'Both,' he replied with a wince.

This, I thought to myself, is going to be an interesting morning.

I was covering A&E and in that department, you see

all sorts. Humanity is laid bare in its most vulnerable, raw form. The cases that walk, stumble or are wheeled through the door range from the tragic to the ridiculous. I was as yet undecided which category Mr Clements would fall under.

'Well, I'd better take a look at what the problem is,' I said, in as matter-of-fact a way as possible.

Mr Clements hesitated. 'It's a bit embarrassing,' he said. 'I'm not going to have to show lots of people, am I? I mean, can we just keep this between me and you?'

'Don't worry, I understand. You just need to show it to me,' I said, utterly unaware how wrong I would be. Mr Clements gingerly removed the blanket.

'What,' I asked, as I let out an audible gasp in horror and put my hand to my mouth, 'has happened there?' Mr Clements shifted slightly in his chair. The offending object quivered slightly.

'I put this round it and then it started to swell,' he said, pointing to a thick stainless steel ring around the base of his genitals. His entire genital area was now so swollen around it that the ring was barely visible.

Now, I have thought long and hard (yes, I'm aware that both of these words are unfortunate given the story) about how to write about this ring without being indelicate. I'm pretty sure I'm about to fail, so if you're easily offended you might want to cover your eyes while you read the next few passages. The colloquial term for the object is a 'cock ring'. The name sort of gives away what you're meant to do with it but if you've never heard of one before then you should take this as an indication that you're not the sort of person who should do a Google search on it. Usually, when discussing such delicate matters, I descend into the doctor's trick of using a Latin word to obscure what I'm really talking about. But I'm not sure the Romans used cock rings and, if they did, the word certainly wasn't on the GCSE Latin syllabus, so I don't know it.

The purpose of a cock ring is to restrict the blood flow out of the penis and therefore maintain an erection for long periods of time. Usually they are made of leather with a fastening or rubber, and are therefore easily removed. Stainless steel, however, is less giving, and as Mr Clements discovered to his chagrin, removing them can be difficult as the penis becomes more and more engorged with blood. Given time, if the cock ring isn't removed, it can restrict the blood flow so much that the tissue in the penis doesn't get enough oxygenated blood and it starts to die. Whatever someone's reason for using one, you can bet it's not a dead penis.

'It got stuck,' he said. 'I tried to take it off but I couldn't. Some of the lads tried, too, but it was no good.' He looked at me furtively. 'I was at, erm,' he paused, as though trying to find the appropriate word, but appeared to give up, 'an orgy.'

I didn't like to say to him that I'd already guessed he hadn't ended up in this predicament from swopping knitting patterns at a WI convention.

'But how long has it been like this?' I asked. We were

both still staring at it as though it were a third person in the room.

'Well, I'd say about,' he paused as he looked at his watch and counted, 'thirty-six hours.'

'What?!' I said in utter disbelief. 'You mean it's been like this for a day and a half? Why didn't you come in sooner?'

'Well, I was having so much fun, I didn't want to leave.'

Fair point, why spoil a party just because part of your genitals starts to look like something that is usually stuffed and served to vegetarians as a main meal?

'But please, can we just keep this between ourselves? No one else needs to know, right?'

I looked at the enormous purple object in the room. 'I think I might need to get the consultant to have a look, but let's try to get it off with some lubricant.'

The ten minutes that followed do not qualify as my happiest moments as a doctor. A large tube of K-Y Jelly, clenched teeth (both Mr Clements and myself) and a good deal of screaming and shouting (ditto) were tried, but to no avail.

'It's no good, it's too swollen,' I said, wiping the perspiration from my forehead and a tear from my eye.

A nurse popped her head round the curtain. 'Everything alright? I heard shouting,' she asked.

I turned round and she looked at me, quizzically, and I watched her gaze drift to the trolley where Mr Clements was lying. Her eyes widened to the size of dinner plates.

'Oh!' she exclaimed. 'That looks,' she hesitated for a moment and I wondered if she'd say that it looked like an aubergine, 'well, erm, painful,' she said, tactfully.

'I can't get the ring at the base off,' I explained.

'Let me have a go,' and she moved towards Mr Clements.

He braced himself and the monolithic member quivered slightly once more.

Nothing, the ring wasn't budging.

'I'm going to get the consultant,' I said with resignation.

Dr Banna looked at me with utter disinterest as I explained the problem in the office.

'Squeeze it hard and then just use lubricant. It'll slip off,' she sighed.

'I've tried that and so has a nurse, it's not budging,' I explained. She sighed once more.

'Do I have to do everything in this place?' she said under her breath as she pushed her chair back noisily and went over to the cubicle.

'Oh!' I heard her exclaim as she pulled back the curtain.

More huffing and puffing and ten minutes later, the ring remained.

'Get urology,' she said, 'the weirdos love this sort of thing,' and she stood back and folded her arms.

I found the urology doctor, who agreed to come down to the department and take a look.

'Oh crikey,' he said as he walked in. Mr Clements put his head in his hands.

'Don't worry, this is a urologist, he specialises in this sort of thing,' I said, 'he'll be able to sort it out.'

The urologist looked at me with a pained expression then frowned and sucked in his teeth in the manner of a mechanic who is just about to rip you off on the price of a carburettor.

'Have you tried squeezing it?' he asked.

'Yes,' I sighed.

'Lots of lubricant?'

'Yes,' chorused the A&E consultant, the nurse and I.

'I'm going to have to get my consultant to see this,' he said, and vanished, returning several minutes later with not one colleague, but two.

'Anyone else want to join in?' said Mr Clements as he looked away. By now he was blushing such a shade of scarlet his face almost matched that of his penis.

'Have you squeezed it and used lots of lubricant?'

'Yes!' we all shouted, including Mr Clements.

More sucking in of teeth followed.

'We'll have to mechanically remove the ring,' decided the consultant.

Several minutes later, the consultant was gently sawing away while all the males in the room watched through their hands, one female nurse poured water on his genitals to keep them cool and another tried to keep the erect penis away from the saw. It hardly made a scratch on the surface of the ring.

By now there were two nurses, Dr Banna, the A&E consultant, three urologists and myself.

Then the fire brigade arrived.

This had been the brainwave of one of the nurses, although quite how she'd sold this to them when she called, I never ascertained. If ever you're asked how many firefighters it takes to remove a cock ring, I can definitively tell you: four. So there were now twelve of us surrounding poor Mr Clements.

We moved to a larger cubicle to accommodate the work force. In an attempt to preserve his dwindling dignity, we all tried to shield his penis from prying eyes, by surrounding the bed and shuffling along as it was pushed to the next cubicle while holding up a blanket and sheet to cover his less than modest modesty.

By now the urologists had decided to try to relieve the pressure by doing a 'needle decompression' on the penis. Now most men will agree that the words 'needle' and 'penis' should never be used in the same sentence and the pained expressions from the male staff suggested we felt it almost as much as he did. This procedure involved inserting a needle into the penis to siphon off the excess blood. It offered some relief. However, the penis was still too swollen and now in rather a fragile state, so the firefighters set about trying to remove the ring with an angle-grinder. For twenty minutes.

Eventually, hey presto, and the cock ring was off. The urologists were convinced that the penis had been saved. The assembled doctors, nurses and firefighters broke out into spontaneous applause. OK, so we hadn't saved a life, but we had saved a sex life. I looked round at the vast number of people standing round his bed. So much for him just showing me. Just then, a medical student popped her head round the curtain.

'Have I missed anything?' she asked.

After the morning's excitement I decided to phone Ruby and see what she was doing that evening.

'Yes?' said an unfamiliar voice at the other end of the telephone.

'Oh, erm, hello, I wanted to speak to Ruby, is she there?' I could hear a strange noise in the background and wondered why someone else was answering Ruby's mobile.

'I'll put you on speaker phone,' said the voice.

'Hi, Ruby, who was that who answered the phone?' I asked.

'Oh,' replied Ruby, 'that was Anya, one of the theatre nurses. I couldn't answer myself because I'm scrubbed-in.' The strange noise continued in the background. It sounded like a dentist's drill.

'What?' I said, rather confused. 'Do you mean you're in the middle of an operation?'

'Yes,' replied Ruby. 'I'm just doing a below the knee amputation.' It was at that moment I realised that the strange noise I could hear was, in fact, an electric saw. Ruby was using it to cut someone's leg off . . . while she was talking to me. I felt a little sick.

'Erm, don't worry, I'll call back,' I said, feeling faint. I know as a doctor I was supposed to be used to that sort of thing, but a leg amputation is particularly gory and just the thought of it sent me weak at the knees, let alone hearing it on the other end of the phone.

'Don't worry, it's nearly off. What did you want?' asked Ruby.

I really didn't feel that this was the moment to discuss going out for a cigarette.

It may come as a surprise that surgeons are talking on their mobile phones in the high-tech environment of the operating theatre. There is a myth amongst patients that mobile phones are banned in hospitals because they interfere with equipment. Ask any surgeon and they will explain that this simply isn't true. The truth is that doctors have known for years that, except for specific parts of Intensive Care Units where there might be equipment sensitive to electro-magnetic interference, mobile phones are perfectly safe in hospitals. I don't know a single doctor who doesn't use their mobile phone on a ward.

Ruby had told me that when she wasn't doing an operation by herself, but instead assisting Mr Griffiths, her chief task was to hold his mobile phone to his ear when he got a call from his wife. Not only did he assure her that there was no risk of the phone interfering with equipment, but also that its use in the operating theatre was actively saving lives: his.

'If I don't speak to my wife to tell her I'm late, she'll kill me,' he explained.

Amongst doctors it is felt that trusts have not dispelled this mobile phone myth, and indeed, have helped perpetuate it by actively banning mobile phones on the wards, for two reasons. Firstly, there are the very valid concerns around the disturbance they can cause if every patient on the ward has them, as well as concerns around liability if they are stolen or damaged. Secondly, though, by banning mobile phones, all patients are forced to use the bedside phones, which have been introduced over the past few years in hospitals. Trusts are involved in 'revenue sharing' to earn money from the calls made from these phones, which charge a premium rate. Years ago there were payphones on each ward that could be wheeled to a bedside if needed, but with the introduction of bedside 'entertainment suites' these have been removed, forcing everyone to pay a premium.

With hospitals being run more and more like businesses in an attempt to increase revenue, the sick have become insidiously taxed, in a similar way to patients being charged to use hospital car parks. If we are going to introduce market principles into hospitals, then it is only fair that there is competition, and this should extend to communication. I'm not going to say I welcome the widespread use of mobiles on wards with open arms – or should that be ears – but I do welcome the fact that patients who have them aren't at the mercy of companies who have a monopoly on their contact with the outside world.

'Give me half an hour and I'll meet you outside. Give me a call if you're delayed,' said Ruby, the horrendous noise still audible in the background.

'Actually, I think I'll just send a text,' I reply.

* * *

Eventually, Ruby was free and we met for a cigarette in our usual spot by the bins at the back of A&E. Ruby arrived with two cups of coffee, balancing one on top of the other in one hand and wrestling with her pager in the other, while simultaneously trying to light a cigarette. I took one of the cups from her and avoided being burnt by the naked flame that she was waving about while also talking on her mobile. If she wasn't a doctor, she really could be in the circus.

'No, I wouldn't try to pull it off unless it's black,' she said, and took a long drag on the cigarette. She was giving advice to one of the Foundation Year doctors. After a few minutes she hung up and turned to me. 'Poor things, do you remember what it was like when we didn't know anything?' she said, taking a slurp of her coffee. I wondered if I did know anything, except how to look and sound like I did. I decided we had more pressing things to discuss.

Since Flora's shock revelation of her pregnancy several days ago, Ruby and I had barely had time to discuss it. She'd been on call and I hadn't seen her properly away from Flora. The most significant impact it had had on us was that smoking was now banned in the house. Ruby had not appreciated this.

'I can't believe that just because she's got up the duff, we all have to suffer,' she said, sulking. 'And as for getting into the bathroom before work, it's a joke. I've twice had to shower at work. You know what those showers are like in the doctor's mess, you feel dirtier after stepping in them than you did before.'

'It's morning sickness,' I replied, feeling that Ruby really wasn't engaging with the bigger picture. 'But who the hell is the father?' I asked, trying to focus Ruby's mind on a topic that didn't immediately relate to her.

'Well she won't tell me,' replied Ruby sullenly. 'I asked her last night when you'd gone to sleep and she just refuses to say.'

'It's obvious then, isn't it?' I said, shaking my head. 'What possible reason could she have for not telling her closest friends unless it's Housewives' Favourite.'

Ruby sighed heavily. 'I know. All that stuff he said to me after we split up about being a changed man and stuff, I knew that was tripe. He's no different and this time he's gone and ruined someone's career.'

It was true that Flora's pregnancy couldn't have come at a worse time for her. Not only was it highly unlikely that Housewives' Favourite would be taking an active role in the child rearing, but Flora was just at the beginning of her training and on a temporary contract that expired after the year, so she would miss out on proper maternity leave.

'Is she definitely going to keep it?' I asked.

Ruby shrugged again. 'God knows what's going through her mind right now. She's so distant at the moment, I feel like I'm walking on eggshells whenever I'm around her. I'm certainly not going to bring up the topic of termination with her.'

Just then Dr Palache arrived and our conversation had to come to an end.

'What are you two gossiping about, then? Out here, thick as thieves as always,' he joked. For a moment I wondered if we could tell him and get his advice, but I thought better of it. It would be unfair to expect him not to tell Lewis, and once that happened, we might as well have taken out an advert in the national press.

'Oh, nothing much. Ruby was just telling me about an amputation she did this morning.' Dr Palache pulled a face.

'I have no idea what the appeal is,' he said. 'Be a radiologist, it's much better. I just get to look at pretty pictures all day.'

'And you get a lunch break,' added Ruby, sardonically.

'You bet,' replied Dr Palache just as Ruby's pager went off and she scurried back to A&E to answer it.

Shortly afterwards, my own pager went off and I was called to the ward. Marsha was on leave but Tracey, another nurse, was in charge and she'd called me, panicking.

'It's really kicking off, you've got to come up here,' she said, breathlessly.

I immediately put down the phone and rushed to the ward, expecting a full-blown medical emergency when I arrived. I could hear the alarm ringing long before I reached the ward. It was echoing down the long, friend-less corridor and I broke into a jog. I arrived at the ward and was met by Tracey.

'She's being very threatening and I think she might

need sedating,' she said, looking back over her shoulder as she stood holding the door open for me.

The noise of the alarm had disturbed the other patients and several of them had congregated outside their rooms to see what the commotion was about. At the far end of the ward by the nursing station stood several other nurses who were trying to calm a woman who was shouting.

Above the sound of the alarm, I could hear her scream a list of expletives and then, 'I just want a smoke, for God's sake.'

I had only briefly met this patient yesterday on the ward round with Dr Webber. She was in her mid eighties and had Alzheimer's. Last week she had been found wandering late at night by the warden of the block of flats where she lived, and the night prior to her admission she'd fallen down some steps outside her flat during the night. She had been admitted so that the social workers could find somewhere more appropriate for her to live, and so I hadn't had many dealings with her until now.

But I knew exactly what this was going to be about, because it had happened before with other patients. All NHS hospitals went 'smoke free' with the introduction of the smoking ban a few years ago. The smoking rooms were closed and for most patients, this just meant a slightly tedious trip downstairs to stand by the entrance, wafting smoke on to passersby. However, for the more disturbed patients – particularly those on my ward who had dementia and were being observed – they couldn't smoke because they couldn't be allowed outside. There was the offer of nicotine replacement patches, but this failed to appreciate the psychological prop that a cigarette represented for many of them, or allow for the fact that many of them had been smoking for a large proportion of their lives. Being admitted on to the ward was disorientating enough without this one constant in their lives being taken away as well.

Being draconian about people smoking on the wards has worrying possible ramifications. It threatens the relationship between the staff and the patients and erodes the civil liberties of a group of already disenfranchised patients. I worry that a strategy that people have developed to overcome stress will be suddenly taken away from them and, as patients become distressed and angry, increasing levels of medication will be used to sedate them. Patients should be encouraged to give up smoking, but standing there trying to calm the woman, I wondered if this was the time or the place. It definitely shouldn't be used to insidiously enforce a public health agenda. While we are supposed to live in a free, liberal society, things like this set alarm bells ringing.

There are some rather unusual things that a doctor can prescribe for their patients. Years ago people used to be prescribed Guinness, and in fact, while working in surgery in my first year I twice prescribed a tot of whisky for patients. It's very difficult to justify six years at medical school when you're writing 'Famous Grouse' on someone's drug chart. I've always rather liked the idea of prescribing someone gold, which is used in certain cases of rheumatoid arthritis. Unfortunately, unless your doctor likes you very much indeed, it comes in the form of an injection or tablet rather than an engagement ring.

There have been times I've wanted to prescribe a treatment that unfortunately has yet to make it into NHS spending policy – haircuts. If you want to help people, you could do a lot worse than becoming a hairdresser. Unfortunately, I had to settle on becoming a doctor because I have the innate style of an ulcer. The ritual of going to the hairdresser's can be, in itself, therapeutic. Grooming plays an important role in the lives of most gregarious primates, and humans are no exception. Sitting in a hairdresser's and getting things off your chest is pretty similar to sitting in front of me in an outpatient clinic and talking, except I'd be rather put out if you asked for a cup of tea and a copy of *Good Housekeeping*. But it runs deeper than that. Not only is hair of social and cultural importance, but since becoming a doctor I've learnt it can also be a good indicator of how we're feeling. When people's mental state begins to deteriorate, one of the first signs is that they stop combing their hair and, in fact, Dr Webber often said that the time to start worrying about my patients was when I noticed that they've stopped doing their hair. It seems that what's happening on top of your head is a good indicator of what's going on in it.

Mrs Daniel had been in a serious accident the previous year and her GP had become worried that she was developing agoraphobia – a fear of leaving her house – as well as depression. He'd offered her several appointments to see him in his clinic but she hadn't attended. He visited her at home and started her on antidepressants but they'd had little impact. She'd then developed pneumonia and was admitted to the ward and, on hearing this story and knowing my interest in mental health, Dr Webber challenged me to see if I could help her.

'My world has fallen apart,' she told me, as I sat by her bedside.

There were several pictures of her and her husband on the table next to her bed. But the pictures of Mrs Daniel on the table, and the Mrs Daniel that sat in front of me, couldn't have been more different. In person, her eyes looked sunken, she'd lost weight, but the most dramatic change was her hair. While in the photographs her elegant, silver hair was neatly trimmed and coiffured, it was now matted and hung limply around her face. It's not easy talking to people about their appearance, but the GP had specifically noted in the referral letter he'd written at the time of her admission that he was concerned about Mrs Daniel's deterioration in self-care.

'I didn't see the point in making the effort any longer,' she explained when I broached the subject, 'and now I dare not go out looking like this. What would people think if they saw me in this state?'

She rarely ventured outside. It was a vicious cycle and someone needed to intervene. I wondered if, perhaps, as well as increasing the dose of antidepressants, getting her hair done would give her a boost in confidence, and in turn, this would mean that she felt happier leaving the house and would be able to get back to her old self. But cuts in the NHS tend to be more concerned with budgets than barnets, so I was at a loss what to do. It was Marsha who came up with a plan.

'Ask Brendan,' she suggested. He was an occupational therapist on another ward, but apparently used to be a hairdresser. I gave him a call and he agreed to help, so a few evenings later he paid her a visit on the ward when he finished work, scissors and hairdryer in hand. When I saw Mrs Daniel in the outpatient clinic a few weeks later after she'd been discharged, she was transformed.

'He's done such a good job, hasn't he? I've been down the Irish club to show it off to everyone,' she beamed. 'He's wasted in the NHS,' she added, as she walked out of the door. I, however, think that's the best place for him.

My clinic was nearly over. I just had one more patient to see. It was a follow-up from several weeks before. Mr Gillespie. He practically bounced into the room.

'How are things?' I asked while he was enthusiastically shaking my hand.

'Son, things couldn't be better,' he said, beaming.

'You saw the urologists, then?' I asked as he sat down opposite me.

'Yes. They gave me a good going over, tweaked some of my medication and gave me some tablets and now I feel like I'm in my twenties again.'

'Oh right, that's great, so no more, erm, problems down below, then?' I asked, not wanting a repeat of our graphic conversation so soon after lunch.

'Rock hard,' he said. I gulped, feeling that really this was more information than I needed. 'Mavis has been on a cruise for the past few weeks but she's back on Sunday and she's invited me over for dinner, I'm going to show her what I can do. And I've got another date with someone I've been chatting to online next week. It's all go!' he said.

'Well, that's, erm, great,' I said, pleased that I had a happy customer but wondering what I'd unleashed on the unsuspecting public. I saw him out of the room and watched as he practically skipped down the corridor.

It's time to lock up your grandmothers.

6

A Bitter Pill to Swallow

'Drop your trousers then, Max,' he said, like an old friend.

Except he wasn't an old friend. And actually, none of my friends – old or new – would come out with such a request. I hesitated, and looked round the room. No chance of escape.

'Come on, let's have a look,' he said in a disconcertingly jocular tone.

This was entirely self-inflicted as, after all, I had made the appointment. I unbuttoned my trousers as he popped his glasses on and scrunched up his nose. Really, there's no need to squint, thank you very much.

Doctors make awful patients, principally because they're all hypochondriacs, and I am no exception. Having found a little lump, I managed to convince myself that I was going to die. I decided I should do the sensible thing and get it looked at. This was quite an unusual step, as doctors tend to prefer not to rely on other doctors, but instead make their own assessment, which is inevitably a wildly inaccurate worst-case scenario. Ruby, for example, has had bubonic plague several times. Not only is it amazing that she has managed to contract a disease that has been practically eradicated from the western world, but also that it was cured with bed rest and Lemsip.

Of course, it wasn't until I was in the waiting room, feeling slightly uneasy about being on the other side of the sick-role and with no prospect of a stethoscope to dangle in front of my modesty, that I began to panic. But it was too late to back out by then. I swallowed hard and stared at the ceiling while he did what he had to do. Phew. I'm sure he was trying to put me at my ease, but there was something about his demeanour that just made it all the worse.

'Well, Max,' he said, 'nothing wrong there.' And then, as I walked out he did it again. 'See you, Max.'

It seemed that at some point we'd become friends and I wasn't even aware of it. Why else would he be calling me by my first name? I don't want to be friends with my doctors because occasionally they have to do things that no friend in their right mind would do to you. Doctors touch you and prod you and generally do things that are not nice to talk about in polite company. What if he really did see me again? Would he keep up the jocular air? Buy me a drink and talk about testicular lumps in a laddish tone, as one might do about Arsenal's last away match?

'How'd it go?' Ruby asked while she paced the room. The smoking ban was still in place in our flat and no one had dared to go against it, even her.

'Have a nicotine gum. You're making me nervous,' I said. 'It was OK, he doesn't think it's anything to worry about.'

There was a pause for a brief moment as Ruby rummaged through the drawer to find the nicotine gum that Lewis had bought for the flat as a present when Flora first told us about her pregnancy. He's such a GP.

'It was a bit weird, though,' I continued, 'he kept calling me Max while he was examining me.'

'What did you want him to call you? Darling? Honey?' she said as she chewed and smacked her lips together.

'No, I just mean, it made me uneasy him calling me by my first name while he did something so personal. It just didn't seem professional.'

'Oh yeah, I hate that too. You hear that all the time these days. It's like everyone is everyone else's best friend. And what's with patients being called 'clients' now, too? Ewww, I hate that, it's like I'm a prostitute.' She paused for a moment, chewing her gum. 'Except I'm not as well paid.'

It seems to me that in recent years the trend for using first names has become *de rigueur*. I do think that there are times when it is appropriate for a doctor to use first names. Sometimes, particularly with younger patients, it's less intimidating and helps with engagement. When I worked with homeless people at the Phoenix Project I always used first names because surnames only further emphasised the clear divide that already existed between my patient group and myself. There are also times when a long-standing relationship between doctors and patients means it would seem strange to carry on the pretence of things being merely professional. But it's the wholesale adoption of assumed intimacy that gives me the creeps. There's something wholly disrespectful about the bawling of 'Gladys, have you opened your bowels?' across a hospital ward by someone young enough to be their grandchild. It pretends that everyone is on the same level, when clearly they aren't and they shouldn't be. I think it's part of a wider problem whereby no one likes to think that they should be deferential to anyone else.

'I actually like calling patients by their surnames,' continued Ruby. 'It tells them you respect them but also gives a bit of emotional distance, both for them and me. It sort of reminds everyone that it's a professional relationship.'

I nodded in agreement. Doctors have mistaken being caring with being intimate. And as I discovered, when you've got your trousers round your ankles, you don't want your doctor to be any more intimate than they have to be.

It had been several weeks since I last visited Mrs Broadhurst in the nursing home. Since my first visit I had been back once to review her. She was still heavily sedated and when I gently suggested to the matron that this wasn't in the patient's best interests and that we should try to manage her behaviour without resorting to medication, I was met with hostility.

'You can't do that. Since she's been on that tablet, she's been so much better.'

'What do you mean, though? How has she been better?' I pushed.

'It's meant that we can all get on with our jobs in peace without being constantly bothered.'

There was something about the matron that gave me the creeps and this statement only served to emphasise this. Her logic contained a fundamental error, as Mrs Broadhurst's well-being should not have been linked to whether or not the nursing staff had time to get their work done and then sit and watch *Midsomer Murders*. It was becoming rapidly evident that the nursing home was not the best place for Mrs Broadhurst. Dr Webber was right – if I simply took her off the medication, what would I achieve? Having a resident who is no longer sedated and shouts out and is disruptive doesn't mean they are going to start employing more staff and training them in how to care for people with dementia. They'll just get the GP back in to prescribe the antipsychotic again.

At the suggestion of Dr Webber, I went to speak to Jeannie, one of the social workers at the hospital. I found her in an office, surrounded by files and reams of paper, sitting on a swivel chair with her short, squat legs dangling jauntily below. She was in her fifties, plump with a short, beak-like nose and large oval glasses pushed high up onto her face, making her look like an owl. She cooed gently as I told her my concerns.

'Well we can reassess her and claim that her needs

aren't being met in her current placement. But it's a long process and I'm not sure there are even any vacancies in a specialist unit at the moment,' she said, staring absentmindedly at one of the large piles of paperwork, which I assumed consisted of many more people like Mrs Broadhurst.

'What about NHS continuing care?' I suggested. This is an option for those people who have multiple, complex needs that can only be met by specialist nursing input. Rather than a nursing or care home, continuing care is more like a hospital ward. It has resident doctors and nurses and is funded by the NHS, so it's not means tested and is therefore incredibly expensive and only reserved for the very worst patients whose needs cannot be met elsewhere.

'Well, I doubt the panel would think she was severe enough,' said Jeannie, pushing her glasses even further up her face. 'There's a serious funding implication with that option and the primary care trust is unlikely to sanction that.'

I let out a sigh.

'Look, don't be disheartened, go and reassess her and write a report outlining your concerns. I'll see what I can do.'

I nodded and went to leave, turning to thank her but her head was already out of view, buried in the mountains of paperwork.

I walked back towards the wards, past the doctor's mess, deep in thought. I wondered what would happen to me when I became old. I have a fantasy that when I am old, I am going to live in the Savoy like Elaine Stritch. Pragmatists, who would include my bank manager, may point out that this is unlikely, but still I can think of no better way of growing old disgracefully than being waited on by room service and having afternoon tea with a view of the Thames. In fact, years ago, it was quite common for wealthy older people to check themselves into a hotel when living at home had become too much for them. It certainly beats the present prospect of being dumped unceremoniously in an old-folks' home while social services sell off all your worldly possessions to pay for it.

Mrs Broadhurst's situation had shown me that the pitiful options available to older people needing care were not fit for current pensioners, let alone the pensioners of tomorrow. For old people who are unable to live independently and require care, it would seem that the founding principle of the NHS – that care is free at the point of use – has been largely abandoned.

The current crisis has its roots in the early days of the NHS. The post-war Labour government, filled with utopian ideologies, wanted to create the kind of care for older people that previously had been the preserve of the rich. Before state provision, those who could afford it lived in hotels, with private nurses tending on them if needed, while the majority lived at home with only basic care, provided by family members or charitable organisations. The National Health Service Act 1946 and the National Assistance Act 1948 promised that the inequalities of the past would forever be put asunder. Or so it was thought. What it actually did, unintentionally, was create two parallel systems of care, and it was between these two systems that Mrs Broadhurst, and undoubtedly thousands of other older people, were now trapped. The NHS, it was decided, would provide a universal system of health care that was free at the point of access, while the National Assistance Act ensured that local authorities would provide a supplementary system for those in need of 'care and attention' or 'personal care'. The latter category was meant to be for those who, a bit weary and tired of life alone, wanted to move into hotel-like accommodation where they could be looked after, and was therefore means tested. It was never intended that this would include those who were infirm.

While the motivation for these two pieces of legislation were honourable they, unfortunately, left a loophole that subsequent governments would exploit. By drawing a distinction between those who were medically 'sick' and those who wanted 'care and attention', an artificial line was drawn that has been slowly shifted over the past few decades to force more people to pay for their care. With NHS trusts desperate to keep expenditure down, the arbitrary line between what constitutes medical care and what constitutes personal care has shifted. Someone who has had a stroke, for example, may be left requiring help with washing and dressing. This, now, constitutes personal care and is therefore means tested, despite the fact that it's clearly because of a medical problem. If they have an ongoing, complex medical need, however, they may be eligible for NHS long-term continuing care, in which case they wouldn't be required to pay a penny, because it's deemed 'medical care' and is therefore funded by the NHS.

What Mrs Broadhurst really needed was specialist-nursing care. Surely the NHS should ensure that she gets the care she needs? But despite working hard all her life and paying her taxes, the state was refusing to pay for her.

For those who'd like to discuss this further, you'll find me in the Savoy bar, frittering away my money before I get old and infirm.

I had passed the doctor's mess but as I walked up to the hospital, I bumped into Flora walking towards me.

'What're you up to?' she asked.

'I'm on my way to visit a patient in a nursing home. It's a bit of a nightmare, really,' I said, and started to explain the situation with Mrs Broadhurst. 'She's just dosed up to her eyeballs. It's wrong,' I continued, but I could tell Flora wasn't listening fully. 'Are you OK?' I asked, moving closer towards her. She had tears in her eyes. 'What's wrong? What's happened?' I asked and put my arm around her just as she broke into full sobs.

'I'm just so worried Max,' she began. I ushered her towards the doctor's mess. 'I just don't know what I'm going to do about money,' she continued. 'I'm not going to be able to even afford the rent when I give birth. I've got no savings. I'm up to my eyes in debt from medical school. I just don't know what to do. It wasn't supposed to be like this.'

I pushed open the door to the doctor's mess and was relieved to see that it was deserted. She sat down and I boiled the kettle. I was sure that this was about more than just money, but it was easier to focus on money than the other issues that might be really preying on her mind, such as what she was going to do in the long term with regard to her career.

'Look, it's not the end of the world. We'll come up with something,' I said. I thought for a moment. 'What about the spare room? I know it's nice having it for when people want to stay over, but it's a luxury we can do without.'

'How would that work?' she asked, looking up as I put a cup of tea down on the table in front of her.

'If we let out that room, it will reduce your rent. I don't mind paying the same amount and I'm sure Ruby won't. It's small, but we can get enough for it that your rent will effectively halve.' Flora seemed to cheer a little. 'It's not much, but it's a start at least,' I ventured.

'That's so kind. Are you sure you wouldn't mind? It seems a bit of a cheek for me to profit from the spare room and not you and Ruby. Do you think she'll mind?' she asked.

I shook my head. 'Of course not. You know what she's like – she can't smoke it or drink it so I doubt she even realises we have a spare room.' Flora laughed.

'Let's talk about it tonight. We can advertise around the doctor's mess or in the paper,' I suggested.

Flora looked at me earnestly. 'Oh, let's not get another doctor. Let's get someone normal.'

I left Flora with the promise of advertising the room in the local paper and made my way towards the bus stop. Just as I was walking out of the hospital gates, I heard a voice calling after me. I turned round and saw Ruby hurtling towards me.

'You're not leaving, are you?' she said, out of breath.

'Erm, yeah, for a bit. I'm going on a home visit. Why?' I asked.

'I've called a meeting of all the junior doctors this afternoon to discuss the plans to close the A&E department. Everyone's talking about it and we need to do something,' she said.

Ruby was always getting fired up about things like this. At medical school she had single-handedly organised a sit-in protest in the finance department of the university that lasted for a week, after a handful of students had been suspended for not paying their fees on time. She had an uncanny knack for being able to get away with being confrontational and combative towards people she thought were in the wrong. I'm sure part of this was down to the fact that she was quite beautiful and had a striking similarity to Audrey Hepburn, but also because people could see that she really believed in what she was saying. Her protests were never motivated by self-interest, but rather an overwhelming sense of anger at any injustice or inequality. Even for those who found themselves the focus of her ire, this was strangely mesmerising and seductive. She had become a legend at medical school after she interrupted a college formal dinner for great university luminaries and their guests, dressed in surgical scrubs and wearing a Tony Blair mask, to ask them to donate money to the protesting students barricaded in at the other side of the university. After making an impassioned speech about equality of access to higher education she passed round a bucket and, to her amazement, all the guests began emptying their pockets. She left to shouts of 'Good show!' 'Keep it up!' and, 'Don't let the buggers get you down!' and the audience then erupted into applause, drowning out the attempts of the vice chancellor to apologise to his guests for the intrusion.

There was something reassuring about knowing that Ruby had taken up the cause for the A&E department, but I did have my doubts that she might have met her match with the hospital management.

'I'll try to get back in time,' I said, shrugging my shoulders. 'I've really got to do this home visit.'

Ruby stared at me with a look that I had come to understand as meaning that no was not an acceptable answer.

'OK, I'll see you later then,' I said, glancing at my watch.

* * *

I arrived outside the front door of the nursing home and rang the bell. Claire, the domestic, opened the door.

'Oh, hello doctor,' she said, a little flustered, 'is Matron expecting you?'

'No, I don't think so,' I said, knowing full well that she wasn't. Arriving unannounced had been an idea of Dr Webber's to see exactly what was happening in the nursing home without them having the opportunity to prepare for my visit.

Claire showed me into the hallway where I stood, waiting for the matron. I looked into the lounge and again, there was a smattering of old ladies sitting motionless on chairs, their chins resting on their chests. Asleep or dead, I wondered to myself, not sure if there was much difference in this place. The woman nearest the door looked up and I recognised her from my first visit when she had done exactly the same.

'Are you here to see me?' she asked.

I opened my mouth to say no, I wasn't, but hesitated. I looked up the stairs in front of me but there was no sign of the matron, so I turned and went into the lounge. The woman immediately perked up and, with great effort, sat up properly in her chair. I sat down in the chair next to her.

'Oh, hello dear,' she said.

'Hello,' I replied. 'I'm Max, I'm a doctor, I'm just visiting.' This, it seemed, was the only prompt she needed to start talking.

'My father was a doctor,' she began, and with that,

she talked non-stop until the matron appeared at the entrance to the lounge.

She looked wary and scowled at Mrs Lawrence, the woman I was talking to.

'Don't bother the doctor now, Clara,' she said in a clipped tone and then turned to me. 'And to what do we owe the pleasure of your company, doctor?' she asked with a smile stretched across her face so tightly that it almost turned into a snarl.

'I've just come to review my patient,' I replied coldly.

I didn't like this matron and I saw no point in trying to hide it from her. She had obviously thought that with a cup of tea and a bit of banter and sycophancy, I'd be on her side and there'd be no chance I'd interfere or make her life any more difficult that it had to be. She'd clearly been put out when it became apparent that I wasn't going to collude with her in this. I'll admit to being a little afraid of her. But as she stood there and I looked into her cold, dark eyes, it suddenly occurred to me – she was afraid of me. This wasn't something I was used to. In the hospital, the nurses weren't afraid of me because they had seen me at my weakest and most vulnerable. They knew that they could easily complain about me to my boss, make my life a misery on the ward and be obstructive and unhelpful if I didn't respect them. The power dynamic was more even. But here, I represented an unknown force, someone from outside who could potentially upset the status quo and must therefore be mollified, contained and managed as best as possible. As far as she was concerned, it didn't matter that I was still a junior doctor. I might as well be Dr Webber, as she had no power over me. This realisation gave me confidence.

'It was nice chatting, Mrs Lawrence,' I said, not standing up. 'I'll come back later and we can finish our chat.' This had the desired effect and the matron stood, clearly uncomfortable at this suggestion.

'Oh, well she's not your patient, is she doctor?' she said, trying to pass it off as a joke, 'I'm sure you've got lots of other people to talk to who actually are your patients.'

I didn't respond but walked past her and pointed up towards the stairs. 'This way isn't it? Second floor? Don't worry, I'll find my own way.' And with that, I left her.

I walked down the corridors and, again, past the bedroom doors opening into single rooms, each containing a single person, sitting, alone, silently. Each room I passed was very quiet and still and, just occasionally, one of the people sitting by the open door would look up momentarily as I walked past. Mrs Broadhurst was as unresponsive as before. I looked around her room. There was a dresser with some framed photographs of her and her husband, and judging from the ice creams in their hands, probably taken on holiday. I reasoned it was from the 80s. As I looked, I suddenly realised that it was familiar. Yes, just there was where the lifeboats were, and just there, in the distance, was the aquarium on the Cobb. I'd been there, at the very spot where this photograph had been taken. It was Lyme Regis, where my family used to go on holiday when I was a child. In fact, if this was taken in the 80s, maybe I'd been there at the same time. The coincidence was too much and I was proud of myself for having recognised a place I hadn't thought about for years from just a few snippets of scenery in the background of a faded photograph. I instinctively turned to Mrs Broadhurst to share this amazing discovery but she lay, motionless, her mouth slack and her dead eyes half open. I put the photograph back on the dresser and stood, staring out of the window, remembering my childhood summer holidays.

'And now we come through to the bedroom,' said the tour guide. I was eight years old, this was a National Trust property, and we were on our family summer holiday. It had been swelteringly hot so we'd stopped off on our way to Lyme Regis. Clearly, this was not a good combination.

'I'm bored,' I whined to my mum. 'Can we go outside and play bongo ball?' She glared at me. I was silent for a few moments. 'I'm hot, can I have an ice cream?' I asked, changing tack.

She shot me a withering glance and narrowed her eyes. 'Behave and listen,' she hissed, and turned back to the tour guide. I huffed and began a low-grade sulk.

'And of course in this very room, in 1840, Jemima gave birth to her first son, Thomas,' continued the tour guide.

I'm sure I'd been annoying the poor guide up to this point, and now, in a flash of inspiration, came her victory.

She looked directly at me. 'It was a very difficult birth, and Jemima had lost lots of blood. The doctor feared she was going to die, so once the baby was born, they put him in a chamber pot and pushed him under the bed, leaving him for dead so they could concentrate on saving the mother.' It began to occur to me that if I didn't behave, perhaps this woman would push me under the bed and leave me for dead.

'They didn't care about the baby?' I asked, horrified.

'Saving the mother was more important in those days,' replied the tour guide, pleased to have finally got me captivated. 'Several hours later, when the doctor had saved Jemima's life, they heard a noise from under the bed and discovered the baby alive and well.' She concluded, 'it was a very good thing for English literature that the baby did survive, because he grew up to be the novelist and poet Thomas Hardy. But in those precarious times, children were relatively expendable, while the death of an adult could ruin a family and turn them destitute.'

I stood, remembering what the guide had said, through the prism of adulthood and my experiences with Mrs Broadhurst. How things have changed, I thought. Because of a multitude of complex social and cultural shifts, from better sanitation to the welfare state, we have fewer children, and the children we do have represent more investment for us. The old are cast aside, moved out of sight into places like this where they wait and wait until they die.

Only a few weeks ago Ruby had been sitting at the

kitchen table and read out an article from her surgical journal about how we now spend more on plastic surgery than we do on tea. While I'm not suggesting we go back to an era where we left babies to die under beds, it does seem that as a nation, we have become obsessed with youth. Why are so many people now determined to fend off the advancing years by going under the knife? What is so wrong with getting old? As we have ceased to value the contribution that older people make to society, so we see the ageing body as grotesque. We have begun to look towards science and medicine to provide the answers to our metaphysical questions. But these institutions, unlike religion, fail when it comes to death. They cannot reassure us or provide us with satisfactory answers about what happens after we die. As a result, we fear old age, because we fear death. And so the ageing body is further reviled because it reminds us of our own mortality. As a society, youth is paraded as the ideal and we have become obsessed with how we look. It's so undignified. Give me lapsang over liposuction, any day.

I went downstairs and looked around, furtively. There were no staff about, so I resumed my position next to Mrs Lawrence in the lounge. She perked up once more and began talking.

'Do you like it here?' I asked, tentatively. She looked plaintive for a moment.

'There's nowhere else to go, really, but it does get lonely.'

'What about the staff, do they talk to you?' I asked. She laughed. 'Oh no, not really, they're very busy.'

'And the doctor, does he come?'

'He visits sometimes, but I don't really see him. He sits with them in the kitchen and smokes out of the back door. I know when he's here because my window is directly below and I can hear them and smell the smoke. I don't think he's that bothered about us oldies. None of them are, really. Who can blame them?' She paused for a moment. 'They don't feed us,' she said suddenly. Until this point I had assumed that Mrs Lawrence was entirely *compos mentis*, but this comment made me suddenly question whether she, too, was demented. Whatever criticisms I might have about nursing homes, they're not likely to be starving their residents.

'What do you mean?' I asked, guessing that she probably forgot about meal times and thus assumed they hadn't happened.

'Well, the portions are so small and often it's inedible. I'm not a fussy eater, but often I just have to leave what they serve up and go hungry.'

I wasn't sure whether or not to believe her on this matter.

'Do you know who the prime minister is?' I asked, bluntly. She laughed heartily.

'Winston Churchill,' she replied. My heart sank. 'I'm joking, son, of course I know who the prime minister is. He's an odious little man and if I could leave this place and go to Downing Street and give him a piece of my mind, I would. I'm not like some of them here. I know what's going on, I'm not senile.' Perhaps she was telling the truth about the food here.

'Have you told them there's not enough food?' I asked.

'Oh yes, but it makes no difference. The person who cooks is also one of the domestics and she hasn't got time to prepare the food properly. We have a lady who comes sometimes, she brings her dog for us to look at, and I've told her about it. She used to work up in the hospital, a nutrition-something?'

'A nutritionist?' I ventured.

'Yes, that's it. I told her and she said she'd look into but it's not done any good.'

Just then, the matron appeared in the doorway to the lounge. She looked at me with suspicion before fixing a smile onto her face.

'All done are you?' she said, pointedly.

'Yes, thank you,' I said, and stood up and turned to Mrs Lawrence. 'Well, thank you for talking to me, it's been really interesting and I'll see if I can help you.'

'Do let us know when you're going to visit again – if you do decide you need to visit, that is – and we can make sure there's a member of staff to help you so you don't have to hang around next time,' said the matron in a perfectly passive-aggressive tone as she walked me out.

'Yes, I'll try to,' I said, and walked into the bright afternoon sun as the front door slammed behind me.

* * *

That evening I got home to find Ruby sitting at the kitchen table. I'd missed the meeting about the A&E closure and hadn't seen her until then. She didn't say anything when I walked in and I tried to avoid the subject initially, before it became apparent that she was annoyed with me. I decided to broach the subject head on, but not before I made her a cup of tea and had put the nicotine gum on the kitchen table.

'Sorry I missed the meeting this afternoon, I didn't get back in time. I was just so busy I thought I was going to die,' I said, dramatically.

'Its just so depressing,' Ruby said, letting out a loud sigh.

'I'm sorry, really, I had so much to do.'

'It's not just you, it's everyone. Loads of people came but then they all just stood there, shrugging, saying "What can we do?" and that making a fuss is futile.' She took a sip of tea. 'They're all so apathetic. I know they care about it and everyone agrees it's scandalous that closing A&E is even being considered, but no one will stand up and say so. They're all too busy or too tired or too worried about making waves.'

'I know, I know,' I said, still feeling guilty that I was included in her scorn.

'Lewis said he'd help and so did Flora, of course, and one of the vascular surgeons. The A&E doctors were out in force, obviously.'

'Well that's lots of people then.'

'But it's not everyone. I don't understand why everyone isn't determined to do something,' she said, shaking her head in genuine disbelief.

'That's just the way people are, Ruby, you know that. But anyway, what exactly is it we're going to do?'

'I don't know,' said Ruby quietly, 'but we'll have to do something.'

7
Ruby and the Rough

'I'm not having someone called Norman Bates as a flatmate,' said Ruby forcefully.

'You can't pick people based on their name,' protested Flora.

'Erm, yes you can. Next you're going to be telling me you're happy to share a bathroom with someone called Hannibal Lecter. If people were sensible and avoided psychopaths after their first film, then there wouldn't be sequels, would there?'

I wasn't sure Ruby had fully grasped the concept of fictional characters but it did seem to be tempting fate. I had horrible images of him standing there at the kitchen sink, late at night, washing up and then turning to me and saying, 'a boy's best friend is his mother, don't you think?' as I backed out of the room clutching *Freud for Beginners*.

'Right, well you've got to make your mind up one way or the other,' interrupted Lewis.

He had come round to offer a detached, objective opinion while we interviewed prospective flatmates, but instead had scared the most promising ones away by subjecting them to a Stasi-style interrogation about their careers. 'You don't want them defaulting on paying the rent, it just makes sense,' he argued.

'But also, you don't need to demand to see their full CV and last five years of pay slips and request they submit a written report detailing their career aspirations and goals,' retorted Flora.

'I'm just being thorough.'

'Ok, so no to Norman,' I conceded.

'What shall I put down as the reason for that outcome?' asked Lewis, who had drawn up and been busy filling out a colour-coordinated 'assessment and evaluation' table with columns for each person we saw.

'Because he's named after a fictional psychopath and Ruby is worried she'll get murdered in the shower,' I suggested.

Lewis paused for a moment. 'That won't all fit into the box. I'll just summarise it as "psycho".'

'Fine, whatever,' I replied, rapidly losing the will to live. 'What about that Richard bloke?' I suggested.

'Oh no, he smelt disgusting,' replied Flora, screwing her face up.

'Erm, that might have been me,' Ruby said, with a little apologetic smile. This had taken up the best part of the evening and I was beginning to wish I'd never suggested renting out the spare room.

'What about Marinella?' asked Lewis, looking at his list.

Flora shook her head. 'Too skinny.' We all looked at her, puzzled.

'What? I won't be able to borrow any of her clothes,' she explained.

'You're pregnant, Flora, pretty soon everyone's clothes are going to be too small for you,' I remonstrated.

'Except maybe Bernard Manning's,' added Ruby, unhelpfully.

'You can't have him as a flatmate,' said Lewis, in horror.

'He's dead, so no, we can't,' I said, putting my head in my hands.

'Well he's not on my list, anyway,' muttered Lewis with relief.

'Right, look, this is driving me mad. Let's have this one,' interrupted Ruby and she leant across and plonked her finger down on the list of names. We all leant forward and peered at it.

'Terry,' said Lewis, reading the name out loud.

'Yep, him, loved him,' said Ruby with an air of decisiveness. 'Now I'm going outside for a smoke.'

'You just picked any name, you didn't even look where you were pointing,' protested Lewis. 'He's got far more crosses than ticks, according to my chart.'

'No, I love him. Best candidate we've seen,' said Ruby resolutely.

'Do you even remember what he looks like?' asked Lewis.

'Erm, yeah, he was male, wearing trousers, he had hair, sort of cut short,' answered Ruby breezily. We rolled our eyes.

'Well, I suppose he's as good a flatmate as any,' said

Flora with a shrug. 'He was the DJ, wasn't he? I quite liked him. He was very smiley.'

'Right, that's decided then. Terry it is,' said Ruby, and she got up from the table to go outside for a longed-for cigarette. And that was how we came to have Terry as our new flatmate. It was also how Ruby would come to realise that there were worse things than living with someone named after a fictional psychopath – namely, living with Terry.

'So what do you do?' asked the taxi driver.

My heart sank. Please, just drive, I felt like screaming. I knew the way the conversation would go. It always happens like this: I tell him I'm a doctor, then one of two things happen. Either he shows me a part of his anatomy and asks me what I think of it – Is it cancer? Is it infected? Do I think it's going to drop off? – or he launches into a tangential story about a relative's misdiagnosis and how doctors don't know it all, do they. And I invariably have to nod and try to wind up the conversation by the time we reach my destination, or face sitting outside for hours listening to someone's medical history – as if I don't get enough of that at work.

It occurred to me that I could say I was an accountant or something, but I wasn't sure how to explain why I was heading to a hospital dressed in a shirt and tie on a Sunday evening, if this were the case. It's pointless lying, I decided.

'I'm a doctor,' I said. 'I'm just about to work a

nightshift.' And then quickly added, 'and I'm really late already, so I'd really appreciate it if we could hurry.'

'What type of doctor are you, then?' he asked, slowing down rather than speeding up. One in a real hurry, I thought to myself.

'Well, I work in general medicine and geriatrics, but I'm on call this evening covering various wards.' I waited for the usual responses.

But instead he said something rather surprising. 'You believe in God, then?'

I looked out of the window; this was definitely not the road to Damascus.

'Erm, no,' I replied, but thought how at this precise moment in time I'd appreciate some divine intervention with regard to the accelerator. He looked at me in the rearview mirror, puzzled.

'Then how do you do your job? Seeing all that suffering, don't you ever wonder what the point of it all is? I'm a believer, me, and I take a certain solace in it, when I see people suffering, knowing that there's something bigger than us and this world,' he said, thoughtfully.

I suppose the thing about being a doctor is that, while certainly you come up against the major questions concerning the human condition, it's easy to avoid confronting them because firstly, you're often too busy to go to the toilet let alone engage in questions about the meaning of life, and secondly, you'd rather be asleep in bed. But certainly I can understand how people take comfort from religion, especially when faced with the bleak reality of death and disease. A belief in God, of course, is an article of faith, inconsistent with rationalist, scientific understandings of the world. But I can't help but wonder if science itself is an article of faith as well, relying on the tendency of the brain to want answers to complex questions, to believe in the un-believable as much as religion is argued to rely on it. Hard line rationalists argue that religion is a ludicrous set of beliefs spread by the gullible. But I've never seen an electron. For most of us, all of science is an article of faith; something spectacular and beyond comprehension that we take as being true without ever really being able to question it with any authority. It's easy for scientists to throw stones at religion, but surely they are merely the high priest at the altar of another God?

The cab driver arrived at the hospital and I paid and got out. Later that night, I was called to certify a patient dead. Before being admitted he'd been in a nursing home for two years with dementia, and for the last year, I read in his notes, he hadn't recognised his wife – a desperately sad ending to any life. I examined the body, signed the death certificate and left the ward. On the way back to the on-call room I thought about my conversation earlier with the cab driver. And then I went to sleep, but not before remembering a childhood prayer.

The following week, after my night shifts, I decided to get to the bottom of Mrs Lawrence's allegations about the nursing home not feeding the residents properly. I'd finished my report on Mrs Broadhurst and so made my way over to Jeannie's office on the pretext of getting her opinion on it. At the same time, I thought I'd see if she could do some digging.

'Ah, yes, I had heard about this,' replied Jeannie. 'A visitor to the home – I think she was a volunteer – had put in a complaint on behalf of a resident to that effect. The problem was, the resident didn't want to be named, so there wasn't a great deal we could do. A spot-check was undertaken.' Jeannie paused as she rifled through some of the papers on her desk. 'I've got the report here somewhere, I think. Well, anyway, it said that there were some areas for improvement but that overall things seemed OK.'

'It's the attitude of the staff, the matron in particular, as much as anything,' I began.

'Max, you've got to realise, there are some truly awful places out there and we need to focus attention on them. I've been to that nursing home and it's really not the worst. Just last week one down the road was banned from accepting any new residents because the care was deemed so bad.'

'What about the residents that were already there?'

'Well, they remain, but the home has to undergo further investigation before it is allowed to open its doors again.'

'Oh, so it's not just closed down, then?'

Jeannie laughed. 'Oh no, things would have to be really bad before that happened. It just doesn't work like that. No, at best some of the staff are fired, replaced with others.' Jeannie could see my utter disgust at the system she was describing. 'Look, Max dear, we're trying to work in an imperfect system here, we're trying to do our best.'

I could see that this was the case. I didn't blame Jeannie in the slightest. There was little she could really do to increase the accountability of these places.

'If you have real concerns about the place, then put it in writing and we'll see. But bear in mind, Max, if you stay in this job much longer you'll see far worse places than that.'

This, it turned out, was very true. In fact, I didn't have to wait long at all.

I don't know anything about decorating.

This became painfully apparent just before putting the spare room up for rent. We decided it might be a good idea to give it a lick of paint. The landlord wasn't particularly keen on the idea, but we reasoned that to offset the squalor that Ruby tended to generate in the flat and which might put people off moving in, it was an investment that was worth shouldering ourselves.

I thought I'd save a bit of money and do it myself. Looking back, I don't know why I thought that this would be a good idea for someone who has difficulty even pushing a trolley around B&Q. Gloss painting is not as easy as it looks. After an entire weekend spent trying to get emulsion to adhere to a damp patch and trying to remove a blob of gloss from the carpet (neither of which is possible, I've now discovered), Flora intervened and called in the professionals. After all, they know what they're doing, and clearly I do not. That's why we have professionals – they are trained to do jobs that others can't. Imagine taking out your own appendix. Yuck.

A few days previously I had been sent by Dr Webber to review a patient of his in Willowbank, a nursing home near the hospital. He'd received a frantic phone call from staff saying that something was wrong and asking him to review her. She was confused and disturbed and they wanted his advice. He agreed, by which he meant, yes I'll send my minion, namely me. It was clear straight away that Mrs Jacobs wasn't well. She was in her seventies and had vascular dementia. I examined her and it quickly became apparent that the problem was not, in fact, a deterioration in her dementia, but rather that she had the beginnings of pneumonia. It is often the case in people both young and old that when they have a severe infection they become confused, and in Mrs Jacobs' case her underlying dementia just compounded this. So I telephoned Dr Webber and discussed the case with him and we agreed that she should be started on antibiotics. This was hardly rocket-science. I wrote her antibiotics on her drug chart, explained to the staff what was wrong and how I was treating it and left. Fairly straightforward.

But when I arrived back on the ward after seeing Jeannie, Marsha handed me a message.

'It's from Willowbank,' she said. 'They called saying that they're worried about one of their patients who you saw earlier in the week.'

I telephoned and they explained that Mrs Jacobs was getting worse, not better. For a brief moment I looked at the pile of paperwork on my desk and considered telling them to call the GP. But I'd been the one to see her and start treatment, so really I should be the one to follow this up. I left the ward and caught the bus the short distance to the home.

One of the care workers met me at the door and ushered me up to Mrs Jacobs' room. She was short of breath, cold and clammy. I didn't understand it.

'What's her blood pressure?' I asked the carer standing behind me. I was met with a blank stare. No basic observations had been done – blood pressure, temperature, pulse and respiratory rate – for the simple reason that the staff didn't know how to do them or why they were important.

I raced into the office and began to arrange for an ambulance to take Mrs Jacobs to a hospital. She was *in extremis*, and if she didn't receive urgent treatment she would die. It was then that I looked at the drug chart. Where I had written her antibiotics, the boxes that should have been signed to say it had been given were blank. I looked at the carer.

'Has she had any of her antibiotics?' I asked.

He shrugged his shoulders.

Another carer who was in the office piped up, 'Oh, the drugs you prescribed when you came last, they didn't have those at the pharmacy, so we're waiting for them to get them in stock.'

I stood open-mouthed at their ignorance.

But why should they know the importance of the medication I'd prescribed and that you can't wait three days before treating a pneumonia, any more than I should know that you can't wash gloss paint off with water (although it seems that everyone I've told does know this, but you get my point)? The staff at nursing and care homes are paid a pittance and not trained appropriately, when actually they have a vitally important job to do. Their job isn't given the respect it should afford.

I made hasty arrangements for Mrs Jacobs to be admitted to my ward. The ambulance arrived and I hitched a lift in the back, sitting next to Mrs Jacobs.

Looking at her, a sudden feeling of rage overcame me. I knew that she represented a problem that was going on up and down the country to the extent that it was a national scandal. But it's easy to blame the carers when in fact it's not their fault that they aren't given adequate training for the job they're expected to do, and there's no legislation in place to ensure that the owners of these homes invest in their staff.

The ambulance stopped and I got out while Mrs Jacobs was wheeled into the A&E department. I had only been back on the ward for a few minutes after leaving Mrs Jacobs in A&E, when Marsha appeared at my office door.

'Sorry, duck, I've got another message for you. It's the coroner's office about Mr Harris, who you pronounced dead? Remember, he was a patient on the ward, the one with the bed sores?' She handed me a piece of paper with a scrawled number on it.

Why is the coroner's office calling me, I wondered? I stopped dead in my tracks and my blood ran cold. Oh God, I thought, I've caused an explosion. I swallowed hard. Every doctor has a horror story like this to tell. It's always a friend of a friend, or someone somebody once knew and until this point, I had always been convinced the stories were the stuff of urban legend. When you begin work as a junior doctor, your greatest fear is pronouncing someone dead when in fact they're not. I'm sure most members of the public are relieved to hear that the diagnosis of death is something that doctors take considerable time over. But with experience you realise that, if in doubt, leave them for a bit as there's nothing like a bit of *rigor mortis* to confirm your suspicions. As you gain confidence, it is then that you start worrying about something else – pacemakers. This is because, as urban myth goes, if you send someone to be cremated before removing the pacemaker, they explode, taking the crematorium and, presumably, all the mourners with them. While many people don't want their funeral to be a sombre affair, most wouldn't want them to go off with a bang quite like this. Of course, before someone is cremated, various morgue attendants, funeral directors and so on will have checked for a pacemaker just in case the doctor has missed it.

I'd assumed this was a fool-safe process but even so, stories were abound of exploding corpses because of a doctor not making the vital checks before signing the cremation form. I wracked my brains as I dialled the number. Had I checked for a pacemaker? I thought I had, but couldn't actually remember doing it. It had been late at night. I had been tired. To my relief, it transpired this was not why they wanted to speak to me.

I was still a junior doctor and had a lot to learn. That's what the coroner's secretary at the other end of the phone was telling me and I wasn't disagreeing with her. What we weren't seeing eye-to-eye about was Mr Harris. Mr Harris and his like aren't often seen by the public. You have to work in hospitals before you get to see them. He was well into his eighties and bed bound. He couldn't eat solid food, so was given a rather disgusting-looking puréed food that, I was assured by the ward nutritionist, provided all the required vitamins, minerals, carbohydrates, fats and so on to keep a human being alive. The smell was rather off-putting, so I took her word for it and didn't try any myself. Mr Harris had no teeth, and was brought in without his dentures.

Everyone knew he was going to die, and I have to say that since starting work as a doctor, so many people have died that I've gotten rather used to it. Not immune, just used to it. Mr Harris was in a bad way, and it came down to one, really rather sad reason: money. He had several of the rather euphemistically-termed 'bed sores'. Bed sores are open wounds caused by nothing more than the pressure of one's body over extended periods in one position. What they are a sign of is neglect. Mr Harris was too incapacitated to turn himself, and so it was the staff's responsibility to turn him to stop the sores from developing. This, evidently, hadn't happened. Instead, he'd been left in the same position until his skin broke down and the underlying tissue destroyed and you could see the bone underneath. Not a pretty picture. I'd never seen a bed sore before, although Marsha and Tracey assured me that I'd see them again.

He didn't die from bed sores, although it's not unfeasible that he could have – they can get infected and lead to septicaemia and then death. But instead he had a stroke. The issue with the coroner was what I'd written down as the cause of death. In addition to stroke, I'd included neglect. I'd done this because I felt at the time, as did the nurses, that this had contributed to his overall ill health and ultimate demise.

'People don't die from neglect,' explained the coroner. 'Neglect isn't a medical condition. He died from a stroke.'

'Of course they die from neglect,' I replied. 'Mr Harris was neglected and then he died.' To me, this was simple.

But of course I had moved out of the realm of medicine and into that of politics. The two, I was learning, are interlinked, and far from simple. If death certificates don't register 'neglect' as a cause of death then no one can ever officially die from neglect. And medicine, along with politics, has a penchant for things official. Which means it's difficult to assess quite the level of neglect going on in institutions up and down the country.

'He was old,' he said, trying to reason with me. 'You can put down old age as a contributing cause of death along with stroke, if you like.' This seemed rather baffling to me – how could something as subjective and culturally determined as 'old age' be a valid cause of death, when enormous gaping bed sores weren't? But arguing was pointless. I agreed to change the death certificate and put down the phone. I rifled through the filing cabinet and found Mr Harris's notes so I could complete a new certificate. It was then that I saw it. As I copied his date of birth from his admission form, I noticed his address. He had been a resident of the same nursing home as Mrs Broadhurst.

Something in me snapped. Although they were at different nursing homes, all the anger I had felt at the incompetence concerning Mrs Jacobs' pneumonia rose to the surface again and I decided that something had to be done.

First the way Mrs Broadhurst had been treated, then the accusations about the food from Mrs Lawrence and now the discovery that Mr Harris had been a resident there. It was too much. I understood what Jeannie had said about it not being the worst nursing home in the area, but that wasn't a reason to ignore the plight of people who had no one to defend them, I reasoned. I sat down and wrote a formal letter of complaint about the nursing home, raising concerns about their treatment of residents and the care they were delivering, and emailed it to Jeannie. Marsha came in to offer me a cup of tea and I told her what I had just done.

'Oh, good for you,' she said. 'I've already informed social services of the fact Mr Harris came in with a bed sore. That matron should be ashamed of herself, allowing something like that to happen when she's in charge. It ain't right.'

I smiled to myself, pleased that there were people like Marsha who obviously did care.

'Next time you see her, you make sure you give her a piece of your mind,' she said, as she walked out to make the tea.

'I will,' I nodded emphatically. At that moment I would never have believed that when I did in fact see the Matron again, I'd deny any knowledge of the complaint.

I left the ward and made my way to the doctor's mess to collect my things, taking a shortcut through the A&E department. I decided to check on Mrs Jacobs, but she'd already been transferred to a ward. I was about to leave when Andrea, one of the A&E nurses, beckoned me over.

'I know who you've come to see. I just couldn't believe it when I saw him in here again,' she said, wide eyed. I looked at her blankly.

'What do you mean? I'm just cutting through, I'm not here to see a patient.'

'You're not here to see our friend?' she replied with a knowing smile.

'Who?' I asked, confused. She nodded behind me towards one of the cubicles.

'He's only gone and done it again,' she said. I followed her gaze and there, sitting up on a bed with a blanket over his lap, was Mr Clements. He saw me and gave an apologetic shrug.

'You're joking,' I said, aghast. 'Tell me he hasn't come in with the same problem.' Andrea gave a slow nod.

'I've already called the fire brigade,' she said with a sigh.

As I walked out of the A&E department, something else caught my eye. It was a poster, pinned up by the ambulance bay. 'SAVE YOUR A&E!' it said in big red letters. Below were written the words: 'There are plans to close the A&E department of this hospital, putting the lives of local residents at risk. Act now before it's too late and tell the trust what you think.' It didn't give anything more specific than this; no contact details, no union logo. Clearly, it was the work of one person who had typed something up on a computer and printed it off. I turned round and there was another one. And another one.

'Just don't make sense, does it?' said someone behind me, and I turned round to see an ambulance driver looking at the sign over my shoulder. He was holding a polystyrene cup and took a sip from it. 'Where's the sense in closing this department? It's bloody madness.'

'How long have these been up?' I asked, pointing to the poster.

'Dunno, but everyone's talking about it. Whoever it was, they ain't gonna be in the good books of the bigwigs, I can tell you.'

There's only one person who can be behind this, I thought to myself, and went home to speak to Ruby.

I was late getting home, as I bumped into Lewis on the way and we'd gone for a drink. When I finally got in the flat I immediately knew that something was wrong. Terry had been moving in gradually as his tenancy on his previous flat still had a few weeks to go and Flora was working nights. I could see in the gloom that Ruby's coat was hanging on the banister. Yet it was strangely quiet and no lights were on.

'Ruby, you home?' I called out. Nothing. I walked through to the kitchen but as I did I glanced at the coat and noticed it was splattered with blood. 'Ruby?' I called out again. I thought I heard a noise come from her bedroom. I tentatively pushed the door open to find Ruby sitting on her bed, her side light on, surrounded by bloodied cotton wool balls.

'What the hell happened?' I asked as I moved into the room. Ruby turned her face away.

'Nothing, it's nothing really,' she said, but I could see that her head was cut and had been bleeding and her right eye was red and swollen.

'Ruby, what's going on? Have you been attacked?' She was silent for a moment.

'Yeah,' she paused, 'kind of. Well, assaulted I suppose.'

'When did this happen?'

'This evening,' she replied.

'We need to call the police. Have you called the police?' I said in a fluster.

'No, no, I don't want the police involved. It's only going to complicate things at work. I just need to think.'

'Do you mean a patient did this to you?'

'No not a patient,' she said, still deep in thought.

'Who then?' I said, confused.

'My boss,' she replied, looking up at me. 'Mr Griffiths did this.'

8

Difficult Conversations

It took some time before Ruby told me exactly what had happened with her boss. After finding her in her bedroom, I had helped clean her up properly and brought her downstairs. Flora was on nights and we both agreed that this was exceptional circumstances and not a time for nicotine replacement gum, so we both lit up a cigarette while I made tea.

'It just happened so fast,' she began. 'One minute I was standing in the Doctor's Arms, the next, he was on top of me, banging my head on the table. It was surreal, I almost can't believe it happened,' she said, shaking her head in disbelief.

'Hang on, you've got to go back. What where you doing in the pub with him in the first place?' I interrupted.

'Well, we'd finished an operation early and his wife was away, so he suggested that we all go for a drink. We'd spent all day in theatre and I thought, why not? A big group of us went, even some of the theatre nurses, too. We'd had a few drinks, I'd been joking with him. It was all fine. I went to the bar, got talking to some people and made my way back to where we were all standing and I walked past him and he was talking to Housewives' Favourite.'

'I knew he'd be involved in some way,' I said, hitting the table with my hand.

'No, Max, wait, listen.' She paused for a moment and had a sip of tea before taking a deep breath and continuing. 'Mr Griffiths was saying something to him and as I was walking past, Housewives' Favourite winked at me. It was just a bit of fun, that's all. You know what he's like. But Mr Griffiths turned round, all angry. But I couldn't work out why. I like him, he's an amazing surgeon and we get on really well. People find him really hard to relate to, he's almost autistic in that way – he finds it hard to connect to people, but that doesn't bother me. We have great banter when I assist him in theatre and the fact he's a bit aloof and odd is fine by me. He's just inspiring to be around. We've actually got to the stage where we tease each other and I feel comfortable around him and can say whatever I like. But I think, looking back, maybe . . .' her voice trailed off.

'He fancies you?' I ventured.

'I don't know. Maybe. Maybe it's more complex than that, maybe it's just that he's found someone he can connect with and it's not sexual. It's more intellectual. It's as though in recent weeks there's been a tension building up, an intensity, and tonight it just erupted. Anyway, I think he took against the idea that Housewives' Favourite was sharing a joke with me that he wasn't included in. I think he felt undermined – humiliated. As I walked past, he suddenly reached out and grabbed hold of my breast. Not in a sexual way, but in an angry way, as though he wanted to stop me from walking away from him. But it hurt. He's a big man and as I tried to pull away he twisted his grip. It all just happened so fast.' The cut on her head was still bleeding slightly and she dabbed at it with a cotton ball. 'I was holding a glass of wine in one hand and I tried to knock his hand away with my free hand but his grip was too strong and I just instinctively used my other hand to push him away and as I did, I threw wine from the glass at him. It covered his shirt and he just let go and then froze for a second. I stared at him and then the next thing I knew, this look of pure fury came over him. He pushed me face down onto the table behind me and got on top of me and swore at me, banging my head on the table. I couldn't move, I was pinned down.'

'Oh my God, I can't believe this. This is insane. What did everyone else do?'

'It was Housewives' Favourite, he was the only one to step forward. Everyone else just stood there in shock. He wrenched Mr Griffiths off me and punched him in the face. Then, without saying a word he picked me up and helped me into his car. Then he drove me home. He wanted to call the police but . . .' her voice trailed away.

'Ruby, I don't understand. You've just been assaulted by someone – by your boss, for goodness' sake – why would you not call the police?'

'I, I don't know.'

I began to get annoyed. 'Ruby, I think the bang to the head has affected your thinking. You must call the police.'

'And then what would happen? He'd get arrested and charged and then the hospital would suspend him, it would be investigated, he'd probably be struck off. What would that achieve?'

'It would be what he deserves,' I said. I was amazed that I was listening to this from Ruby, of all people. She was the arch-feminist and a man in a position of authority to her had just sexually and physically assaulted her.

'It was just as Housewives' Favourite was leading me out, I turned round and saw Mr Griffiths on the floor, trying to get up, and the look in his eyes, he was so pathetic. He knew what he'd done was wrong. We'd both been drinking. He's had his punishment. I felt sorry for him and I thought, if I make this official, he'll never operate again and all I'll have achieved is stopping a brilliant surgeon from working. He's one of the best surgeons in his field and a few seconds of madness means that thousands of people would be denied his skills.'

She was wrong. What she was saying was true, he would never be able to work again, but I couldn't accept that not going to the police was the right answer.

'I just want him to apologise, for him to mean it.'

'OK, look, just promise me you'll sleep on it, OK? Don't make your mind up yet. Wait and see how you feel tomorrow.'

'OK' she said, but I knew her mind was already made up. 'Housewives' Favourite has said I should take the rest of the week off anyway – I can't really go into work looking like this.'

She went to bed, leaving me alone in the kitchen. I sat in silence, thinking about what she had told me. I knew that it would be a loss to medicine if he never practised again, but surely it wasn't right to let him get away without being punished, even if his behaviour had been completely out of character. It was also one of the few times when I'd seen Ruby appear so vulnerable. It was also one of the few times in all the years I'd known her that I had really questioned her judgment.

'I really don't want to,' I said, the panic steadily rising in me. Dr Webber stared at me impassively then shook his head.

'It's important,' he said emphatically.

'I know, but it just feels . . .' I struggled to find the word.

'Awkward?' he offered.

'Yes,' I agreed, 'as though this just isn't the time to talk about this sort of thing.'

He put his hand on my shoulder. 'We have only a few hours if the organs are going to be of any use to anyone. We don't have the luxury of time.'

I swallowed hard. At medical school I had done a course on how to broach difficult subjects with patients but this was altogether different.

'I'll be in there with you,' he said, trying to calm my nerves, 'you lead the discussion though.'

I began to feel sick.

Earlier that day a woman in her early twenties had been brought in after a road traffic accident. She had suffered multiple injuries and had been rushed up to theatre. I had been involved in the trauma call as I was holding the pager and happened to be in A&E at the time. While their daughter was in theatre, I talked to the family as they waited. They paced about the room, desperate for any news. When it came, it was of the worst kind. Mr Butterworth had been the surgeon on call at the time. He'd been unable to save her life and she died on the operating table. He was not renowned for his emotions, but even he looked grief-stricken. Ashen faced, he told them the news. I sat with them for some time as they sobbed quietly and it was when I emerged from the room that I saw Mr Butterworth talking to Dr Webber. They beckoned me over.

'You've built up a relationship with them,' said Mr Butterworth, 'really, I think it's only right that you do it.' By this, he meant talk to them about organ donation. I imagined that this was the last thing they would want to think about just now.

I opened the door and sat opposite them, convinced that I was only going to make things worse for them.

Yet before I had even finished speaking the mother interrupted me, 'It's what she'd have wanted,' she said emphatically. While I'd imagined they might be angry with me for bringing up such a subject in their moment of grief, in fact they seemed pleased. They began telling stories about how kind and thoughtful and compassionate she was.

The father looked at his wife and smiled. 'She was always so generous in life,' he said, 'it seems fitting that it should continue now she's gone.'

Dr Webber and I left them and gave a gentle nod to Mr Butterworth, who was standing outside waiting to hear the verdict. It occurred to me that I'd been wrong in thinking it would be an awkward conversation. Nothing could take away the pain of having lost their daughter. Yet this last, final act had comforted them and helped them feel that the spirit of their daughter lived on in this act of generosity. Strangely, it was one of the most heart-warming conversations I have ever had.

I remember when I was fifteen years old and studying for my History GCSEs being horrified to read that, of all people in society, it was doctors in Nazi Germany who first implemented mass murder.

It was naive of me to think that doctors should be different from anyone else. The eugenic and anti-Semitic ideas that culminated in the holocaust received strong ideological and practical backing from physicians and psychiatrists, and indeed, the first victims of this were mentally ill patients. Even before the outbreak of war in 1939, it was doctors who ordered the forced sterilisation of 400,000 mentally handicapped and ill people, epileptics and alcoholics. Between January 1940 and

September 1942, over 70,000 mentally ill patients were murdered. These were chosen from a list of patients whose lives were deemed 'not worth living', drawn up by leading doctors, including nine professors of psychiatry. I've never understood how these doctors, who had joined a profession whose main aim is to relieve suffering, could be the cause of it, and on such a horrific scale. Humans, while capable of such bravery, compassion and kindness, stand apart from all other animals in the level of suffering they are capable of inflicting on each other. And doctors, I realised, are no exception to this.

But then we have people like Mr Sinclair. I met Mr Sinclair after he was admitted to my ward. He'd gotten an infected ulcer on one of his legs. He sat, propped up in bed, smiling, as I approached and introduced myself. He was in his late eighties, a bit unkempt and dishevelled. The old man in front of me certainly didn't look very special. But in fact, in the Second World War, that's exactly what he was. After talking to him about his leg ulcer, I sat on the edge of his bed and he began to tell me about his life.

'I'm not originally from this country,' he began, and went on to explain that he had fled from Poland when it was occupied by the Nazis. 'But then the danger really started,' he added. He was recruited into the Special Operations Executive. This, he explained, was an underground army that went behind enemy lines to try to bring the Nazis down. 'I don't talk about it so much; there are things I don't want to remember. But it is important for your generation to know.'

Mr Sinclair had gone throughout occupied Europe, along with countless other members of the SOE, sabotaging Nazi plans. The risks were very real. The life expectancy of an SOE wireless operator in occupied France, for example, was six weeks.

'But more than the fear for your own life, the thing that was hard – that's still hard now – is knowing that people died because of your actions. It doesn't matter that they were the enemy, they were still human beings,' he said.

All his family were killed in concentration camps. He went on to tell me some of the things he did, the operations he was involved in, and then started to tell me of some of the atrocious things he saw. How he saw his friend blown up by a grenade. How he found the bodies of a mother and child, both shot at point-blank range. It was obviously very painful for him to relive this, and I was honoured that he felt me worthy to hear it.

'Thank you for listening,' he said as I got up to go, when in fact it should have been me thanking him. And as I went to shake his hand, I noticed that he had started crying gently. As a doctor I know that I'm supposed to be removed from my patients to some extent, but as I walked away, I found myself close to tears as well.

I went to visit Trudy for a slice of cake and a chat. I wondered if she'd heard any more about the planned closures from A&E and, more importantly, if she'd heard about Ruby's assault. Of course, I knew she would have, but I wanted to know specifically what she'd heard and from whom. I went into her office and she was engrossed in a newspaper, which was spread out on her desk.

'What a relief, we're not here,' she said, still scouring the newspaper and not looking up.

'Do you mean about the A&E closure?' I asked.

'What? No, it's a report that's been published naming and shaming the worst hospital wards for cleanliness. It's some Department of Health thing.'

'You mean it's like a league table for dusting?' I asked as I looked around for evidence of cake.

'Yeah, kind of. And I tell you, the wards that have done worst are all your sort. You know, psychiatry.' Because it was widely known in the hospital that I wanted to specialise in mental health, and this was felt to be a rather 'exotic' choice, anything even remotely related to mental illness was directed to me.

I peered over and looked at the list. Sure enough, the worst offenders – those deemed 'unacceptable' – were psychiatry wards. The more I looked at the list, the more annoyed I got, not for what it was saying about the state of hospital wards in this country, but about what it wasn't saying about psychiatric wards.

Psychiatry is often referred to as the Cinderella profession. It's still waiting for the fairy godmother to make an appearance. Services run on a shoestring. There isn't even adequate funding to provide basic services like psychotherapy for many patients. Who's worried about finding money for a new vacuum cleaner when resources to provide patients with actual treatment are stretched? Psychiatric services are at the bottom of the pile when it comes to funding because it's not a vote winner.

But underfunding for psychiatry isn't all to blame. The general decline in hospital hygiene is because of the cleaners. Not the actual cleaners, but the way cleaning services are run. Only a few years ago, when I first started going into hospitals as a student, things were different. I remember to this day the name of the cleaner on the surgical ward. Everyone knew her. She took pride in cleaning the ward. She knew the patients, the staff. She was part of the team as much as the nurses, physiotherapists and doctors. But now, the job of cleaning hospitals has increasingly been given over to large companies that are only interested in profit. The companies cut corners. The cleaners change daily and are no longer part of the team. And if you treat cleaners little better than the dirt they're paid a pittance to sweep up, they don't do the job properly. In fact, while the shift to using contractors was aimed at reducing costs, I suspect that the increase in infection rates over the past few years has had the opposite effect.

Looking at the list, it also occurred to me that if you're going to emphasise the importance of anything on a psychiatric ward, there are more pressing issues than whether there are balls of fluff in the corners of the rooms. No one has open wounds that can be infected. What actually matters is that the environment is stimulating. There is a wealth of research to suggest that one's external environment affects the way one feels. If we want people on a psychiatric ward to be happy – and trust me, it would be a welcome change – then we need to spend time making wards look less like Victorian prisons and more like places where a person's broken mind can be put together again. The government is interested in dirt because it knows that this is what wins votes. But the real problems are swept under the carpet. While politics may be dirty, who'd have thought that dirt could be so political?

My pager went off and I had to leave Trudy alone with her paper, but not before swiping a slice of Swiss roll. I made my way past the doctor's mess and just as I did, I saw Supriya walk out. She looked ghastly.

'Are you OK?' I asked. She didn't reply but kept walking. I caught up with her. 'You alright, Supriya?' I repeated. She turned and looked at me with a pained expression.

'Oh Max, something awful has happened.' Supriya was usually very good at remaining calm but she was clearly panicking.

'What is it?' I asked as we walked together towards the main hospital.

'Haven't you heard? Last week, I was on call and I saw this man in A&E. He'd been referred because he'd taken a massive overdose of amitriptyline. You know how dangerous that is and there was something about him that made me nervous. His wife had come home early and found him and called the ambulance. In the department he was saying to me how much he regretted it not working and that he still wanted to die. Well, I was worried about him, you know, really worried. I had to write up my notes and page the psychiatry team and I needed to check how long he'd need a heart monitor on for, so I asked the security guards to keep an eye on him, just while I was away. I was only gone for a moment, I just turned my back and . . .' she stopped walking and closed her eyes as she remembered. 'One minute he was there, the next he was gone. I knew there was something about him, I knew he was going to try it again.'

'What happened, why didn't the security guards stop him?'

'Apparently they're not allowed to anymore. The security is outsourced now to some private company and the guards aren't allowed to stop the patients leaving the department. They haven't done the training or something. They just watched him walk out and when I returned, they just shrugged and pointed me in the direction he went off in.'

'Did you find him?' I asked.

'Yeah, we found him. He was brought in by ambulance an hour later after he'd thrown himself off the flyover. He was dead on arrival.'

'Oh Supriya, that's awful.' I knew exactly what she was thinking. 'It's not your fault. What else could you have done?'

'I can't help but blame myself. I just wish I'd stayed with him a bit longer, maybe said something to him that would change things.' She looked down at her shoes as she explained how she would now have to go to the coroner's hearing and how the hospital were refusing to accept liability because she'd left the patient unattended. 'I feel so guilty and I don't know what's going to happen. His wife will be at the hearing and I can't face seeing her. What should I do?'

Just then, both our pagers went off and we had to run to the hospital, leaving her question unanswered.

Doctors would like to think that they have the necessary knowledge and skills to make people better. But gradually I've realised that this isn't always the case. Sometimes, there isn't a cure and doctors don't have the answer, but that doesn't mean there isn't hope.

Christian was not a patient on our ward but appeared one afternoon. He was wearing a hospital gown and had a patient tag and had obviously just come over from the paediatric ward, which was further down the main corridor.

'I'm here to see the dog,' he said.

Marsha assumed this had been arranged and dutifully allowed him onto the ward to pet the dog that one of the hospital volunteers brought in each week. Christian was nine years old and had cerebral palsy because when he was born his brain was briefly starved of oxygen and this left him with brain damage. Medically, there was little that could be done for him but he and his parents coped well with his disabilities. Despite having learning difficulties, he went to a mainstream school and did well in lessons. He'd had to undergo several painful operations to help his walking, but last year he fell while at school and since then, he had been confined to his wheelchair. The surgeons investigated why he was still having difficulties walking. They had done a series of X-rays but were still baffled as to why he wasn't walking. He was sent for physiotherapy but after four months he had not progressed and was still using his wheelchair. He was seen by paediatricians, neurologists and rheumatologists. The braces, which encased his legs and helped him stand, were changed, but still no improvement. While he used to run around with the other children at break time, he now just sat and watched them. The concern amongst the doctors was that the longer he remained in the wheelchair, the weaker the muscles in his legs would become. They were considering doing another operation on his legs to see if this helped. But before this could happen, he was admitted with a chest infection. After several days of lying in bed with intravenous antibiotics, he began to improve.

We learnt all this because when they came to his bed on the ward round that afternoon, he wasn't there. There was brief pandemonium on the ward as the nurses searched frantically for a boy who, the doctors assured them, couldn't walk. Another one of the children said they'd seen him slip out behind a porter and it wasn't long before they found him safe and sound on our ward. They all stood in amazement as they watched him running round, laughing and shouting with the dog. His mother, who had been frantic, arrived on the ward behind the doctor but didn't seem surprised to see him on his feet.

'He just suddenly started walking a few weeks ago actually,' she said nonchalantly. The consultant paediatrician frowned. 'Our neighbours have got a new dog and it keeps getting into our garden and that was when he started walking. One minute he was sitting down and the next he was outside playing with it,' she continued.

The consultant smiled and said, 'Well, looks like that dog has done what none of us could do.'

'I don't understand,' said Marsha, as she ushered Christian towards his mum.

'Neither do I,' confessed the consultant, 'but I suspect that Christian's confidence was so knocked after having that fall that he needed a reason to overcome his fear and start walking again.'

'So he doesn't need another operation then?' asked Christian's mum.

'No,' replied the consultant, smiling, 'I'd say he needs a dog of his own.'

And with that, Christian, his mum and the doctors walked back to the paediatric ward.

9
A Week of Nights

The brain is an amazing organ capable of incredible things and it's cheering to know that if you wish hard enough, it might just give you what you want.

I stood in A&E at the beginning of my first night of a week on call, and thought back to when I was a teenager, sitting in my bedroom revising for exams, desperate to go to medical school but knowing that the only thing that stood in my way was the little problem of A-levels. Of course, my knowledge of photosynthesis, inorganic chemistry and how to use a Bunsen burner are now vague memories (though setting fire to Anne-Marie O'Connor's cardigan with aforementioned Bunsen burner is pretty clear, but that's another story). Despite the almost overwhelming desire to sunbathe, I spent hours cooped up in my bedroom memorising reams of facts to regurgitate in the exams, in order to make my dream of being a doctor come true. At the beginning I couldn't believe my brain would retain the amount of information I was expected to learn. There were times when I thought my head could burst with the detritus I was cramming into it.

But it held fast, and come the exams it served me well. Nearly a decade later, here I was, standing in A&E with the two letters 'Dr' gracing my name badge.

I'd not even had time to get a cup of tea before my first patient was referred to me. I'd been asked to see Mr Simcock, who, according to the A&E doctor, was saying some strange things. He had pneumonia and needed to be admitted.

'He won't stay, Max,' explained Andy, one of the doctors looking after him, 'he says he's got to get back to see his wife.'

Mr Simcock is in his late seventies and it's perfectly understandable that he's anxious about leaving his wife alone in their home. Perhaps she's bed bound or can't see well.

'Seems reasonable to me,' I suggested, and began to leaf through the directory for Social Services' telephone number.

'Max, she died four months ago,' he said, starkly.

'Oh, right, I see,' although I'm not sure I do. 'She has, I mean, she is, you know, buried or whatever . . .' I said tentatively.

'Oh, well yes, but he says that he sees her every evening, and wants to get back to her. Good luck!' he said, giving me the notes and heading off to tackle the steady stream of walking wounded cluttering up the department.

Mr Simcock used to be in the army.

'The Royal Air Force,' he corrected me, and then waited expectantly for me to amend the notes accordingly. He was married to his wife for nearly fifty years, 'and no time off for good behaviour,' he chortled.

He was sitting upright on the trolley, a gown stretched tightly over his corpulent frame. He had a thick, fat, white moustache, which seemed to be growing out of control and now covered his top lip and there were stray, mad, whiskers on the sides of his jaw where he hadn't shaved properly. When his wife died suddenly in the autumn, he didn't know what to do with himself. He paced around his bungalow for days after the funeral, not believing that she'd gone.

'And then, she'd probably been buried a week when I saw her,' he says, as if it were the most normal thing in the world. He went on to explain that she visits him most evenings, just as he's dropping off to sleep. Sometimes they talk, and other times they don't. 'She was always a bit of a nag, so I suppose she feels she needs to keep her eye on me. It's nice to know she's still there for me,' he said.

Post-bereavement hallucinations, where people see their dead loved ones, are a very common response to grief, particularly in older people. It's wish-fulfilment – the brain's way of giving the bereaved person what they so desperately want. Mr Simcock was worried that if he stayed in hospital he wouldn't see her. I suspected he'd spent much of his life telling other people what to do and wasn't going to do something just because I told him to. But I couldn't let him leave the hospital.

'What would your wife say if she thought you were risking your own health for her?' I asked.

He was silent as he contemplated this.

'I suppose you're right,' he replied slowly, and then looking round, 'and if I'm honest, it would be nice to get away from the old battleaxe for a bit. Over fifty years, and no time off for good behaviour,' he said again, still chortling.

With that settled he was admitted to a medical ward and I made arrangements for him to be followed up by the psychologists.

The night shift finally came to an end and Andy and I walked out into the bright morning sun, tired and hungry. My body ached and my head hurt and all I could think of was going to bed, yet I knew that in twelve hours time I'd be back, ready to start all over again. Anyone dreaming of becoming a doctor should be careful what they wish for – they might just get it.

By chance both Ruby and I were on call together that week. Usually a week of on calls meant that we'd see little of each other, as whenever one of us was arriving home, the other was off to work. But this gave us the opportunity to discuss recent events, even if it was in snatched moments in between patients. Ruby was back at work after the incident with Mr Griffiths. She'd had a meeting with the head of surgery, who had heard about what had happened and said he would support her if she wanted to make an official complaint about Mr Griffiths, but Ruby declined. She seemed to think that it was best to ignore it, although I wasn't sure the rest of the hospital would see it in that way.

'Look, you're not going to change my mind, so it's pointless going on about it,' she said irritably as we smoked a midnight cigarette round the back of the A&E department.

'We're just all worried about you, that's all,' I said, trying to pacify her. 'You seem to have taken it in your stride but I just worry that you're bottling it up. If it's your decision, that's fine, it just wasn't the decision I thought you'd make.'

'Well, just goes to show you never know someone entirely, doesn't it?' she said waspishly. I changed the subject.

'Terry seems nice,' I said, and Ruby nearly choked on her coffee. Terry had finally moved in properly and was proving to be a hit with Flora and I, but less so with Ruby. He liked to present the image of being a trendy DJ, dressing in oversized hoodies and long shorts, but this was ruined by the knowledge that in fact he worked in an office and his accent, despite his best efforts to conceal it, was clearly public school. He was more suburb than ghetto.

He was short and dark, with thick black hair and an eleven o'clock shadow. Some people might call him swarthy. Ruby called him a prick. This was because, despite liking to promote the image of himself as a bit of a lad, he was fastidiously tidy. He had only been in the flat for under an hour before he presented a rota for emptying the bins.

'Do they need emptying?' protested Ruby, 'We've never had to empty them before.'

'That's because I always do it,' said Flora pointedly.

'We'll, now there won't be any squabbles about it, because we'll all know who's turn it is,' said Terry breezily.

'There weren't any squabbles before you turned up,' Ruby muttered under her breath and Flora and I looked at each other and smiled. Washing-up was next on the agenda and this too got the Terry rota treatment.

'It just makes sense that either we each take responsibility for the washing up or we take it in turns to do it each day,' he said, apparently unaware of the havoc his suggestions were having on the social fabric of the house.

'What a sensible idea,' said Flora, clearly relishing this injection of much-needed domesticity to our lives.

Around the back of A&E, Ruby continued to complain about him.

'Oh he drives me mad,' she continued, as she ate her supper of a packet of Jelly Tots, 'he's always got an opinion about everything. And if he tells me one more time about recycling, I'll shove his plastic bottles . . .'

'Oh I think he's alright. I like it that he tries to make the place look nice. You must admit it's a pleasant change to come home to somewhere clean and tidy, and with toilet paper.'

Ruby softened slightly. 'I suppose so,' she conceded. 'It's just his manner, as though we're all in some minor public school and he's the head boy.'

We were joined by Tanya, one of the A&E nurses. Her dress was several sizes too small for her but she seemed not to be bothered by this.

'Have you heard?' she said as she lit a cigarette and eyed up Ruby's Jelly Tots. 'They're trying to close this place down.'

There had been talk of little else in the department since the news had gotten out. We stood around discussing and were joined by Malcolm, another one of the nurses.

'Have you heard?' said Tanya, turning to him.

He shrugged and took a sip of coffee.

'Someone should tell the local paper,' Tanya continued, 'it's a scandal. Them bloody managers, they don't know what they're doing. They won't be happy 'til there's no patients in this hospital at all and it's just us lot sitting about on our arses filling out forms.'

Ruby and I laughed.

'I dunno,' said Malcolm with resignation, shaking his head and sighing. We waited to see if he would make any further pronouncements, but nothing came, which was not unexpected. A contemplative 'I dunno' was usually the total sum of his input in most conversations, which, when discussing the A&E closure, was fine, but when discussing whether or not a patient had gone for their scans or was about to die, was slightly more irritating.

'We should do something though. Someone's got to make a stand, you know, kick up a fuss,' said Ruby with wild eyes, showing for the first time since the assault her usual spark.

'Oh, I couldn't agree more,' said Tanya enthusiastically, before adding, 'I can't though, obviously. I've got annual leave coming up and besides, I've never really been one to make a scene.' She gave a little laugh and looked up to the heavens whimsically. I could sense Ruby's irritation at this, but thankfully Tanya finished her cigarette and went inside before anything else was said.

Ruby's pager went off shortly afterwards and we both went back inside. I stood by the notes trolley and watched as she went over to her next patient. It was funny to think of how we'd all grown in competence and confidence since we first met at medical school.

Just then the door of the ambulance bay flew open and the paramedics rushed a trolley into resus. Everyone flew into action, including Ruby, who, as the on call trauma surgeon, immediately took the lead. There were two patients: a mother and her six-month-old son. The child was carried hurriedly in behind the trolley in the arms of one of the paramedics who looked at me as he passed with a pained, drawn expression. The child was obviously dead, his still, grey face evident when it was placed on a trolley next to his mother. Ruby worked frantically to try to stabilise the mother, but she was haemorrhaging from a torn blood vessel somewhere inside her body and had already lost a lot of blood from her leg, which appeared to have been crushed. There were no details at that time of exactly what had happened, although we later learnt that the woman had been in a car that had sped out of control and collided with a lorry, but the injuries were horrific. Arrangements were made for the woman to be transferred up to the theatre for an emergency operation, but before this could happen she went into cardiac arrest. She died. The two dead bodies lay in resus, surrounded by us all standing grim and silent. Ruby went to clean herself up and write up the notes.

'You ok?' I asked Ruby while the nurses cleaned the bodies up as best they could.

'Yeah, fine,' she said, not even looking up from her notes. We stood in silence for a few moments.

Tanya came up and waved a set of notes in front of Ruby. 'There's a six-year-old with suspected appendicitis in cubicle four,' she said, and put the notes on the side. Ruby finished her writing and picked up the notes.

'It never stops, does it,' she said with a shrug and walked over to the child. 'Hello. Oh dear, does your tummy hurt?' I heard her chirp as she drew the curtains round cubicle four, 'Well you're being very brave.'

'It all happened so quickly. One minute I was standing there talking, the next minute a fist was flying through the air and I was knocked to the ground.' Rob winced as I prodded the laceration on his scalp.

'We can glue it rather than use sutures,' I said, 'head wounds often look worse than they are. The cut is quite small, actually, you were lucky.'

'You can't believe what some people are like, can you,' said a nurse as she walked past and patted Rob on the shoulder, 'blooming thugs.'

Rob nodded earnestly and his colleague, Darryl, who had just returned from getting a cup of coffee, smirked at her knowingly. Rob was a special patient and this wasn't the usual type of fistfight that takes place on a Saturday evening and ends up in A&E. For starters, Rob was not a late night drunken reveller who had been assaulted. He was a paramedic and had been attending a 999 call when he was attacked. Ambulance staff are on the absolute front line. While everyone is running away from an emergency, they are the ones who are running towards it. Unfortunately, this sometimes means that they find themselves in sticky situations.

'Hardly a thug though, was she?' said Darryl as he stirred his cup of coffee. Rob looked at the nurse sheepishly.

'It's the eighty-year-olds you have to watch out for, I've always said that. Anyway, she caught me off my guard,' Rob said defensively.

Rob and Darryl had been called to the home of an elderly couple after the man became worried about his wife, who was complaining of chest pain. She also had dementia and had a tendency to be aggressive towards strangers. As Rob had leant forward to attach the blood pressure cuff, she'd taken a swing at him, causing him to lose his balance and catch his head on the side of the chair. While not nice, it was forgivable, as she didn't know what she was doing. But the sad truth is that it's far from unusual for us to have to treat ambulance crew in A&E as they're often on the receiving end of people's aggression who have no such excuses. This is despite the paramedics being there with the sole intention of trying to help. The nurse was right; you can't believe what some people are like. Just then, an elderly woman was wheeled in by another ambulance crew.

'Quick! Evacuate the department!' shouted Darryl as he slapped Rob on the back. Rob rolled his eyes and gritted his teeth. It occurred to me that if Darryl kept this up for much longer, he might end up with a head injury of his own.

'Where's my patient?' asked Ruby, looking around the department frantically, 'I've lost her. She was here a minute ago.' She stood by the cubicle where her patient had been, scratching her head.

'Maybe she's self-discharged?' I suggested while I checked some blood results on the computer.

'She's fractured both her hips, so I doubt it,' said Ruby sardonically. 'I only turned my back for a few moments.'

Now, it's not unheard of for people to lose things in a hospital: a handbag, perhaps, even your sanity, but a patient? Surely an A&E cubicle would be the one safe place to leave a patient? Apparently not, as Ruby and I discovered.

'Oh, here she is,' I said, looking on the inpatient system on the computer, 'she's not in the cubicle, she's upstairs.'

'How did she get up there? She can't walk, how can she make it up stairs?' replied Ruby, perplexed.

'She's in a bed in the acute assessment unit. Someone's moved her,' I replied.

'What?' shouted Ruby. 'But she's not medically stable. She's not ready to go to a ward. There must have been a mistake.'

After several frantic phone calls it transpired that there had not been a mistake. The decision to move the patient out of A&E and onto the ward had been taken not by a member of the medical team but by a manager, because the patient was about to breach the A&E waiting target of four hours. With the introduction of targets came financial penalties for those hospitals that failed to meet them. Of course, targets were introduced with the best of intentions; to improve patient care. But they have metamorphosed into a stick with which clinicians are threatened by the increasingly powerful non-clinical management.

'Oh, this is beyond a joke,' fumed Ruby as she picked up the telephone. She waited to be put through to the bed manager, muttering under her breath. It was futile though. The decision had been made and there was no changing it now.

This was not Ruby's first run-in with the bed managers. She often came home complaining that her patients had been discharged before they were fully ready and, against the recommendations of the occupational therapists and physiotherapists due to pressure on the beds, in the full knowledge that they would have to be readmitted. Far from seeing this as a problem, the hospital welcomed it, as not only did it mean getting through patients faster but it also registered as two separate 'clinical encounters' on the official documentation and therefore made them look twice as busy. All this has been possible because there has been a subtle shift in power within the NHS over the past few years away from the clinicians – who are presumably far too bothered about the welfare of patients to run things efficiently – and towards managers, who have no such concerns.

'Well don't interfere with my patients again,' sniped Ruby, although we both knew that one angry doctor wasn't going to change things. She slammed down the telephone and turned to me. 'It shouldn't be patients that we're losing in this hospital. It should be managers.'

Technology is great. Without it we wouldn't have been able to put a man on the moon, explore the ocean's depths or have microwave sausages. Computers have revolutionised our lives and have the power to educate and enlighten. But sometimes this empowerment can be a curse, creating more problems than it solves.

Every doctor has had to spend time reassuring patients who have come into their surgery waving a print-out from the Internet, convinced that they have some incredibly rare and obscure disease when in fact the truth is far more prosaic. They don't have cancer or smallpox – it's just a throat infection. Being a graduate from the 'Google school of medicine' does not guarantee accurate self-diagnosis. And sometimes, rather than turning people into hypochondriacs, it does the opposite.

Mrs Almond had come into A&E after feeling faint after a trip to the theatre. She was put on a drip and blood tests were arranged and I set about taking a history from her to try to find out what was wrong.

'Oh, I know what's wrong,' she said calmly, 'I've got glandular fever. I know there's nothing you doctors can do about it and I've just got to wait until I get over it myself.'

This was true of glandular fever, but as a matter of routine I ordered a chest X-ray. An hour later I looked at the blood results and the X-ray. Something wasn't right.

'Did your GP do an X-ray when you went to see them?' I asked Mrs Almond.

'Oh, I haven't been to the doctor for years. I read about glandular fever on a website and the symptoms fit so I knew that's what I had.'

Some of her symptoms, like the chronic cough and the weight loss, didn't fit with the diagnosis, but she'd just ignored this. I looked at the X-ray again and some more blood tests confirmed that this wasn't glandular fever, but tuberculosis, something that most certainly does need treating and can be fatal.

She was lucky we caught it when we did. Mrs Almond went pale when I explained she'd have to be on antibiotics for the next six months to ensure that it was fully eradicated. It was a salutary lesson in attempting to self-diagnose.

'I'm so embarrassed,' she said, shaking her head, as I explained that all the people she has come into close contact with will have to be traced and tested.

Mrs Almond was referred to the respiratory team for follow-up and I went to the doctor's mess to type up my notes on the computer. It wasn't working so I had to wait for the on call IT support person to call me back.

Typical.

Maybe I should have a microwave sausage while I wait?

My final night on call and so far, it had been free of drama.

'I don't know what's wrong with me, Doctor, but I think I'm dying.' The man looked at me earnestly while he sipped a cup of tea from a paper cup. He didn't look like he was dying to me. The man obviously noted my faint air of scepticism and coughed for good measure.

Julie, his girlfriend, who until this point had been sitting quietly, sighed loudly and rolled her eyes.

'Steven, what exactly are your symptoms?' I asked again, trying to see if I had missed anything that would suggest this man's sudden demise.

'Oh. It's awful. Headache, but not just any headache. This is the worst headache I've ever had. Ever.' I nod sympathetically. 'And aches, all over my body.' He went on to describe the classic symptoms of flu but with lots of hyperbole thrown in.

I gently suggested this diagnosis to him and also reminded him that there is little we can do for him in A&E and that really, he should be tucked up in bed, taking paracetamol and drinking plenty of fluids.

'No,' protested Steven, 'it can't be flu.'

Julie interrupted. 'I've told him already he's got flu. It's the season for it. Lots of people have got it. He's just making a fuss and I told him it was a waste of time coming here bothering you all.' With this she let out another sigh, folded her arms and looked out of the window into the dark.

'I've had flu before, lots of times,' interjected Steven, 'it's never been like this.'

This, I realise, is a classic misunderstanding. There are certain people (which, if you're female, you might identify as 'men') who refer to every cough or cold they have as being the flu. Colds sound rather boring, whereas flu, well, that's something a bit more dramatic. It's worthy of sympathy. Maybe even an excuse to get out of the washing-up for a while. But of course the problem is that genuine flu is rather unpleasant and if your point of reference for this illness is actually the common cold, then when you're hit with it you think you're dying, especially if you're prone to a spot of hypochondria.

'Yes, what you've got,' said Julie pointedly after a slightly awkward silence, 'is what I had last Christmas and yet I still managed to drag myself up out of bed and make Christmas dinner for all your family who were staying with us, remember?'

Steven looked a little sheepish at this remark.

'Yeah, I remember.'

'Well, now you know how bad I felt. And did I complain? Did I moan?' asked Julie.

Steven thought for a moment.

'Yeah, you did actually,' he concludes, 'constantly.'

He turned to me and rolled his eyes.

I left them to it.

10
A Moving Patient

'Where's my money? You've stolen my money, haven't you? I saw you take it,' said Mr Berridge as he wandered into my office.

I sighed. I hadn't stolen his money.

'It's in your pockets, isn't it?' he asked again in a surprisingly convivial tone considering that he was accusing me of stealing £7,500 from him. This was his entire life savings, which he had been keeping in the bread bin in his kitchen before he came into the hospital. I showed him the contents of my pockets: a half-eaten packet of wine gums, a pen lid, a mobile phone, my keys and fifteen pence in coppers. He seized on the coins and quickly counted them, frustrated to find that it fell somewhat short of the missing amount. I looked at him wearily.

'I told you I hadn't stolen it,' I replied. He returned my stare with a blank look.

'What? What you talking about?' he asked, bewildered.

'Your money, I was saying how I hadn't stolen it,' I explained. Much more of this and it would be me who was going to go demented.

'What about my money? Where is it? Have you stolen it?' he asked.

I took a deep breath and opened my mouth to start all over again. Just then, Jocasta, one of the ward physiotherapists, poked her head round the office door.

'It's time for your assessment,' she said, smiling warmly. Jocasta stood with balletic poise, gently ushering Mr Berridge out of my office. I seized the opportunity to duck out and hide in the nurses' office. From in there, I could hear Mr Berridge chatting away to Jocasta as she asked him to walk up and down the ward corridor with his walking sticks, but inevitably conversation turned to his money, and I smiled quietly to myself that I'd managed to secure some respite from the constant accusations.

There is much talked and written about the damages that alcohol does in excess. It's hard to appreciate sometimes quite how poisonous it really is. Physically, there are all the problems it causes to the liver, with all the further associated problems this brings. And of course there's the link with depression, suicide, homicide and violent crime. But there is another problem it causes, which doesn't get so widely publicised but which is dreadfully debilitating and means sufferers require nursing care for the rest of their lives. Mr Berridge suffers from Korsakoff's, which sounds, ironically, like a brand of cheap Russian vodka but is, in fact, a syndrome of irreversible brain damage caused by alcohol excess. It is characterised by short-term memory loss and confabulation, where the sufferer fills in the gaps in their memory with fictional explanations.

Mr Berridge was found confused and wandering the streets a few months ago, and was brought into the hospital. He remembers that he has savings, but can't remember that his social worker opened a bank account for him and that his money is safe. Because he can't remember, his mind becomes creative and imagines that it's been stolen. If you push him further, he elaborates on this to include all sorts of fanciful scenarios, from the belief his daughter is being held by the IRA and he needs the money to secure her release, to it being stolen by nurses who broke into his flat wearing bunny-girl outfits. And no matter how many times you explain, within a few minutes he's forgotten again. Anyone needing a reminder on the evils of drink should spend a day on the ward having to explain, repeatedly, to Mr Berridge what has happened to his money. I can only last a few minutes and so I have the greatest admiration for the nursing staff on the ward. This admiration, I decided after a few minutes hiding in the nurses' office, was best experienced from a distance.

I had a patient who had been transferred to one of the surgical wards so I decided now was a good time to review her. I sneaked out of the ward and on to the main corridor.

As I walked on to the ward, I got the strange feeling that someone was watching me. A woman in a uniform was standing bolt upright in the corridor and as I looked over at her, she quickly looked down at her shoes. Strange, I thought to myself, and ignored her. I walked towards the nursing station and searched on the board for the bed number for my patient. The uneasy feeling of being watched returned, and I suddenly became aware of another figure standing, motionless, on the other side of the ward. I turned and looked at her. She was also wearing a uniform and intently studying her clipboard. The ward was buzzing with activity. A bed was wheeled in with a prone patient on it, a porter came and plonked a pile of notes on the desk. I looked around for a nurse but there was none that I could see, so I wandered round the ward until I saw some curtains drawn around one of the beds.

'Hello?' I called out. 'It's Max, one of the doctors from ward nine. Do you know where Mrs Delgado is?'

There was silence for a moment and then a nurse pulled the curtain back briefly, and I gave a weak smile to the woman who was still sitting on a commode by the bed, before the nurse moved forward and the curtain fell back. The nurse was holding a urine bottle and an empty catheter bag. She contorted her head to mop her forehead against the top of her tunic.

'Sorry, I know you're busy,' I began, but the nurse was harassed and not listening.

'Erm, I'm not sure, love, I think she's in bed twelve but give me a moment.' The nurse went off and came back a few minutes later, still carrying the urine bottle and catheter. 'Yes, bed twelve, over there,' she said, gesturing further down the ward with the urine bottle, making its contents splash precariously against the side.

I walked down the ward and passed yet another shadowy figure standing motionless by the wall. OK, enough is enough. What is going on here? I turned around and looked down the ward, counting four figures standing silently with clipboards. No one else appeared to be paying them any attention or be at all disconcerted by their presence. And then from behind me, another appeared. She was walking over to me. She was looking intently at me. I frantically looked around me for an exit, but I was trapped.

'You're wearing a watch,' she said, looking down at my wrist. She showed me her badge, and suddenly everything became clear.

What I had just inadvertently stumbled into was a government audit. The people standing motionless up and down the ward were nurses recording how many people were adhering to the government guidelines about hygiene in hospitals. I'd just been given a black mark because I wasn't 'bare below the elbows'. Under the dress code policy that hospitals have now had to adopt, doctors are not allowed onto a ward wearing a coat or outer garment of clothing, and they must have their shirt sleeves rolled up to their elbows, with no watches or other jewellery. This purports to be an attempt to reduce hospital-acquired infections being spread by staff (bizarrely the guidelines do allow you to wear a wedding ring, as if bugs respect the sanctity of marriage). No one would question the importance of hand washing in clinical settings. But as doctors we are encouraged to practise evidence-based medicine so I would expect that before a draconian rule is implemented, there would be some evidence that a blanket 'bare below the elbows' policy works. I apologised to the woman, explaining that I hadn't known about the ban, and took my watch off and rolled up my sleeves. And then I started talking to her. She openly admitted that, unlike hand washing, there was no evidence that it had any impact on infection rates.

'But it's what the public want,' she explained. 'They think it looks cleaner if everyone has their sleeves rolled up.' Presumably somebody somewhere had done a focus group. What this policy amounts to is little more than a PR stunt; utterly meaningless and a waste of time and money that won't help make hospitals any safer. If the government were genuinely concerned about infection rates, it would stop reducing the number of beds in hospitals, as bed occupancy rates have been shown to be the single biggest factor in MRSA and clostridium difficile outbreaks. Really, focusing on shirt sleeves and watches is a way of deflecting attention away from the fact that the government has relentlessly pushed its agenda of Private Finance Initiative, under which bed numbers have been drastically reduced, despite warnings from doctors and scientists that it will result in risks to patients. I looked back up the ward at one of the nurses ticking her form as someone rolled up their sleeves and wondered if this was the best use of her time. I caught her eye, and she looked at her shoes again.

I finished seeing Mrs Delgado and made my way back to my ward. As I opened the door to the ward I was met by a shout from Marsha and then a thunderous clatter coming from my office. What now, I thought? I looked around the office door and was confronted with all of my furniture piled, precariously, in one corner of the room. Marsha was attempting to wrestle one of the office chairs from Mr Brownlee.

'Put the chair down Dennis, come on,' she said.

'Right then,' he said.

'What have I told you about piling the furniture up like this?' she remonstrated with him. He was tall, spritely and in his fifties, but slim and no match for the brute force of Marsha, who successfully prized his fingers open and whipped the chair away.

'Right then,' he repeated, standing back with his hands on his hips. He sucked in his teeth and shook his head as he surveyed the scene, oblivious to the mayhem he was causing. He paused for a moment then began to try to move bits of furniture from the pile, but he did so without any method and, pulling on a box embedded in the pile, sent a chair and a box file tumbling and crashing to the floor.

'Right then,' he said yet again, sucking in his teeth once more. Mr Brownlee had been admitted the day before precisely because of this behaviour. It had driven his wife to distraction over the past five months and within twenty-four hours had managed to do the same to me.

The reason for this behaviour was Creutzfeldt-Jakob disease, or CJD. It is a degenerative neurological disorder that is the human form of bovine spongiform encephalopathy – or BSE, which first caused panic over beef in the 1980s and was dubbed 'mad cow disease'. It is caused not by a bacteria or virus, but by a prion, a tiny strand of abnormal protein that builds up in the brain and kills the brain cells. The death of the brain cells causes a whole host of horrific symptoms – like personality changes, dementia, problems with movement and difficulty speaking. Ultimately, it is fatal. It's a tragic illness and there is no known cure. The concern, since the 80s, has been that the cow form of the disease – BSE – had been shown to mutate so that it could affect humans. But for some unfortunate people it can also occur spontaneously and this is what had happened to Mr Brownlee. He had rapidly begun to deteriorate and now could barely communicate, save for saying a few clichéd phrases. His wife had been determined to care for him for as long as possible at home, although the community team and the GP had warned her that he would soon need nursing care as his physical health deteriorated and he became increasingly incapacitated with difficulty swallowing, incontinence and seizures.

However, before this happened, she had begun to notice him behaving strangely. Ultimately, it was his behaviour, not the deterioration in his physical health, which she could no longer cope with.

Since the age of sixteen, Mr Brownlee had been a removal man. He was unable to recall any aspect of his life, but somewhere, deep down in the recesses of his mind, he must have remembered the job he had done day in and day out for nearly forty years. At some point during his illness, as it ravaged through his brain, he had slipped into a world of singular familiarity. While he remained oblivious to where he was, the time of day or what was happening around him, he believed that he was at work, on a removals job. His wife had woken up countless times to find him emptying the lounge, lugging heavy bits of furniture out onto the front lawn in the dead of night. Once, when she left him for a few hours to go shopping, he had cleared the entire downstairs and she came home to find the washing machine on the drive with an armchair balanced on top. This was not only incredibly disruptive, but also dangerous. He had no awareness of what he was really doing and would pull at electrical objects, ripping out the wall sockets in the process, piling objects on top of each other, breaking and smashing things. He had already severed a tendon in his hand trying to wrench a glass cabinet off the wall when the screws gave way and it fell on him.

Despite her noble efforts to care for him at home, his current behaviour meant it was no longer feasible. Mr Brownlee had been admitted to the ward to provide his wife with respite while his future care was decided and his physical health monitored. Marsha gently coaxed him out of the room and attempted to distract him while

I set about dismantling the pile of furniture. I listened to her talk to him, her voice rising and falling gently with its Irish lilt. The nurses working in geriatrics and especially those trained in dementia care are a special breed. It is incorrectly considered a dull, dead-end job, reserved for those who can't hack it in the more exciting, dynamic areas of medicine. Yet nothing seems to faze them. They are calm in the most extreme situations. They make sure that everyone is comfortable, they offer support and help and have awe-inspiring patience and they are there, relentlessly, on the ward with the patients. It's non-stop work, all day, every day. I honestly don't know how they do it.

Just then, I heard Mr Berridge return from his assessment with Jocasta. He was still talking about his money. Fiona, the deputy ward sister, peered out of the nurses' office after a few minutes.

'Poor Jocasta, she's had long enough I reckon,' and without batting an eyelid walked out into the corridor and I heard her call over to Mr Berridge. 'You let Jo get on with her rounds now. Come with me and we'll get a nice cup of tea,' she said.

'Where's my money. You've stolen my money haven't you?'

It's enough to drive you to drink.

'I thought you said you were going to cook me dinner,' said my sister that evening as she leaned against the kitchen worktop, sipping a glass of wine. Was that a slight sneer I detected, creeping across her face? From my sister? Surely not!

'I am cooking dinner,' I said as I took the container out of the microwave. 'There,' I said triumphantly, as I spooned out the sloppy contents onto two plates. I opened a packet of salad and plonked it in a bowl. 'Ta-da! Dinner is served.'

Flora was on call, Terry was at a gig and Ruby had taken a few days annual leave to visit an aunt, so I thought this was a good opportunity to have my sister over. No doubt she'd have a list of medical complaints she'd want me to look at. But just now, her primary complaint wasn't so much a rash, but my rash approach to cooking.

'That's not cooking,' said my sister, shaking her head in disgust as she carried the plates to the table.

'Erm, yes it is,' I protested innocently. 'The food was cold and now it's hot. That, I think you will find, is cooking.'

She rolled her eyes. 'No, that's called reheating,' she said sardonically. 'Cooking is when you take the ingredients, cut them up, and turn them into a meal.'

This was quite a revolutionary concept. I thought for a moment. So – given that since university I have survived pretty much entirely on things I can microwave in under five minutes – I haven't been cooking. Slowly it dawned on me, I don't think I've ever properly cooked something from scratch, at least, not unless toast counts. Oh dear. That would explain how I had always managed to get by in the kitchen without a cookbook . . . or in fact any kitchen utensils. This wasn't helped by the fact that neither Ruby nor Flora had any ability, or interest, in cooking. In fact, Ruby's culinary skills didn't extend very far beyond being able to open a packet of Hula Hoops.

It was a little bit rich taking culinary criticism from my sister – she was, after all, the person who was caught eating worm castes at a birthday party. OK, she was four at the time, but even so.

'You're a doctor,' said my sister, helpfully, as though I didn't already know this and spent my days taking blood and putting my fingers up people's bottoms for fun, 'you're supposed to be healthy.'

'I am. I get lots of fresh air now we have to smoke outside,' I replied earnestly.

'You should know better than to eat this sort of thing,' she continued.

This was, though it pains me to admit it, perhaps true. But, in my defence, despite a growing appreciation within medical circles of the importance diet plays on physical and mental health, the attitude that 'cooking' constitutes reheating pre-packaged food has infiltrated into places where good, basic nutrition really is needed.

Anyone who has stood watching as patients are fed in hospital will bear witness to the fact that often the food is of a shockingly poor standard. Cooks are now a rare commodity in hospitals. Instead, the responsibility for providing hospital food has been increasingly outsourced to catering companies. Meals are now mass-produced off-site and transported in to the hospital where these 'cook-chill' dishes can then be reheated on the wards, in trolleys or their own individual containers, or, more ominously, 'regenerated', Dr Who-style, using self-contained high-pressure steamers. This is all being done in the name of 'efficiency', but while it might be cost-effective to outsource catering, it doesn't produce very appetising results. It's a false economy – patients who are undernourished either because they aren't eating the food or get food of poor quality, take longer to get better. There is one simple answer to this problem: reinstate hospital kitchens and staff them with trained cooks.

'Revolting,' said my sister with a smile as she put down her knife and fork next to her half-eaten meal. 'Next time, let's go out for a meal, yeah?'

I nodded in agreement.

'Now, I've got something to show you,' she began. Any hope of it being a winning lottery ticket she was planning on sharing with me quickly dissipated as she bent down and slipped off her shoe to reveal a manky (I'm aware that is not official medical terminology) infected nail. 'What do you think of that?' she asked, sitting back in her chair and waving her foot in my direction.

'Revolting,' I replied.

While Ruby had returned to work and from the outside appeared fine, we all remained worried about her. She continued to refuse to take what had happened any further, and Mr Griffiths had apologised, which for her was adequate but for the rest of us seemed an insignificant gesture given what he had done. Yet, while we could understand – although not necessarily agree with – the logic behind her decision, Terry was disbelieving and thought that we were all colluding with Mr Griffiths because of misguided professional allegiance.

'I can't believe you're all just accepting that she's not going to do anything. It's like listening to a room of Patsy Clines' he said, much to our bafflement.

'Do you mean Patty Hearst?' ventured Flora.

'Erm, yes, you know what I mean. It's like you're all under some spell. Just because he's a doctor doesn't mean he should be allowed to get away with that sort of thing. I don't care how many people he helps, he should be prosecuted.'

Ruby looked at him philosophically but refused to buckle.

Flora was more pragmatic and pointed out that, although he appeared contrite now, what would happen in a few years' time when Ruby was applying for a consultant job? Would he really want someone with the knowledge of what he had done as a colleague? Would he not do everything he could to ensure that her progress through the ranks was curtailed?

Ruby, it seemed, was damned if she did and damned if she didn't and I felt deeply sorry for her. The situation had not been of her making but could have serious repercussions. There had already been a rumour going around the hospital – entirely false and that Lewis had alerted us to – that Ruby and Mr Griffiths had been seeing each other and he had found out she had been having an affair. Her refusal to make a formal complaint was being seen as an admission that she was not entirely an innocent victim. Lewis had also made the point that even if she had made a complaint, the incident would be so scandalous in the world of surgery that she would forever be known as the woman who grassed up her boss and it would overshadow her career.

With all this uncertainty and pressure, it hardly came as a surprise to us that she sought solace in the arms of her registrar. He had been there the evening of the assault and visited the flat several times to check up on her over the next few weeks. What did come as a surprise was that it ended as suddenly as it began.

'I thought you liked him?' I asked as the two of us had a cigarette at the back of A&E.

'I did, it just, well, I know he wants to settle down, and I don't want that. You know, the idea of being in a proper relationship, it's just . . .' her voice trailed off and she took a drag. 'It's not the idea of a relationship as such,' she said after some time, 'it's just what comes with that.'

'What, long woodland walks and a preoccupation with the Ikea catalogue?' I suggested.

Ruby laughed. 'No, it's the inevitable question that comes up, you know, about having children. It's not something I want but there's an expectation that it is, that it should be.'

'Is it Flora that's brought this on? I mean, it's different for her; it's more complicated. She's not in a relationship and her contract is only for a year.'

'No,' interrupted Ruby, 'I've always felt like this. I've watched the people I went to school with get pregnant, get a flat, settle down. I've always wanted something different.' She paused again, lost in thought. 'My mum had a place at veterinary school, but just before she could take it up she fell pregnant with me. She never went. She never let me forget what she gave up because of me and I think, deep down, she never forgave me. We were always poor, always living hand to mouth. I remember, as a little girl, watching her going off to work, doing menial stuff she hated, with her sense of resentment for never reaching her potential, and thinking, I'm never going to let that happen to me. I'm not going to make the same mistake. I'm going to escape.' Ruby rarely talked so candidly about her emotions. I knew that she had worked hard to get to medical school, that her family was poor and she had not come from the usual world of privilege that most of our contemporaries at medical school did. She had always seemed so driven, so hungry to achieve, and now I started to understand why.

'Well you have escaped. You've got a good degree, a good career,' I ventured.

'But I'm not sure I have escaped, not fully. It's as though I'll never be satisfied; as though I can't get far enough away because I'm always carrying a bit of it with me. The more success I have, the more guilty I feel about abandoning my mum. As though my success was to the detriment of hers.' She took a sip of tea and leant against the wall. 'There's just something about the idea of settling down, having children, which brings all this into sharp focus. I can't bear it.'

It struck me that medicine was the perfect career as it provided a ready, all-consuming distraction from this; the perfect excuse not to stop and deal with her feelings of guilt.

'I have worried,' continued Ruby, 'about the whole Mr Griffiths thing, if this isn't all mixed up with it.'

'What do you mean?' I asked, 'Ruby, you're not to blame for what happened at all. You didn't do anything.'

'No, I mean my reluctance to report him. With my head, I'm sure I'm doing the right thing. He's apologised, we should all get on with our jobs. The alternative would be too tedious, me being cast in the role of the victim, the poor little woman.' I knew where she was heading with this, because quietly, it had occurred to me too.

'You mean about your Dad?' I asked. Years ago, just after he'd died, Ruby had gotten drunk and told me that she'd spent her childhood witnessing him beating her mother. He would threaten to kill her and many times her mother fled the house when he went through the drawers to find a kitchen knife, leaving Ruby hiding in her bedroom upstairs.

'Yeah,' replied Ruby. 'I just hate the idea that I'm the victim. But then I hate the idea that I might be complicit in what he did; to condone it.' The contemplative air was disturbed by the sound of her pager and she jolted back into her usual bravado. 'Well, anyway, you're the one who's going to be a psychiatrist, you work it out. I'd better get this.' She stubbed her cigarette out on the wall and turned and went back into A&E.

I made my way across the grass and over to the administration block. I popped my head round the door of Trudy's office, but she wasn't there so I went into the main office, but the three Marys were also absent. There was just Craig, sitting, listening to his iPod and dictation while he typed.

'Alright?' he mumbled as I walked in. By now I had become accustomed to inarticulate grunts and could decipher pretty much anything he said.

'Where is everyone?' I asked.

'Ain't you heard?' said Craig, iPod in situ, 'the local paper's turned up. Trudy and that lot 'ave gone down to 'ave a look.'

'The local paper? What do you mean?'

'Some reporter turned up to speak to the chief executive about the A&E closure. He weren't having none of it, called Trudy down to get rid of 'em and the Marys went too, just to stick their noses in.'

'How did the paper know about that?' I asked.

'Dunno, someone must 'ave tipped 'em off.'

'I wonder who?' I asked, but knew full well it must have been Ruby. I'd assumed she'd been too preoccupied with what had happened with Mr Griffiths to think about her plans to try to save A&E, but obviously I'd been wrong.

I left the administration block and made my way back across the grass to the back of the A&E department.

'Do you work here?' asked a man in his twenties who was standing outside one of the doors.

'Yes' I replied, then noticed he was holding a notebook.

'Can I ask you what you think about the plans to close the A&E department of this hospital? Do you think it will compromise patient welfare?' I hesitated for a moment. 'You can speak off the record if you want,' he added, seeing my wariness. I thought of Ruby and knew I should stand firm along side her.

'No, it's OK, you can quote me,' I said, and showed him my name badge. 'Yes, I think it's a disgrace. It's dangerous and ill-conceived,' I began, not imagining what I was doing was in any way reckless. I went on to explain how it was a short-sighted attempt to cut costs, but at the expense of the welfare of the local residents and part of a wider agenda to fragment healthcare.

'That's great,' said the reporter as he scribbled down everything eagerly. 'Thanks so much. No one else I asked would say anything to me.'

As I walked away I began to feel slightly uneasy about what I had just done. I couldn't get in trouble for speaking my mind, could I? We lived in a democracy, free speech and all that, right? And anyway, I was standing shoulder to shoulder with Ruby. It wasn't until later that evening that I began to really worry.

'No, I didn't have anything to do with it,' said Ruby, when I asked her about it as we sat around the kitchen table.

'What?' I said, my mouth suddenly going dry as I began to panic.

'I don't know what you're talking about. I was going to write to our MP about it, but haven't got round to it yet. I was thinking about a petition, too, but again, I've just had so much on my mind.'

'Oh, right, OK,' I said slowly, it now dawning on me that not only had Ruby not put her head above the parapet, she wasn't even in the same trench as me. My diatribe to the reporter was rapidly appearing to be not an act of solidarity but an act of madness. Just then Flora came home.

'Do you want some tea?' said Terry, getting up from the table and giving her his seat as she walked into the kitchen. She didn't reply but plonked herself down on the chair heavily and leant forward across the table.

'You'll never guess what I've just heard about Mr Griffiths,' she said, wide-eyed. Ruby looked up immediately and fixed Flora with an intent stare.

'Has he resigned?' she asked, pensively.

'Resigned?' spluttered Flora, 'Not at all. He's only gone and applied for the post of Head of Surgery at the hospital.'

The table fell silent.

'That man's got some nerve,' said Terry from by the sink.

I watched as Ruby silently got up from the table and went to her bedroom.

11
A Gay Old Time

It was spring, in my first year of life as a doctor, when I met him. I was walking back from the supermarket, my arms weighed down with shopping bags.

As I crossed the road I briefly found myself walking parallel to an old man. He was frail and walking slowly but he turned to me.

'I bet there's been some advances since my day, hasn't there?' he said.

I wasn't sure what he meant. I looked at him quizzically.

'You're a doctor aren't you?' he continued and beckoned to our front door. 'I've seen you coming out of that flat where the doctors live, and don't tell me you carry that around for fun,' he said, pointing to the stethoscope poking out of my bag. 'I used to be a surgeon – years ago. I'm eighty-nine now.'

He held out his hands for me to see, as though they were in some way evidence of his past profession. They were mottled and shook slightly. He put them back in his pockets.

'So you must have been practising when the NHS

was born,' I said. 'What an amazing time to have been a doctor.'

'Ah, it was, that's true. I was just a junior, but it was exciting times. Not all the doctors were in favour of it to begin with. Right up until the last minute it was touch and go whether or not it would happen.' We had reached my front door and the old man hesitated. 'I live just over there,' he said, taking a hand out of his pocket and gesturing to a small block of flats to the left of ours. 'Why don't you come in for tea sometime? I'm Anthony,' he said.

So a few days later I found myself sitting in his flat eating custard creams. I'd been there an hour when the front door opened and another man in his eighties walked in, carrying shopping bags. 'This is my brother-in-law, Geoff,' he said, introducing me. We talked about the theatre and books and a bit about medicine. A few days later I happened to mention my visit to our next-door neighbour. She had lived on the estate ever since it was built in the 70s and knew everyone.

'Yeah, course I know them old men. Quite sad, the tall one hardly ever leaves his flat, you know.' It transpired that Anthony found it difficult to walk and Geoff, who was now his carer, was too frail himself to push a wheelchair.

I had mentioned all this to Flora one evening and she took this as a challenge. Not having any grandparents herself, from then on she adopted them. Between the three of us in the flat, we would run the occasional errand for them, do some shopping and occasionally visit when

we had the time. Six months ago Anthony had been diagnosed with bladder cancer. It had spread. He had talked
candidly to Flora about the diagnosis and it seemed he
actually enjoyed talking in medical parlance once more,
even if the subject matter was painfully close to him.

All this was how I came to be pushing Anthony in a
wheelchair around the park when he finally confided
in me and told me his secret. I hadn't seen him since
starting work back in hospital and had been telling
him about my visits to nursing homes.

'I hope Geoff never ends up in one of those places,'
he said. 'We've lived together for sixty years, you know.
I dread to think how he'll manage when I'm gone.' He
fell silent for a few moments then motioned for me to
stop pushing him.

'Max, I've got something to tell you. Something I
think you should know. I'll understand if you . . .' his
voice trailed off. 'It's about Geoff. He isn't my brother-
in-law,' he said with trepidation.

'Oh I know,' I interrupted, 'he's your partner.'
Anthony looked at me warily.

'You knew?' he asked.

'Yeah,' I said breezily.

I declined to mention that the entire block knew and
in fact our next-door neighbour had told us when we
first mentioned them to her.

'It's their secret though, so don't let on you know,'
she explained. 'They're very sensitive about it and
don't understand that times have changed.'

I sat on the park bench with Anthony next to me in his wheelchair and he began to talk. As I heard about the harassment and persecution that he and Geoff had experienced as a result of their sexuality, I realised why they were so sensitive. Anthony had to keep his private life a secret for his entire working career. He had lived lies for so long that now he found it hard to accept that attitudes have changed. Even when homosexuality became legalised in this country, he explained, there was still dreadful prejudice towards gay people, particularly within the medical establishment. Despite being a world expert in his branch of surgery and a pioneer in new surgical techniques that have now become commonplace in operating theatres, he feared that he would lose his job if his secret came out, and he had been blackmailed by a colleague for years. Eventually, it became too much and he resigned from his post. He had ended his working life as a clerk in the town hall. He told me all this in hushed whispers. It was so sad to see this frail, weak old man, still bowed down by a secret that had dogged him his entire life. He had never been able to relax and enjoy his life with Geoff, and now it was nearly over.

That evening, sitting around the kitchen table, I told Flora that Anthony had finally confided in me what we had known all along. Terry was there too and although he'd never met them, he immediately took an interest.

'Surely when Anthony dies, Geoff is going to lose

the flat? He won't be able to afford the death duty so he'll have to sell. Then what will happen to him?' This hadn't occurred to me.

'They need to get married!' declared Flora excitedly.

Once Flora managed to convince Geoff and Anthony, she and Terry hatched a plan. Civil partnerships were conducted at the local town hall and Terry got the papers. Flora's sister was a solicitor and she helped with the legal side of things. Lewis was even roped in as wedding planner. This was going to be the wedding of the century.

The secret plans to close the A&E department had made it onto the front page of the local newspaper, along with my comments. Seeing them there in black and white, my name clear for all to see, my initial anxiety returned. This, it transpired, was well founded. In the doctor's mess, several people came up and congratulated me on speaking out and I quietly wished that they would offer to give a quote to the paper, too, so I wasn't so alone.

It was shortly after this that I checked my email and there, staring back at me, was a message from the chief executive's office asking that I attend a meeting to discuss 'concerns' they had over 'misconduct'. I swallowed hard. Later that day I found myself sitting, like a naughty schoolboy, on a chair outside an office on the top floor of the administration office. I'd never been up there before and part of me was quite intrigued to see the lovely thick carpet and freshly painted walls with tasteful art hanging from it. This was the 'Executive Suite' and it certainly was plush. Even the water cooler worked. The other part of me, however, was too petrified to care about any of this. A blonde woman with an Australian accent opened a door and called me in. I wasn't sure who she was but assumed she was a secretary and would leave after summoning me, but she stayed and wrote copious notes through-out the meeting. I had wrongly assumed this would be an informal chat, but quickly realised this was far more serious. There were four people in the room excluding the Australian woman, and everyone was wearing suits. One was obviously from HR and I recognised the medical director and the chief executive. I didn't know who the other man was but he was scowling, so I assumed he wasn't on my side. They were all wearing grey suits and stern expressions. There was also a copy of the newspaper in front of them. I tried not to look at it. Everything seemed to go very fast and I was left not knowing what to say. The upshot of the meeting was that I had brought the trust into disrepute and that this was a breach of my contract. It occurred to me that it was in fact they who had brought the trust into disrepute by attempting to close down A&E without appropriate consultation or thought. This point, I reasoned, was best to keep to myself given the circumstances. They assumed that I was also responsi-ble for leaking the story to the press in the first place, and for the posters in A&E, and my denial of this only served to annoy them further.

'We have decided that the best cause of action is to give you an official warning which will go down on your record,' said the scowling man, who was still scowling. Of course, I should have had a union representative with me so that they would have gone through the formal channels, but as they had already demonstrated, they obviously had a flagrant disregard for procedure and protocol. I left the office, not really sure what was happening. Back at home, everyone sat round the table in horror.

'Max, you've got to be careful. They've been shown up and humiliated by this getting into the press. There are already petitions going round and people talking about it on the radio. You're in a really vulnerable position,' said Flora.

'I know,' I said, feeling very alone.

'Get on to your union,' suggested Terry, trying to be helpful, but I just wanted it all to go away. I went upstairs to my bedroom, a knot in my stomach. I was scared about what might happen, what the implications were for my future career, but also, part of me was ashamed. I wished I had been the one who had informed the papers and I wished, rather than sitting, cowed and afraid, I had stood up to them in that meeting. I wished I'd had the courage of my convictions to denounce the plans to their face rather than mutter apologies.

A few days later I popped some groceries round to Geoff and Anthony, expecting to find them excited about their big day. Instead they appeared withdrawn and scared.

'Why aren't you looking forward to it?' I asked, surprised.

Geoff looked at Anthony and then back at me, 'I know you're all trying to help, and we're really grateful, honestly we are, but we're just so . . .' he paused, lost for words.

'What if people find out?' said Anthony. 'What if there are reprisals? What if people find out where we live?'

I laughed. 'Nobody, and I mean nobody, cares,' I said emphatically. But, I looked at them both, cowed and afraid, and was overcome by sadness. The world they had known, the world of living in shadows, afraid of backward glances, might have gone but it lived on in their minds. It was almost impossible to get them to understand that society had changed since they were young.

'Maybe we should cancel all this. Yes, I think that's a good idea. It's for the best,' said Geoff.

I looked at Anthony imploringly. 'Please, I promise you, it will be fine,' I said. 'Geoff, you'll have to leave this flat. Just think of it as a bit of paper you've both got to sign. We don't have to make a fuss if you don't want to.'

They looked at each other, unsure of what to do.

'No guests, just us as witnesses, no fuss. No one has to know about it if that's what you prefer. Flora has gone to so much effort, she'll be so disappointed if it's cancelled,' I pleaded.

Geoff looked at Anthony once again, 'Well . . .' he hesitated.

'No one else needs to know?' asked Anthony.

I reassured them.

What actually happened, however, was quite the opposite.

The day of the ceremony arrived. Given Anthony's failing health, Flora had convinced the town hall to squeeze us into a booking space on a Saturday so we could all attend. She had booked a taxi, and Geoff, Anthony, Flora and Terry went to the town hall together while the rest of us made our own way there. Ruby, Lewis and I arrived before them and waited outside on the steps leading up to the entrance. Gradually we noticed more and more people coming out of the building and standing around with us. Eventually, an official-looking woman came over to us.

'Are you waiting for the civil partnership between Mr Guthrie and Mr Penstone?' she asked.

'Yes, Geoff and Anthony. Are all these people waiting for them too?' said Ruby, a little surprised.

'Yes,' she replied with a smile then turned to the dozen or so people waiting, 'they should be here any minute.'

I spotted a photographer and someone else with two bunches of flowers.

'Erm, who are they all?' I asked.

'Oh, they all work here at the town hall. They heard about the ceremony and I know they didn't want a fuss, but, well, it's such a lovely thing. Sixty years they've been together. Sixty years! We couldn't believe it. It's a record for the town hall, we couldn't let that go without a celebration.'

'Where did the flowers come from?' I asked, beginning to worry that my promise of a low-key affair was looking unlikely.

'The Mayor paid for them. There's more inside. He should be here any minute, actually.'

Ruby and I looked at each other a little stricken but before anything could be done, the taxi pulled up and the door opened. Flora and Terry stepped out and turned to help Anthony out of the taxi, and Ruby and I went to help. The crowd assembled on the steps cheered and clapped. Anthony looked up in horror and scrambled to get back in the car.

'What, what's wrong?' asked Flora, putting her head back into the taxi.

'There's a crowd out there. Someone must have told them,' replied Anthony. He was visibly shaking and close to tears. Geoff held on to him.

'Quick, close the door before they do anything,' said Geoff, panicking.

Flora put her hand on Anthony's arm. 'It's OK,' she said soothingly.

'They're from the council. They work here. They just came out to say congratulations. They're happy for you, that's all,' explained Ruby.

Anthony shook his head. The crowd began to look at each other, wondering what was wrong.

'He's not feeling well,' I said to them. Geoff and

Anthony were adamant that they should not get out of the taxi and should go home.

'We never should have done this,' said Geoff, berating himself.

Just then the official-looking woman appeared.

'Mr Guthrie, Mr Penstone? I'm the registrar and I'll be conducting the ceremony. Is everything OK?' I'm not sure if she had guessed what the problem was, but she spoke softly and kindly. 'I know you didn't want a fuss, but we've splashed out on some flowers for you.' And with that, she handed over two bouquets. Anthony and Geoff smiled slowly.

'You're sure it's OK?' said Geoff, looking at Flora.

'Oh for goodness' sake, you pair of queens, get out of the taxi and let's get this over with, then we can all get pissed,' interrupted Ruby in her indomitable style.

This appeared to settle the matter. A cheer went up once more as the pair stepped out of the taxi and people came forward to congratulate them. Despite what they had said, they began to enjoy all the attention. They smiled and nodded to everyone as they passed, like visiting dignitaries.

'I can't believe all these people have come out just for us,' said Geoff incredulously, as they walked into the entrance. The mayor came over to shake their hands and congratulate them both. The ceremony had been intended to be a brief formality, but buoyed up by the attention and affection they had received, both Geoff and Anthony made spontaneous speeches.

'Thank you for sharing your life with me,' said Geoff, turning to Anthony. Until that moment Anthony had looked small and frail. He had become painfully thin and was easily lost in the large cavernous room with its high ceilings and gilt cornicing, but at Geoff's words he sat upright and his face seemed to glow.

We went back to their flat and Lewis brought bottles of champagne and smoked salmon canapés. Geoff was delighted to see Anthony eat, although in truth he couldn't manage more than a few meagre mouthfuls.

'Do you remember when we met?' said Anthony, sitting back in his chair. 'It was raining, you were waiting for a friend by the statue of Eros in Piccadilly Circus, do you remember?'

'Of course I remember, you wouldn't stop pestering me,' replied Geoff as he sipped his champagne.

'You lived in digs opposite the Natural History Museum with that woman who used to sit by the door, always knitting. You weren't allowed visitors after eight, and I used to have to wait till she was asleep and sneak past her.'

'And do you remember that day when you borrowed the car from someone – I can't remember who – and we drove to Epsom and went to the Downs and could see right across to London.'

'I rented the car, I think, to try to impress you. You said you loved strawberries but we couldn't find anywhere that sold them and the next day I came to your digs with punnets and punnets of them.'

'Yes and I couldn't eat them all and I had to give

some of them to that Italian man who lived over the way, the one with a limp who wore a wig.'

'No, you're thinking of the Irish man,' replied Anthony and they went back and forth, reminiscing, apparently oblivious to us all sitting listening.

'You know, this has got me thinking,' said Lewis later that evening as we sat around the kitchen table, 'I'm going to tell my family about me and Mark.'

'What, they don't know?' asked Ruby incredulously.

'God no,' replied Lewis. 'They're from Ghana, it's not tolerated there at all and all my family are very religious. I've always kept it from them.'

It was strange hearing Lewis talk like this. At medical school he had always been out and it never seemed an issue for him. Of course, I now realised, we had only ever seen him in the context of university or work and it was only now that it became apparent that he had been living a double life all this time.

'But don't they ask about girlfriends?' asked Flora.

Lewis looked a little sheepish. 'Well, when I was a medical student they thought I was too busy with studying, and since I've become a doctor,' he paused for a moment, 'well, I've let them think that . . . maybe they think that you're my girlfriend.'

The table erupted into laughter.

'They think what?' asked Flora with wide eyes.

'Well, I haven't actually ever said so, but I talk about you a lot, they know we go out together, so they have just assumed and I haven't corrected them.'

'Who do they think you live with?' asked Ruby.

'They think I'm Mark's lodger. It's an untenable situation. My cousin has already seen Mark and I out shopping once and started asking questions. I'm sure he's guessed. My parents still haven't been to the house in case they start asking questions about where I sleep. It really is a pressure and seeing those two today, it's fired me up. I'm not going to live a double life anymore. Life's too short. I'm going to tell my parents and I don't care what the consequences are.'

Lewis went home and Flora and Terry tidied up while I went to bed.

I lay, staring at the ceiling. I thought back to how scared I'd been when confronted by the panel of suits in the Executive Suite and wished I had some of Lewis's bravery.

As the name might suggest, for Care in the Community to work, two things are needed. Firstly, there needs to be a level of care provided, and secondly, there needs to be a supportive community in which the person is cared for. This may seem obvious, but it would appear that these simple facts eluded those who drew up the policies that saw numerous large psychiatric institutions close. Judging by how the reforms were implemented, the primary motivation for these policies cannot have been compassion for people locked away for indefinite periods of time. It must have been money. They set out to save money spent on expensive beds by reducing the number of people in hospitals. And so psychiatric patients up and down the country who had been institutionalised for large parts of their lives, were allowed to return to their communities to receive their care there.

While I don't agree with the motivations, it is undoubtedly true that it was monstrous to keep these people locked up, denying them their liberty and freedom. But it seems so cruel to firstly take away someone's freedom indefinitely and then to give it back so carelessly. Problems arose because many who were discharged didn't have any community to return to. Mental illness is stigmatising; families cannot always be supportive and communities, particularly in inner cities, are fragmented and disparate. These men and women had lost whole decades of their life while in asylums and then spent their remaining years, once released, lonely and isolated.

But out of this mess came some wonderful stories of compassion. Mr Cullen lived with his brother, William, in a tiny council flat in a very rough part of town. We had received a referral to the outpatient clinic but a home visit had been suggested by the GP. Before I went to visit them, Dr Webber asked if I would like a security guard from the hospital to escort me, but I reasoned that if two men in their eighties can live there, I was sure I could last a few hours.

Mr Cullen had been looking after his brother on his own since their parents died twenty years ago. William had been interned in a local asylum for thirty years because he suffered from schizophrenia. On his release, Mr Cullen took him into his home. When his mother died, Mr Cullen promised her, on her deathbed, that he would look after William for the rest of his life. With the help of his brother, William had lived a relatively normal and stable life in the community. He is an example of how, when given a loving and supportive community, someone can flourish.

Although William was the one with schizophrenia, he was not my patient. It was Mr Cullen. He'd been refusing to return to his GP after he had some tests a few months ago. It looked as though Mr Cullen had cancer, and I'd been asked to assess him and to try to persuade him to attend a hospital outpatient clinic.

'I'm not going to leave him, I promised my mum,' explained Mr Cullen when I visited. I sat precariously on the edge of the sofa, surrounded by furniture, ornaments and photographs. 'I don't want to be rude, I'm very grateful for all that you doctors have done,' he continued.

'It will only be for an afternoon,' I tried to explain, 'we can arrange for someone to come in to look after your brother while you're at the hospital.'

'No,' he said emphatically, 'because if they find something, then that's it, isn't it. There'll be no one to look after my brother, and you'll take him and lock him up again, won't you?'

It was illogical to think that by refusing to get a definitive diagnosis he'd be able to remain looking after his brother indefinitely. But whoever said humans were logical creatures and I couldn't help but admire his dedication to his brother.

I walked out into the bleak grey estate on my way back to the hospital and wondered what hope there was for William. If his brother were no longer able to look after him, then the community team would care for him. And that's the problem, because what was needed to complete the equation was the one thing the NHS couldn't provide. It can provide care, but not a community.

Over the past few weeks Mr Brownlee had remained steadfastly disruptive with his removals antics. He had been started on low doses of medication at night to help him re-establish a sleeping pattern and minimise his agitation. However, it was becoming apparent that the dose was going to have to be increased so that he was sedated during the day, for the safety of everyone. In this state, any hope of his wife continuing to care for him at home would be lost.

I'd become so used to regular interruptions from Mr Brownlee, usually dragging a piece of ward furniture, including, on one occasion, a chair with a confused and bewildered old lady still sitting in it.

I stopped typing for a moment.

Silence.

I had been back from visiting Mr Cullen and his brother for several hours and I suddenly realised I'd been able to get on with things undisturbed. I went back to work but after another fifteen minutes, I began to worry. Maybe he'd fallen over or had some accident? I got up and went out into the corridor. From there, I could see into the lounge and sure enough, there was Mr Brownlee sitting in a chair, quietly, peacefully watching television and drinking a cup of tea. I had never seen him sit down for more than a brief moment, but on this occasion he stayed put. Marsha was sitting next to him and occasionally he would begin to stand up and she would say something to him and he would sit down again. I beckoned her over.

'What have you done to Mr Brownlee?' I asked, incredulously. 'He's not sedated but he's just sitting there calmly.'

'I know!' exclaimed Marsha. 'The answer was so simple in the end. I just watched him for a while and then it suddenly struck me.' Mr Brownlee went to stand up. 'It's tea break,' she called to him from the doorway and he looked over, nodded and sat back down. 'He thinks he's on a never-ending removals job, but it occurred to me that even removals men have breaks. You just tell him he's on a tea break and he understands and stops trying to carry things.'

I was open-mouthed. It was so simple, yet so effective. 'You're a genius,' I said, still disbelieving that a solution had been found without resorting to medication.

'I know,' replied Marsha, 'and devastatingly beautiful to boot,' she said with a laugh and went off to the sluice.

There are times when 'health and safety' makes me sick. I'm sure that this is not what it is intended to do. But as with all things dreamt up by people in boardrooms wearing suits and drinking skinny lattes, they can end up harming the very people they intend to protect.

Mr Hazlit wanted to go outside.

'You can't,' came the reply from the nurse on the ward. The sudden glorious weather that week had seen patients flocking outside to escape the oppressive heat of the hospital. Well, the heat along with the smell of bleach and burnt toast that seems to pervade through every ward.

Mr Hazlit was under the care of the surgical team after having had an operation for bowel cancer. It was the second operation he had had, as the tumour had returned after the first. I'd been asked to review him as the surgeons wanted advice about managing his heart medication and his blood pressure, which had been very erratic. He was also clearly depressed. I wasn't surprised. His heart was very weak and beginning to fail, the surgeons had failed to remove the entire tumour and he was growing increasingly weak. He was going to die. He couldn't walk and was confined to a side room in the hospital. He had no visitors.

'Waiting to die is interminably boring,' he said, managing to laugh. 'It gets you down being in here day in and day out.'

I looked at his medication chart and wondered if there was anything I could do. There was little point in starting this man on antidepressants and there were no magic pills or potions that would make things better for him. He knew he wasn't going to get better physically. But what he really wanted to do was to go out in the sun and feel the warmth on his face, and to breathe fresh air. Now that seemed to me to be a pretty fair request.

'It's against health and safety,' came the reply from the ward sister when I suggested that this would be the best thing for him.

This is the blanket reply for anything that deviates from accepted protocol. I wondered exactly where the prohibition on taking sick men outside into the sunshine was written. But the nurse was bigger than me so I didn't push the point. The problem with health and safety is that it has become applied to the wrong things. It is now a general idea rather than a defined list of protocol, and those working with patients live in its shadow. The ever-increasing litigious nature of our society has meant that doctors and nurses are increasingly scared of getting sued, and this concern has now taken over when deciding what is best for patients.

'Well, OK, I'll take him myself, then,' I offered.

'You can't,' came her reply, 'you're not insured to push a wheelchair.'

I'd come up against this one before. A number of times while I was working in surgery I had sick patients who needed a scan when porters weren't available, so I pushed them myself – much to the anguish of the ward sister who failed to see that if the patient didn't get their scan they were far more likely to die or sue than if I pushed them to the X-ray department without insurance. It also missed the point that I appeared to be allowed to do far more risky things in my day-to-day work than pushing a wheelchair. But Mr Hazlit wasn't my patient, and while I was sure that health and safety didn't specifically cover this case, I knew that now it had been officially vetoed, there was no further discussion to be had.

'I'll take full responsibility for anything that happens,' piped up Mr Hazlit, who had been listening from inside his room.

'No, it's against health and safety,' came the reply yet again.

I tried to reason with the nurse, but to no avail. I wrote in the notes and left the ward. There was nothing that could be done for Mr Hazlit and indeed a few days later he died.

Officially he never did get to go outside. But of course the thing about health and safety is that it can only be enforced while you're at work. I'm sure you can guess what happened, unofficially, at five minutes past five when I wasn't officially working and the nurse was on her break.

12
Who's the Daddy?

'I'm not going, I'm ill,' I said, as I made myself Lemsip and settled down to watch some black-and-white films on TV and feel sorry for myself.

My mum gave me one of her withering looks of disapproval.

'You're not coming over here and moping around,' she said sternly.

Whatever happened to motherly love? She glared at me and I decided now was not the time to ask her this.

'Get up. They'll be so pleased to see you and she's come all the way from South Africa,' she said sternly.

It wasn't fair – I wasn't even allowed to be ill in peace. I began to wish I'd stayed in the flat, as I'd get more sympathy from my goldfish.

I dragged myself off the sofa and coughed loudly as I walked past my mum, to emphasise just how close to death I was.

'You've only got a cold, not the black death,' she called after me as I stomped upstairs to get changed.

'I feel really ill,' I called out in protest.

'You'll survive,' replied my mum dispassionately.

This was the standard response from my mum about any medical complaint I might have, and said in a way to make it sound like a threat, rather than words of encouragement.

Eventually we arrived at the party, which was at the house of some family friends to celebrate their mother's seventieth birthday. They were South African and although the children had emigrated to the UK, the mother, Mrs Kumalo, still lived there and had come over especially to celebrate her birthday here. It had taken the family a year to save up enough money to pay for her flight.

Her daughter and son-in-law came to the UK five years ago with their children, and one year later they were joined by Mrs Kumalo's other daughter. Three adults and two children lived in a small two-bedroom flat on the other side of the town from where my own mum lived. It was cramped and basic, but they would rather this life than the one afforded to them in Johannesburg. There, the division between the rich and poor is great; the opportunities available small. The family were mixed race, and because of this, continued to be subjected to insidious racial division. And the crime caused by crushing poverty meant that it was not an environment conducive to bringing up children.

I stood in their small lounge and looked at all the smiling people. Despite their slender means, the house was full of people enjoying themselves. Mrs Kumalo came over to me.

'It is such an honour that you have come for my birthday,' she said, and I felt embarrassed to think I nearly hadn't. The afternoon went with a swing. There was singing and dancing and I almost forgot about my cold.

As the afternoon drew to a close, I began to help clear away. In the kitchen, Mrs Kumalo stood, doing the washing-up.

'Oh, leave that, I'll do it,' I said, horrified to think that she had travelled thousands of miles to celebrate her birthday and had ended up cleaning dishes. She shook her head.

'No, you go and have fun,' she replied.

I was resolute. 'I'm not going back out there while you are still in here,' I exclaimed with a laugh. I picked up a tea towel and began drying the dishes.

'You shouldn't be doing this,' she said emphatically. I held the tea cloth for a moment, not sure what she meant. 'You're a doctor, it's not right you should do such chores,' she said, shaking her head in genuine worry.

I was acutely embarrassed by this and not sure what to say. Her deference to me was both flattering and also appalling. She had known hardships that I could not dream of, and besides, she was old, a guest in my country and it was her birthday. Of course I should be helping. But for her, the fact that a doctor had deigned to attend her birthday at all was an honour and the notion of him doing housework was incomprehensible. She was clearly very uncomfortable with the idea of me standing there and repeatedly asked if I wanted to sit down. I resolved the matter by saying that my mum would be angry to think I hadn't helped. This was the same mum who at that moment was sitting playing charades and eating gateau in the other room.

I looked at Mrs Kumalo's hands as she washed the plates. They were gnarled and swollen with arthritis. She walked slowly and tentatively, her frame twisted slightly and bent to one side. She still worked as a housekeeper in South Africa although the pain from her joints meant that she was finding it increasingly difficult to manage and, she explained, she feared that soon she wouldn't be able to work any longer.

The poverty that I encounter in the UK sometimes surprises me, but it does not impact on the healthcare people receive. It has become something of a national pastime to criticise the NHS, perhaps because it provides a diversion from complaining about the weather. But the reality is that across the world there are millions of people without access to even basic medical care simply because they are poor. The UK is unique in providing world-class healthcare for free at the point of use.

'There are pain killers, but they are too expensive,' she explained. In fact, she did take some painkillers, which she bought on the black market from a friend who had health insurance through her job. 'But they make my stomach hurt so I can't take them all the time,' she continued.

I listened to this with alarm. This is a well known,

and dangerous, side effect of the anti-inflammatory painkillers that she was taking. It can lead to life-threatening ulcers and in this country doctors routinely prescribe other medication to counteract this side effect. But that was a luxury she couldn't afford.

She smiled and shrugged her shoulders. 'In my country, we are used to things being difficult. It makes us strong and grateful for the good times. I have so much to be grateful for,' she said, gesturing back towards the lounge. This was a woman who had experienced apartheid, poverty and ill health and yet she did not complain.

In the taxi home I felt humbled to have met such a courageous and stoical woman and I thought how lucky we are in the UK to have the health service that we do. And for the rest of the weekend I didn't complain about my cold.

I arrived home after my weekend at my mum's to the sound of shouting. I closed the front door and peered through to the kitchen. Ruby was standing up by the sink and Flora and Terry were sitting round the table. Lewis – who had recently become a permanent fixture in our flat with Mark away on lots of conferences – caught my eye and rolled his eyes. He mouthed something at me and shook his head. Ruby saw me standing in the doorway and silence descended.

'Hi,' I said timidly with a smile. Nobody spoke. 'Sorry, have I interrupted something?' I asked gingerly.

'They were just . . . rather Ruby was just . . .' stumbled Lewis.

'Basically,' blurted out Ruby, 'I think it's ridiculous that Flora won't tell us who the father of her child is. Or rather, she won't tell us it's Housewives' Favourite, which we all know anyway. It's stupid. I don't see what your problem is, we're supposed to be your friends,' said Ruby, spitting out the last word.

Lewis was silent, but gestured that she'd been drinking.

'Ok, right . . . I might go upstairs,' I said, not wanting to get involved in a drunken row. I stood back up again.

'OK, fine,' blurted out Flora, looking at Ruby.

I sat back down again.

'You want to know? It's not Housewives' Favourite, it's nothing to do with him, he just happens to be helping me. It's Abdul.'

There was a moment of perplexed silence. I looked at Ruby, baffled.

'Abdul?' said Ruby 'who the hell is Abdul?'

'He was a medical student,' replied Flora stiffly. 'He was attached to Housewives' Favourite's team when I joined it at the beginning of the year.'

'But when did all this happen?' asked Ruby, still confused by the news.

'He's had various placements in the hospital over the past year, I got to know him a bit when I was doing my last job and then when I started this job and we found ourselves on the same team, it just sort of happened.' Flora was clearly getting upset speaking about this.

'So it wasn't Housewives' Favourite?' said Ruby. 'Then why were you seen skulking around with him, behind the back of A&E and stuff?'

'I told him I was pregnant, he was the only person I told except you lot, and he was helping me to apply for a permanent post so I'd get maternity leave. He was so kind to me, I don't know what I'd have done without his support.'

'Hang on, do you mean he knew it was this Abdul who was the father?' asked Ruby.

Flora nodded.

'You told him and you didn't tell any of us!' said Ruby incredulously.

'Not exactly,' replied Flora slowly.

Lewis shifted in his chair and Ruby and I looked at him.

'You knew!' shouted Ruby, pointing at Lewis.

'Erm, well,' he spluttered.

'It's not his fault,' said Flora. 'I had to tell him. Remember that day, when we all went out to the Doctor's Arms?'

'When you didn't come home?' I asked.

'Yes, well I was with Abdul,' said Flora slowly, 'and in the morning I was so upset and confused, I needed Lewis to act as an alibi, so I told him where I was and made him promise not to tell anyone and to cover for me.'

It transpired that the morning I had seen them both

in the doctor's mess, Flora was confiding in him what was happening. Flora explained that Abdul had texted her while she was in the pub saying that they needed to talk and, after spending the night together, had made it clear that he couldn't see her again.

'He's Muslim,' continued Flora, 'he said his parents wouldn't approve of me and he couldn't keep seeing me.' She was silent for a moment and Ruby poured herself a glass of wine. 'By the time I found out I was pregnant, he'd already left and begun a placement in another hospital. He just didn't want to know. He's not even bothering to reply to my texts anymore.' A single tear delicately traced its way down Flora's face and Terry put his arm around her. 'He's literally left me holding the baby,' she said, trying to compose herself. Flora got up and was shortly followed by Terry.

'I knew it wasn't Housewives' Favourite,' said Ruby, pouring herself another glass of wine.

'Haven't you had enough?' I said warily and she scowled at me.

Supriya had been oddly quiet the whole time and I turned to her, 'You OK? You don't seem yourself,' I said.

She sighed heavily. 'Just stuff at work. Things have been getting on top of me.'

Supriya, as I had witnessed first-hand in our first year of work, was not one to allow things to get on top of her. She was ultra organised and efficient, focused and determined. She wasn't herself, and then I suddenly remembered. 'When's the Coroner's hearing for that patient who killed himself?' I asked, as I realised that it had been hanging over her for several months and must be soon approaching.

'It was last Friday,' she said.

I felt a dreadful pang of guilt that I hadn't thought to mention it before. Supriya was quiet and dignified, and certainly not the sort of person to make a fuss. While she was eminently good at listening and helping with other people's problems, she preferred to keep her difficulties to herself as much as possible. I should have known to ask rather than assume she'd tell us.

'Oh Supriya,' I said, 'I'm so sorry. What happened? How did it go?'

'It was,' she said, closing her eyes, 'just awful.'

'Who went with you? Did your consultant go?'

'No, no one,' she said quietly.

'That's awful. He should have been there to support you,' I said, aware that it was not just him I was criticising, but me also.

'I was so nervous. I know there was nothing else I could do, that it wasn't my fault, but standing there I felt so guilty. The trust submitted a report trying to absolve themselves of any responsibility, even though I had clearly written that the patient shouldn't be allowed to leave the department. How can I be blamed for the fact that the trust won't provide appropriate security? But I was in the position of having to defend myself and all the time, his family was standing there, staring at me. His mother didn't stop crying throughout the whole thing. It was awful.'

'Supriya,' I said, looking at her directly, 'I'm so sorry. We should have remembered and been there to support you. What happened is not your fault. You can't blame yourself.'

'I know. It's the system's fault, the result of cutting corners and not training the security guards properly. I know that. But it just feels like the blame gets handed round like pass the parcel and all along, someone is dead and that person was my patient. I just can't stop thinking about his family.' I put my arm round Supriya.

Ruby sat down heavily next to us, 'Have a glass of wine.'

The next day, Mr Brownlee's wife came into the office.

'Doctor, I just wanted to thank you personally for everything you've done for my husband.' She was holding out a box of chocolates and a card and pushed them into my hand.

Outside I could hear Marsha saying goodbye to Mr Brownlee.

'I'm so grateful. I just want to care for him at home for as long as possible and when he was admitted this time, I really thought that I'd never get him home again. I can't believe he's coming home. You're a miracle worker.'

I looked down at the chocolates and the card, a little embarrassed. I really couldn't take the credit for the fact he was now being discharged. While the small doses of medication at night-time ensured he went to sleep, he was now manageable during the day thanks to the skill of the nursing staff, Marsha in particular.

Mrs Brownlee could now easily manage her husband at home with the simple words 'tea break'.

Of course, in some ways medicine had utterly failed Mr Brownlee. There was no cure for his condition and in a few months he would be dead. The best we could hope for is that it would be a quick and peaceful death. But out of the dark, bleak prognosis, Mrs Brownlee's determination to care for her husband right up until the end shone through. It was breathtakingly admirable. It would still be difficult for her. She would still have to continue to witness the man she loved ebb away from her until the person she was faced with was little more than a shell of the man she married. Mr Brownlee's future was full of unknowns, the only constant being his wife's love and dedication. And thanks to Marsha, his wife could care for him a little bit longer and that was something worth celebrating.

Just then Mr Berridge interrupted us. 'Where's my money?' he said.

I sighed. 'Marsha, can you help?' I called out.

Not everything, however, was good news on the ward.

After my visit, Mr Cullen's health had deteriorated rapidly. It transpired his prostate cancer had spread to his bones and he had begun to experience extreme pain, which needed morphine to manage it. He was admitted to the ward.

'They are looking after my brother, aren't they?' he said as soon as I saw him. In fact, while he was on the ward, he said little else.

'Yes, don't worry, social services are caring for him,' I tried to reassure him.

'It's all been so sudden. He'll be so lonely and scared. He's never been on his own before,' he replied.

'You'll see him soon, try not to worry about him. You need to focus on yourself for a bit,' I said, trying to reassure him. But it was no use.

'I promised my mother I'd always look after him,' he replied, still agitated.

A few days later Mr Cullen developed pneumonia. Then one morning when I went onto the ward there was a lady sitting up in the bed where he had been. He'd died during the night. I'm not sure who told his brother or what happened to him. It was all so sudden.

'Concerns have been raised about your professional conduct,' said the man in the grey suit, staring at me across the table.

I swallowed hard.

I had received another email requesting that I attend a meeting about 'concerns', as they called them, and had dutifully gone back to the Executive Suite, which seemed an unfortunate term given that all the executives here seemed anything but sweet.

'You were seen taking a patient outside against the express wishes of the nursing staff and in breach of health and safety, who then died,' he continued, not looking up from the piece of paper he was reading from.

'Erm, yes. But he was going to die anyway. He

wanted to go outside and . . .' I began to explain but
he interrupted me.

'And there was also an incident when you refused to
perform a procedure on a patient.' I wasn't sure what he
meant and looked at him quizzically. 'You were sched-
uled to perform ECT on a patient but then refused and
left without explanation,' he said, looking up.

'I did explain,' I protested, 'and I spoke to Dr Webber
about it.'

'Yes, Dr Webber,' he said slowly, raising an eyebrow. I
was aware that Dr Webber was considered to be a thorn
in the management's side and I immediately regretted
bringing his name up. 'Certainly he seems not to have
any concerns about your behaviour. Quite the contrary.
However, it might be an apposite time for you to consider
your career options with regard to employment in this
trust,' continued the man. 'Obviously these incidents
must be seen in the light of other concerns raised about
your conduct,' he said.

Ah, I thought, so this is what this is about. Flora, Ruby
and Lewis had been worried that the trust would not
forgive me for leaking the story about A&E, even though I
actually hadn't. I knew denying it was pointless, as far as
they were concerned, the fact I'd talked to that reporter
proved my guilt. This was obviously an attempt to punish
me and get me out so I couldn't further sully the trust's
reputation. I said very little, principally because they didn't
seem that interested in anything I had to say to defend
myself. They had obviously already decided and would
now make my life increasingly difficult until I resigned.

I left the meeting to consider my options and went down the stairs to the floor below where Trudy had her office.

'I know where you've been,' she said before I'd even sat down. 'Bastards. Don't let them bully you. I saw their emails and they're just trying to do damage limitation as they call it. Don't let them get to you.'

'They want me to resign,' I said.

'Tea?' said Trudy, getting up, apparently dismissing my concern. 'Look, they're running scared. What they've done is wrong and they know it, you know it, and now everyone else knows it. You've got the upper hand, don't forget that.'

'Thanks,' I said to Trudy, knowing that she was trying to help, but still feeling very alone.

'You know the local MP has been on at them?' she continued. 'He's kicking up a right stink. This kind of thing is so political, people really care about it.'

'There's already a campaign group been set up by the locals and there's stuff all over Facebook about it. Thanks to Craig getting round the hospital Internet security, I've been looking at the postings and everyone is furious about what's going on.'

I gave a weak smile.

'Here, have some Angel cake,' she said, handing me a slice.

I took it but wasn't hungry. I need a guardian angel, I thought, not Angel cake.

* * *

I left Trudy and went in to see Craig.

'Alright?' he said, looking up briefly and giving a nod before returning to his typing. I went over and sat on Mary 1's desk.

'Looking down in the dumps today,' she said. There was no hope of sympathy here.

'Yeah, just work stuff,' I replied.

'Oh, don't let that get to you. Take a leaf out of her book,' she said, pointing to Mary 3, 'just don't do any and then there's nothing to stress you out.' Marys 1 and 2 both laughed at this, although Mary 3 looked wounded.

'I do work. I work harder than both of you two put together,' protested Mary 3 earnestly.

This was a frequent debate between them and it occurred to me that they would be more productive if they collectively just got on with work rather than bickering about who did the least.

'Oh yeah, guess what?' said Craig, taking out his earphones and looking over to me. He didn't bother to actually turn off his iPod so we were all treated to the tinny, distant thumping sound of drum and bass which they emitted while they dangled from around his neck. 'I got an interview at medical school,' he said nonchalantly.

'Oooh, boffin!' exclaimed Mary 2 mockingly.

'That's amazing news. Ignore them,' I said, gesturing over to the three Marys who were pulling faces.

'I do,' he said bluntly, 'just thought you might be interested.'

'Seriously, well done,' I said. I hadn't really thought

Craig was serious about wanting to be a doctor and certainly hadn't entertained the idea that he might actually get an interview. 'Well, let me know if you want any help with preparing,' I said, but he'd already put his earphones back in. 'I said . . .' I repeated.

'Yeah I know, I heard you, thanks mate,' he replied.

I walked back out and past Trudy's office.

'Oh, I forgot to tell you,' she called out. I poked my head round the door. 'You know Mr Griffiths has applied for the Head of Surgery?' said Trudy.

'Yeah, we heard. Ruby was quite upset. He's got some nerve, considering what he did.'

'I know. Well hopefully I've put a stop to that.'

'How?' I asked, reminding myself once again never to mess with Trudy.

'Well, I'm getting married now and I quite like the idea of being married to a Head of Surgery,' said Trudy, showing off her engagement ring.

'Is Mr Butterworth applying?' I asked. Certainly the man had the social skills of a gall bladder, but he was infinitely more preferable to Mr Griffiths and actually, since he'd been in a relationship with Trudy, he'd warmed up considerably.

'Interview is next week. And don't you worry about having to resign. It will be OK,' she said with a mischievous smile.

I went back onto the ward and bumped into Dr Webber, who was having a meeting with Marsha. I told him what had happened at the meeting earlier.

'Don't worry old chap,' said Dr Webber, waving a hand dismissively. 'They haven't got a thing on you. If they did, they'd suspend you and refer you to the GMC. They're just making it difficult for you, putting the pressure on, you know, to try to make you leave and take all their problems with you.' He laughed. 'Well done, though, good show. I'd have done the same if I were in your shoes.'

'But I actually didn't do anything. I just spoke to a reporter. I didn't leak anything to the press,' I protested, but he wasn't listening.

'Right, I've got an outpatient clinic and I'm sure you've got work to be getting on with,' and with that, he turned and left, leaving me standing alone.

'How are you feeling?' I asked.

Mrs Leslie sighed and turned her face to the wall. She pulled the bed sheets up to her chin.

'Do you think you are depressed?' I ventured.

She shrugged. I sat down at the bottom of her bed and she continued to stare at the wall.

'I miss Robbie,' she said after some time. I nodded. Mrs Leslie had been widowed two years ago and was totally alone.

'Yes, it must be very hard,' I replied. 'How long were you and Robbie married?' Mrs Leslie looked at me, puzzled, then shook her head.

'Robbie's my Jack Russell,' she said. 'I was married to my husband for forty years but, God, I don't miss him.'

'Oh, OK' I said, a little taken aback.

'My neighbour has been looking after him, but they're not dog people and apparently he's keeping them awake all night howling. He never howls when he's with me.'

Mrs Leslie had been admitted to the hospital after a stroke. It is common after a stroke for patients to suffer depression. This is not only because they have often lost some function and maybe experience a degree of incapacity, but also because damage to the brain can disrupt some of the neural circuits that regulate mood.

'What if I never get out of here? What if I have to go into a home? What will happen to him then?' she continued with tears in her eyes, 'I don't know what I would have done sometimes without that dog.' She went on to explain that although she might be alone, she had never felt lonely because she always had Robbie. He was fourteen years old and blind in one eye, but he clearly gave her life meaning and structure in a way that no prescription tablet I could prescribe ever would.

Mrs Leslie was right to worry, though. If she were to go into a home, it's likely that Robbie wouldn't be allowed to go with her, despite the fact that there is clear evidence to show that pets help people's physical and psychological well-being. The most important thing in her life would be taken away from her and she would spend the rest of her days alone. It was clear that, regardless of her stroke, just a short period of time being alone and away from her dog had contributed to a depressive illness and I wondered what a future without any pets would do to her.

I didn't start Mrs Leslie on an antidepressant. Instead, I spoke to Dr Webber and the district nurse and we concluded that it was in her best interests to be at home. A week later she was discharged back to the care of a certain Jack Russell.

13
Going Bananas

Fruit isn't renowned for making people go bananas. However, on our ward round at the beginning of the week, it was indeed fruit that pushed Dr Webber over the edge.

Jamie Oliver's sterling efforts to overhaul dinners in schools have yet to reach other institutions such as hospitals. In the past there has been furore over children being served up deep-fried, reconstituted, reclaimed pap, with the nutritional content of ply board, and this is quite right. How are children supposed to learn if they don't have adequate nutrition? But on our ward, it wasn't what was on the menu that was the problem, rather, it was what wasn't.

Poor Mrs Lund, as well as having the beginnings of dementia, had a list of medical problems. She was eighty-two years old and her appetite wasn't good at the best of times. But she loved fruit. So much so, she'd taken to hiding bananas under her pillow. And now she thought that another one of the patients had taken one. She was so upset we could hear the noise during our ward round. We all peered out of the office and into the lounge.

'You've eaten it already,' Marsha was trying to explain.

'I haven't, he's taken it,' she shouted, pointing to another patient, Mr Murray. Everyone looked at Mr Murray.

'I never touched her bloody banana!' he shouted back.

'Don't worry,' said Dr Webber in an attempt to pacify Mrs Lund, 'we'll get you another banana.' He looked at the nurses. Embarrassed silence.

'Erm, no, we can't I'm afraid, we've had all the ones we're allowed for today,' replied Marsha, 'that's why she hides them under her pillow.'

The shortage of fruit on the ward, Marsha went on to explain, was because the trust had recently decided it needed to make cut-backs. One of the significant casualties was the food budget.

I'd love to have sat in on the meeting when the managers decided limiting the amount of fruit that was allowed would be a good idea. How anyone can justify withholding fresh fruit from sick people is beyond me.

Our ward of fifteen patients was allowed three bananas a day. Demand, obviously, outstripped supply. The nursing staff had taken to either cutting them up so that everyone could get some or rationing them for each patient over the week. The ward also got two apples a day, but as most of the patients had dentures or bad teeth, they were traded with other wards for more bananas. An orange had yet to make an appearance. In the fruit hierarchy, this was obviously out of our league. Patients had begun to adapt to the fruit ration in ridiculous ways, with some patients taking their piece of banana into the bathroom in case someone else ate it while they were away. Marsha informed us that a black market in fruit had sprung up on the ward. The going rate for a whole banana was five cigarettes. Here was a group of people for whom fresh fruit would do a world of good, and who actually wanted it – in fact were clamouring for it – but it was being severely rationed. You'd be forgiven for thinking we were in the Second World War.

Dr Webber was furious. He quite rightly pointed out that patients stuck in hospital were wholly reliant on what was served to them at meal times to provide the vitamins, nutrients and energy needed in order to get better. They might be in hospital for months on end. Many of them couldn't easily go outside, and they certainly couldn't do their own shopping. Few of them had visitors who would bring them food.

'We have tried to raise the issue with catering, but there's little they can do,' added Marsha defensively.

Dr Webber remained silent, and it wasn't clear to us who he was angry with.

The next day, however, Dr Webber returned to the ward with a basket of fruit, which he had paid for out of his own pocket. Mrs Lund was beside herself with excitement.

'I'm not going to let this lie. It's a disgrace,' he fumed, at which point Mrs Lund burst into applause.

I smiled to myself, pleased that there were doctors who, despite reaching the top of their profession, still remained idealistic and angry at injustice, ready to defend their patients and stand up for their welfare. Certainly he had a reputation in the hospital for being cantankerous and irritable. He was authoritarian and insisted that everything was done correctly and was quick to lose his temper when it wasn't. Marsha said he was once in the Foreign Legion but left because it was too free and easy. But without someone like Dr Webber, his patients – old and often confused, dismissed and forgotten – would have no one to defend them. After dishing out the fruit, he left the ward to find the hospital managers, and I was pleased I wasn't in their shoes. I suspected it was going to take more than an apple a day to keep this doctor at bay.

The issue of food continued all week. Amazingly, after Dr Webber's outburst regarding the fruit (which Trudy said she could hear from the other side of the administration block), it had begun appearing in abundance on the ward. Clearly the man from Del Monte had finally said yes. Who said shouting never got you anywhere? But, as I learnt from a patient later that week, simply having good, nutritious food wasn't the panacea I had thought. Things, as I had learnt to expect from medicine, were more complicated.

It all started with a loud crash. The nurses and I winced. Someone suppressed a giggle while someone else helpfully handed Dr Webber a tissue. He had porridge all over his trouser leg now. He carefully dabbed at it, then froze. He looked up at the patient who was lying in her bed and stared at her for a few minutes. Then he picked up the toast from where it landed on the floor when he knocked over the breakfast tray.

One of the ward nurses accompanying us leant forward, 'We've got biscuits if you're hungry,' she offered, tactfully.

'Sorry, someone should have been in to take the tray away,' said another nurse, removing the breakfast things and putting them outside the room.

'This toast is hard,' he said, not addressing anyone in particular and then added, 'the porridge has gone cold.'

And clearly, he's gone mad I thought.

'It's obvious what's wrong with Mrs Hudson, isn't it?' asked Dr Webber, surveying the scene. The nurses and myself stood around the bed, utterly bemused. How could he have made a diagnosis simply by looking at her and knocking over her breakfast tray?

Mrs Hudson had been admitted to the surgical ward after having a fall and breaking her hip. She didn't seem to be making much progress and the surgical team was at a loss to explain why. They had run tests, examined her, prodded and poked her, but still couldn't see why she was so weak. Technically, the operation had been a success, yet she still lay in bed, losing weight and unable to walk for more than a few paces before collapsing.

Of course, I realised later, I had missed a number of vital clues as to why Mrs Hudson was so frail, because while I was looking, I wasn't seeing.

Much of being a doctor is detective work, Dr Webber had often told me. Reaching a diagnosis is not dissimilar to the deductive process employed by any good sleuth. Possible suspects are drawn up and eliminated until one culprit remains and, hence, the diagnosis reached. Dr Webber had often argued that it was no coincidence that one of the greatest fictional detectives was created by a doctor. Sir Arthur Conan Doyle based the character of Sherlock Holmes on a professor named Joseph Bell for whom he had worked as junior doctor. Bell used to amaze Conan Doyle by his careful analysis of apparently unrelated observations to help elucidate his patients' conditions. You can clearly see the way that this was used in the creation of Holmes.

'Every good doctor should read Sherlock Holmes,' insisted Dr Webber.

Until now I'd never been convinced. Thinking about it, though, the techniques of observation and deduction form part of the training at medical school and are employed by all doctors to some extent. A thorough examination of a patient, for example, always starts with looking at the hands for telltale signs that will help with a diagnosis. Red palms suggest liver disease; upward turning nails indicate possible iron-deficiency anaemia, and so on. Mrs Hudson had cataracts and arthritis. But what was the significance of the open box on the side table, which contained dentures? What had cold porridge and hard toast to do with this? Dr Webber rolled his eyes at our apparent inability to understand what was staring us in the face. The answer, it transpired, was alimentary, my dear Watson (sorry, I couldn't help myself).

'Of course she's not getting better, she's not eating enough,' Dr Webber concluded. She didn't have her dentures available, her eyesight was poor and the food was out of her reach. Her arthritis meant that she couldn't cut up her food properly, and the tray was merely removed uneaten without question. The quality of the food being served is irrelevant if the patient doesn't even eat it.

Dr Webber gave strict instructions for the nursing staff to supervise Mrs Hudson at meal times and ensure she was eating properly. I was surprised, though, as we walked away from the ward, that he hadn't been angry with the nurses. I had braced myself for him exploding with rage at them, but instead he was polite and conciliatory.

'It's not their fault,' he said as we walked away from the ward, 'it's a common problem in hospitals. The neglect isn't out of malice, it's because increasingly nurses' time is taken up with reams of paper work rather than the job of actual nursing.'

We walked past the paediatric ward and I thought for a moment. 'But it's not as if older people are the only ones in hospitals who have difficulty feeding themselves,' I said, 'yet you don't see rows of under-fed babies because they've been left with a bottle and told to get on with it.'

Dr Webber smiled at me. 'That's very true,' he said, 'and I suppose that's at the very heart of the problem. It's recognised as being vital, and therefore it's prioritised. Mrs Hudson's malnourishment is just symptomatic of the way that society as a whole ignores older people.'

Another case of looking without seeing, I thought, and we made our way to the canteen.

As I paid for my lunch, Jeannie, the social worker, came up to me. I was balancing a tray on my arm while trying to silence my beeping pager and simultaneously taking my change from the cashier.

'Oh, I've been meaning to email you. I've got some good news, of sorts,' she said as she picked up a bag of crisps. 'The matron from the nursing home where your patient is has resigned.'

I looked at her, surprised.

'We started investigating the allegations and as soon we started sniffing around, the owner announced she was leaving.'

'She resigned? I asked. 'Why would she do that?'

'Well, to be honest, it's likely she wasn't given a choice. In reality, she'd have been told to leave – fired – but to keep things low-key and avoid any scandal or suggestion that things are wrong, the official line is usually that they resign in these situations.'

'That's great news, isn't it?' I said.

Jeannie gave me a gentle smile. 'It would be lovely to think that things were that simple, wouldn't it?' she said. 'From my experience, one person leaving doesn't change things. The problems are bigger than that. The owners will do a bit of window dressing, pay lip service to any recommendations, re-jig the staff around, but there'll be no fundamental changes. It's a business for them, nothing more.'

'What will happen to the matron now?' I asked.

'She'll get a job somewhere else, I expect,' replied Jeannie.

At that point my pager went off again. I put my tray down on a nearby table and went off to answer it, leaving Jeannie to her bag of crisps.

That weekend Lewis came round for a drink as he'd just finished a week of nights.

It seemed that everyone except Lewis had something to contend with recently. Ruby had the prospect of Mr Griffiths becoming Head of Surgery. Flora had her pregnancy and the difficult questions this raised about her career. Supriya had been badly shaken by her experience at the coroner's hearing and the realisation that, when the chips were down, the trust was more concerned with looking after itself than its staff. I had the prospect of being asked to resign looming over me.

'We need a holiday,' I suggested. Everyone round the table looked at me wearily. 'Come on, it will be fun,' I said, trying to chivvy them along. Terry was the only one who seemed keen.

'Yeah, it could be like a team building exercise,' he said gleefully.

Ruby glared at him and, remembering it was her turn, stood up to do the washing-up. Lewis, who I had counted on to be enthusiastic about the idea – and to organise it – didn't say anything.

'What's wrong with you?' I asked, noticing that he was staring off into the distance.

'Oh, sorry,' he said with a jolt, 'I was just thinking.'

Ruby abandoned the washing-up after just one plate and belligerently went outside for a cigarette.

'Our job is quite strange sometimes, isn't it?' he said, enigmatically.

'What do you mean?' replied Flora as she looked up from the newspaper.

'We see some really awful things.'

'Oh yeah, all that blood and guts,' said Terry, screwing up his nose in disgust. 'I don't know how any of you do it.'

'No, that's not what I mean,' corrected Lewis, 'I don't mean the blood, I mean the way we witness peoples' lives just unravel in front of us. I remember when I started, I used to hate all the gore. But actually, that's the easiest bit to deal with.'

'Well, it's good that the things you see effect you, everyone wants their doctor to care,' said Terry.

Lewis turned to him, 'But that's the whole point. You – the public – want us to care, but only about you. That's the difficulty.'

'Surely you should care about all your patients,' protested Terry.

'No, don't you see, you want us to be empathetic and concerned, but if we came to you from seeing another patient and burst into tears and you had to console us before we could treat you, you wouldn't like that. So we have to care about our patient at that moment we're with them, then switch it off and turn round, pause and smile for our next patient.'

I knew exactly what he meant and this was something that all of us had to contend with.

'What's brought this on?' asked Flora.

'Nothing,' said Lewis, but this was out of character for him and I knew something must have happened to make him speak like this. 'Well,' he paused 'there was just this man, the other night when I was on call. He was brought in. Crashed his car. In resus, not breathing, we worked really hard to bring him back.'

'What happened to him?' I asked.

'It was pointless,' said Lewis, shaking his head. 'We did an X-ray of his spine and he'd been decapitated.'

Terry let out a gasp at this and closed his eyes firmly. 'What? But that's . . . that's horrible. Couldn't you tell just by looking at him?'

'No, that was the thing,' Lewis replied, 'it's called an internal decapitation – the head is severed from the spinal cord but the skin remains intact. It was just such a horrific thought when I looked at him yet he seemed so peaceful.'

'Oh Lewis,' said Flora 'that is horrible.' She put her hands up to her neck and shivered. 'Oh, just the thought of it.'

'Don't you get counselling for things like that?' asked Terry. This provided a brief respite as we all burst out laughing at his suggestion.

'It's difficult enough getting patients counselling,' said Flora, 'let alone us.'

'The thing that threw it all into sharp relief was that before I could even think about it, a nurse came up to me and gave me another patient. I just turned round with the notes in my hand and walked into the cubicle to see this middle-aged woman who had chest pains.'

'It's alright if you're upset,' said Flora tenderly, and she put her hand on his arm but he shrugged it off.

'No, it's not that. I'm not upset. I've seen so many dead bodies. It's just that sometimes I want things to pause, just for a moment, so I can try to understand them. It's as though we bear witness to such monumental things and yet they flash past and hardly even register.'

There was a brief silence.

Ruby walked back into the kitchen and looked at us all sitting there, sombrely.

'God, who died?' she said.

The next day I had a new patient on the ward.

Mrs Maddox had been doing her weekly shop in her local supermarket when she developed chest pains. Not wanting to make a fuss, she leant against the wall and held on to a nearby shelf. But rather than the pain subsiding, it got worse. She slid down the wall and collapsed, bringing the shelves crashing down around her. The groceries on the shelves fell to the floor and several tins hit her on the head causing some nasty gashes. When the ambulance crew arrived and picked their way over broken eggs, smashed ketchup bottles and packets of cornflakes so they could kneel down to assess her, the only thing she kept saying was, 'Is someone going to look after Manuel?' She continued to repeat this in the A&E department, even after a tracing of her heart showed that she had suffered a heart attack.

'We're going to have to admit you,' the casualty doctor had explained as the cuts on her head and hands were sutured. Mrs Maddox had shaken her head.

'But what about Manuel?' she said aghast. 'I can't come into hospital, I have to look after him.'

Reading through her notes I could see that the casualty doctor had had some difficulty persuading Mrs Maddox to stay in hospital, despite the seriousness of her condition. But eventually she had relented and agreed to be transferred to my ward.

Sitting on her bed and talking to her for a few minutes, it was no surprise that she had had a heart attack. Manuel, her husband, had Parkinson's disease and dementia as well as kidney problems and she, at the age of eighty-three, was his sole carer. Every morning she got him up, emptied his catheter, washed him, got him dressed, made his breakfast, then took him out in his wheelchair. She had to ensure he was drinking enough otherwise his catheter became blocked. The combination of her husband's mobility problems and memory impairment meant he was unable to do anything for himself. He often did not know who she was and became aggressive and hostile towards her. Yet she was dedicated to his care to the extent that she was more concerned for his welfare than her own and it was obvious that the demands of the job were taking a toll on her health. I thought back to Mr Cullen and his brother. Mr Berridge, too. In fact, there are thousands upon thousands of individuals up and down the country who are caring for loved ones. The amount of money they save the taxpayer is more than the total budget for the NHS. Yet the toll that this work takes on these people is great. Not only are they twice as likely to be permanently sick or disabled than the general population, but the work they do is also incredibly emotionally draining.

Mrs Maddox was trying to be stoical, but as I sat on her bed talking to her, she began to break down. She clenched her jaw, trying not to cry.

'There are just some days when . . .' her voice cracked and she cleared her throat, 'when I really don't know how long I can carry on. It just gets too much sometimes. Don't get me wrong, I want to care for him, but it's just so relentless sometimes.'

'What about respite care?' I asked. 'Surely a break would be a help?'

'Yes, I have thought about that, but it's so complicated getting it arranged. The forms you have to fill in, the hoops you have to jump through. It's almost not worth the stress it causes.'

I had seen the forms that carers were expected to complete and knew what she meant and had heard many people saying the same thing. The health service would be crippled overnight without carers, yet the very things that are intended to help them are difficult to access.

'Look, while you're in here, why don't I ask one of the social workers to come and have a chat with you, see how she can help?' I suggested.

Mrs Maddox looked at me and nodded frantically.

'Oh yes, please, anything,' she said, and I left her to make a phone call to Jeannie.

As I dialled the number, I wondered if it had really gotten to the stage that a person must be admitted to hospital with a heart attack before getting the support they need?

No wonder surgeons act like they're God. After all, there's a definite air of the messianic about what they do.

'He was blind and now he can see,' says the ophthalmic surgeon.

'He was lame and now he can walk,' says the orthopaedic surgeon.

Unfortunately, in my job, there are few miracles. Much of it is managing a situation, trying to make adjustments to the social circumstances and tweaking medication to make things a little bit better. One of the most important jobs I can do for some of my patients is to act as their advocate. The stigma that affects people suffering with mental illness comes in many forms and it's surprised me to realise that it doesn't necessarily end when they come into hospital. People who are mentally ill also get physically unwell but a diagnosis of mental illness, in whatever form, can cast a shadow over every other illness the patient has. Forget the fact that they might have other things wrong with them. There's a feeling that 'mad' people must be making things up. Doctors who ordinarily would never consider a psychosomatic origin for a symptom suddenly feel this can be the only explanation when confronted with a patient with a physical complaint in conjunction with an underlying mental illness. Perhaps this is because some doctors don't listen to people who have mental health problems, or because they don't want to have them on their ward.

Mr Maggs had been transferred to our ward from the assessment ward next to A&E. He'd had schizophrenia since he was twenty-three years old and was now in his early seventies. Several years ago he had developed diabetes as a side effect of the antipsychotic medication he had been prescribed. He was not very good at managing his medications; sometimes he would not take his insulin and then compensate by taking too much. On the day he was admitted, he'd injected too much and fallen unconscious. Thankfully, his community psychiatric nurse was visiting and found him on the floor of the bathroom. He was rushed into hospital and admitted to the assessment ward after being stabilised in A&E.

However, while he had recovered from the overdose of insulin well, he was difficult to manage on the ward, crying out throughout the night, shouting at the nurses and doctors when they walked past. But then again, I'd shout out too if I'd fractured my shoulder in three places. No one had thought to examine him properly, so this wasn't discovered. His doctors assumed he was shouting out because he was mad, and as soon as it was obvious his diabetes was now stable, they transferred him onto the geriatric ward under Dr Webber's care. He'd been in hospital for three days with an untreated broken shoulder, which he'd sustained after collapsing from the insulin.

Before he'd even had his wash bag unpacked, though, Marsha knew something was wrong with him. Within an hour he was sitting in the X-ray department. It took her to see he was crying out not because he was mad, but because he was in pain. With the X-rays showing that he had broken bones, the orthopaedic surgeons were duly called. I had thought about calling Ruby, knowing that she'd be sympathetic to his plight, but orthopaedics, like many areas of medicine and surgery, is further divided into sub-specialities and her team only did lower limbs. After phoning around, I found the specialist team for shoulders. I sent Mr Maggs down to the fracture clinic, assuming that they would now deal with him. Later that day, though, I noticed he was back on the ward.

'What's happened with Mr Maggs?' I asked Marsha. 'Did he see the surgeons?'

'Yes, but they just sent him back up here. I don't think they're going to do anything.'

'What?' I asked incredulously. 'He's broken his shoulder. Did they see the X-rays?' She nodded. 'Did they send him back with a letter?' I asked. She shook her head. There must be some mistake, I reasoned, so we sent him again, but the same thing happened. I was beginning to tire of this, as all along, Mr Maggs was unable to use his shoulder and was in pain. I telephoned the registrar and began to get the distinct feeling that they weren't going to operate on Mr Maggs because they didn't want to, because he was mentally ill.

'We don't want him being disruptive on the ward,' he explained.

'He's not disruptive,' I tried to reason with them, as if good behaviour was now a prerequisite for surgery.

'Someone like him will manage fine with limited movement anyway,' he continued, although he didn't wish to expand on what 'someone like him' meant. No one seemed to want to help Mr Maggs. After all, he wasn't going to write a letter of complaint or try to sue. But while I couldn't fix his shoulder myself, the one thing I had learnt from Dr Webber was that it was our duty as doctors to stand up for our patient and I couldn't accept the idea that Mr Maggs would just be left with a broken shoulder.

'Not all orthopaedic surgeons are the same,' said Dr Webber when I phoned him asking what I should do, and he suggested I telephone the consultant directly.

He was a professor and I didn't fancy the chances that a lowly junior doctor such as myself would persuade him. To my surprise, though, he looked at the X-rays on his computer while I was on the phone to him explaining all the problems we've had getting people to take Mr Maggs' problems seriously.

'There's no reason why this man shouldn't have an operation,' he said, and then added, quietly, so I could only just hear it, 'My sister has schizophrenia, you know.'

And two days later Mr Maggs was transferred to the orthopaedic ward for his operation. Thank God.

14
A Private Dilemma

I looked at the man lying down in front of me. I moved my hands away from his temples as his feet began to twitch and the assembled nurses and doctors watched him. After about thirty seconds the twitching in the feet stopped and the anaesthetist stepped forward to bring him round. The consultant looked at the readings being spewed out of a machine on a seemingly never-ending ribbon of paper. It cascaded onto the floor as he scrutinised it carefully.

My hands were still shaking slightly. I was aware that what I had just participated in was controversial, not least because of the last time I had attempted to do this.

The man woke up and opened his eyes. 'Is it all over then?' he asked me with a calmness that would make it easy to forget that he had just had a current of electricity passed through his brain.

'Yes, that's it Mr Jones,' replied one of the nurses and helped him off the bed.

'Thank you very much,' he said to the assembled team and pottered off back to the ward.

Was that really it? I thought to myself. What had particularly surprised me was that Mr Jones, having spent years battling depression, had actually been eager to have this done. He had already undergone a few weeks of ECT and was ecstatic about the difference it had made already.

'It's the first time in my life when I can honestly say I feel normal. I now wake up in the morning and I don't wish I were dead,' he had said to me earlier when he was waiting outside.

But the road that had led me back to this had been long and not one I had readily walked down. I had done what Dr Webber had suggested and read through the literature concerning ECT. I had looked up the research, read accounts of people who had had it done and thought long and hard about it as a treatment option for people with severe depression. Given the connotations of institutional barbarism that this procedure conjures up, I wanted to assess the evidence base myself, to contemplate this carefully and, above all, not to feel I was being forced into something before I'd had time to think about it.

While the professor had clearly had difficulty understanding my position, Dr Webber was more accommodating. He had encouraged me to talk to some of the patients on the ward who had undergone ECT in the past to see what they thought about it. I was overwhelmed by the positive response. Without exception, they told me how when they were in the quagmire of despair and all other treatments had failed, it had saved their lives. While their responses are in no way substitute for sound, empirical research to support its use, they did go some way to challenging the image I had of some screaming patient, tied down, being electrocuted until they were gibbering wrecks in some grotty backroom of a 1950s asylum. The reality couldn't be further from this. It takes place in an operating theatre surrounded by doctors and nurses. The patient is anaesthetised and given a muscle relaxant to stop them jerking during the seizure. The patient doesn't shake wildly, doesn't scream, there aren't any bolts of electricity flying around the room. In fact, there's barely anything to see.

I tried to approach the subject rationally. I studied the research and read about the evidence base and alternatives. And I was amazed to learn how safe and effective it was. ECT still has its critics, but I wonder how many of them have seen the practice in its modern context. It's a bit like condemning leg amputations carried out by orthopaedic surgeons because of images of sailors having their limbs cut off in the Napoleonic Wars.

In fact it has far fewer side effects than many of the drugs I happily prescribe. Certainly the science behind how it actually works is not fully understood, but this is the same for many of the treatments that we use.

From my reading one sad fact emerged: depression kills. Suicide in the UK constitutes nearly one per cent of deaths from all causes annually. After road traffic accidents, it is the single biggest killer of young men.

The Confidential Enquiries into Maternal Deaths found that suicide was the leading cause of maternal mortality in the UK. Depression also destroys lives insidiously, dismantling them piece by piece until little remains. Depression represents a significant public health issue. But depression is treatable. The development of talking and pharmaceutical therapies has meant that the lives of millions of people have been transformed. But there remains a small cohort of people for which standard treatment does not work. It is in this group that ECT is sometimes used. In fact, empirical evidence has shown it is the most effective treatment for severe depression; meaning people can resume work and relationships and start living their lives again.

It is particularly useful in older patients who present with depression so severe that they refuse food and drink, appear confused or paranoid, or experience severe nihilism. For these people, ECT can mean the difference between returning to their life at home and ending their days in an institution.

While the public perception of ECT is frequently one of an archaic, barbaric, inhumane treatment and conjures up images of dark, ominous corridors in friendless asylums, this is not the reality. The electrical current lasts for no more than a few seconds. All patients consent before undergoing ECT treatment, and can withdraw this consent at any time. Very occasionally someone is so ill that it is felt they are not capable of consenting. In these circumstances, two doctors and a social worker must assess the patient to detain them in hospital under the Mental Health Act, and then an independent psychiatrist, sent by the Mental Health Commission, must assess the patient and agree that the treatment is necessary.

As with any treatment, there are side effects, although ECT is amongst the safest medical treatments given under general anaesthetic. The most commonly reported ones are headache, dizziness and memory problems. The latter is the one that receives the most attention. It tends to refer to memories formed in the period directly after the treatment, but memory usually improves within a few hours to a few weeks, if problems occur at all. While the exact mechanism by which ECT works is not fully understood, and it's likely the result of several complex processes, it is understood that the seizure produces changes in the brain, at a molecular as well as cellular level, which 'resets' the neuro-chemical equilibrium.

It's not a cure-all. It should be used carefully and only when clinically indicated. But, from talking to patients who had it done and reading the evidence for myself, I began to understand that ECT is an invaluable weapon in the arsenal used to fight depression. Having depression is nothing to be ashamed of, and neither is having ECT. Depression kills, and sometimes, ECT saves.

A few days later I walked onto the ward and saw Mr Jones sitting there, drinking a cup of tea. He smiled and waved at me, and I waved back. I thought back to my initial refusal to do ECT all those months ago. I didn't regret my initial reticence and wariness; it's vital that doctors question the treatments they give and don't bow to pressure. But looking at the man now, I was confident that ECT had been the best treatment and it would have been wrong to withhold this from him based on misconceptions and prejudice. This was a man who had battled with suicidal depression for years, for whom no tablet or talking therapy had worked to penetrate the black cloak that surrounded him day in and day out, but who was now, finally, getting better. In fact, he'd made such a dramatic improvement after just a few sessions of ECT, there was talk of discharging him home soon. It was all a far cry from the images in *One Flew Over the Cuckoo's Nest*. It's clear that, for a patient like Mr Jones, ECT was not controversial. It was a lifesaver.

Marsha came into my office and handed me a note.

'It's from Dr Webber. I think he wants to see you,' she said, then grimaced.

I started to panic.

Marsha walked out of the office and then poked her head back round. 'Do you still have that box of tissues I gave you?' she asked.

I looked around my office. 'Yes, somewhere, why?'

'Oh, because you'll probably need them if Dr Webber wants to see you,' she laughed. I didn't find this funny, although I did take a tissue and put it in my back pocket, just in case.

As I knocked on his door, I wracked my brains as to what I could have done wrong, but could think of nothing. Inside he was sitting, surrounded by books and piles of paperwork. The keyboard on his desk was precariously resting on a pile of paper and there were boxes piled up on top of each other around his desk. By a filing cabinet in the corner I noticed a microwave and, incongruously, a lawn mower. There was an area towards the rear of the room with a coffee table and two low, upholstered chairs, but they were swamped in piles of paper and clutter with yet more boxes scattered around. Along one wall was a series of shelves piled high with books, and a number of books were on the floor directly below, which had obviously fallen off and lain there for some time.

'Excuse the mess,' he said, observing me look round the room. 'After my divorce I moved into a one bedroom flat and I didn't have the space for everything so it ended up in here.'

'You wanted to see me?' I asked, nervously.

'Ah, yes. We need to do your appraisal,' he said, searching around the room. I breathed a sigh of relief. 'There's a form I have to fill in somewhere,' he said vaguely. 'Erm, I think it's over there. No, it must be over here.'

He moved various piles around and eventually gave up and printed a fresh form from his computer.

'Meaningless,' he said, as he ticked various boxes. 'All this rubbish came in after Shipman, as if a few tick boxes ever stopped a psychopath. It's just a complete waste of everyone's time, but still, we need to pick our battles and if this is what the public want us to spend our time doing, then so be it.'

I smiled benignly and wondered if he would feel obliged to mention my run-in with the trust managers on the form.

'Professionalism,' he said, and I looked at him. 'Excellent.' and he ticked a box. 'Any cause for concern?' He read aloud, 'Nope,' he said to himself. 'There, that should do it,' he said finally, and handed me the form. I breathed a sigh of relief and was touched to see all the positive things he had written. 'Now, about this business with the trust,' he began. 'Do you know there's a TV crew outside A&E?'

'No!' I exclaimed. 'Because of the closures?'

'The management are really feeling the heat with this, but you mustn't let it prey on your mind. Just get on with your job and keep your head down, these things have a habit of blowing over.' I nodded, but wanted more than just bland reassurances. 'Just whatever you do, Max, steer clear of A&E today and don't speak to the TV crew.'

I smiled and nodded.

I walked along the corridor and into Trudy's office. She was sitting at her desk, speaking on the phone and eating a lemon slice.

'I'll call you back,' she said, putting down the phone receiver and beaming at me. 'Have you heard?' she said as she swallowed the last bit and swept the crumbs onto the floor. 'The results of the interviews for Head of Surgery are out.'

'And?' I asked.

'And you are now looking at the fiancée of the new Head of Surgery.' She pouted and flicked her hair back.

'That's great news,' I said, thinking how delighted Ruby would be. I knew that Mr Butterworth would keep an eye on Mr Griffiths and support Ruby as she climbed the career ladder. I smiled. Good old Trudy.

'Anyway, what you doing over here?' she asked distractedly as she admired her engagement ring.

I explained that I'd been to see Dr Webber for my appraisal and about the TV crew outside A&E.

'Oh, you're not still worried about all that are you?'

'Of course I am. I'm going to have to give them an answer soon and I don't know what to do. If I stay, they'll make my life a misery and watch my every move and if I go, then they've won.'

'I've told you already, I'll sort it out,' she said with a shake of her head. 'Trust me.'

I wanted to believe this, but seriously doubted what a secretary could do. I smiled and said thank you anyway, not wanting to hurt her feelings.

I left Trudy and went downstairs to the lunchtime academic meeting. These were a weekly occurrence for all the doctors in the hospital. The junior doctors took it in turn each week to present interesting cases and then open it up to a discussion. It was intended to be educational, but frequently descended into little more than an opportunity for the consultants to show off to one another and attempt to settle old scores by disagreeing with what another had said. Before this, though, we would have a twenty-minute teaching session on pharmacology. But this wasn't like the sort of lectures I had at medical school. It wasn't education, more indoctrination.

A student's view of life is essentially horizontal, and medical students are no different. I spent every possible moment as a student in bed, and now that I've had a few years exposed to the horrors of the working week, I'm pleased I misused my youth so wisely. I would wait until the last possible moment before dragging myself out of my lovely, cosy bed each morning and into the draughty, dusty lecture hall.

There was one exception to this: when Dr McAllister and Dr Robin were lecturing us. I never minded getting out of bed for them. They were a riotous double-act, the Morecambe and Wise of the clinical pharmacology world, two doctors who single-handedly managed to teach me nearly every bit of pharmacology that I know, and that now I'm a doctor, I use every day. At the time I didn't appreciate quite how important a role they would have in my medical education, or indeed how lucky I was to be training at a hospital with such a strong clinical pharmacology department. I just turned up because they were outrageously funny. In addition to knowledge about drugs, they also imparted a healthy scepticism with regard to any claims made by pharmaceutical companies. They argued that as doctors we had an absolute responsibility to give our patients the best possible treatments informed by the best clinical data and, in addition, we were guardians of the public purse. They instilled in us that it was our responsibility to never squander money on medications that don't work or that don't work as well as cheaper alternatives. This attitude of scepticism, however, is not encouraged in this hospital. In fact, it is actively discouraged.

The reason for this is that drug companies pay for the lunchtime spread of sandwiches and cakes. The pay-off for this apparent act of altruism on their part is that we're obliged to sit for twenty minutes and listen to a lecture from one of the drug reps. Now, in most other jobs where public money is concerned, this sort of thing would be frowned upon. MPs, for example, are supposed to declare any interests that might affect the way they vote and yet doctors never have to provide a list of drug companies they've been schmoozed by when they hand over their prescription to you. Of particular concern, however, is that this lecture is given to us as 'education', when in fact what they provide is marketing material. They are not objective, because they have a drug to sell and therefore shouldn't be involved in informing doctors about therapeutic options, just as we wouldn't have someone from Vauxhall's marketing team presenting *Top Gear*.

But while we're expected to endure the drug company reps' spin, Ruby had decided to make it a one-woman mission to make life for them as difficult as possible. Both Ruby and I refused to eat the sandwiches they bought, but we were still expected to listen to the lecture.

The man stood up and began his presentation. He was only a few years older than us and he stood, waiting a few minutes for people to stop talking. I sat back and started texting people but Ruby sat forward, avidly interested in what he was saying. Occasionally I'd look up and see the PowerPoint slides, all bright colours and pictures of smiling people. It was about some new drug for lowering high blood pressure. It was fifty per cent more effective than the current treatment, he explained. He flashed up some impressive looking graphs.

The problem with this kind of presentation is it doesn't actually present all the statistics, which means no one can really appraise the quality of the research or evaluate the real benefits of the drug being discussed. Everything has to just be accepted. There are a whole host of ways that data from drugs trials can be presented to make them sound more impressive, and multiple ways drug companies can skew the results of research in favour of the new drug they are marketing. Without actually sitting down and reading the paper, there is no real way of knowing for sure if the research supports the company's claims.

Suddenly Ruby piped up. 'Yes, but that's the relative risk reduction. What's the absolute risk reduction?'

Sensing everyone looking towards me, I put my phone away and tried to look engaged.

'Erm, I don't have that data,' said the man and began to continue with the presentation.

Ruby was not deterred. 'Well, if we are to know

exactly how effective this drug is and if it's worth prescribing, the very least we need to know is the absolute risk reduction.'

Several people could be seen shifting uncomfortably in their seats. What she was asking was perfectly reasonable. Statistics has a reputation for being difficult. But actually, most of the concepts are quite straightforward; it's just that complex words are used to describe fairly simple things.

For example, take a hundred people who have high blood pressure and put them on standard medication to lower their blood pressure. One of the consequences of high blood pressure is that it can cause strokes, and this is something that doctors want to avoid for their patients. If two people have a stroke despite being on this medication, but with a new medication only one does, then this new medication can be argued to reduce the risk of stroke by fifty per cent or, alternatively, to be twice as effective as the standard medication. This is the 'relative risk reduction' and sounds really impressive. It's the kind of thing that gets reported in the press and has people knocking on doctors' doors asking for the new, super-duper, all-singing, all-dancing medication. When said in a room full of doctors pacified by a tomato and houmous baguette, it's intended to make us all switch to prescribing the new drug.

However, viewed another way, it has only reduced the risk of a stroke in people with high blood pressure by one per cent. Suddenly, not so super-duper. This is called the absolute risk reduction and is far more useful as it gives more information about the actual figures involved and the real extent of any benefits. But this is precisely the kind of thing that drug reps don't like discussing because it doesn't sound as impressive. This is before we even get into the fact that drug companies can cherry-pick the data they present, manipulate it, exclude inconvenient findings, ignore important side effects and so on.

The drug rep was unable to answer any of Ruby's questions and his presentation began to unravel under the weight of her scrutiny. While several of the other junior doctors were delighted by her direct challenges, a number of the seniors looked at her as though she were accusing Mother Teresa of being the Antichrist.

'This isn't acceptable,' insisted Ruby after the meeting had ended. 'You can't insist that we sit through little more than an advert and tell us that it's educational,' she said to Mr Butterworth, who was standing eating a gratis Kit-Kat courtesy of the drug rep. Mr Butterworth, his head bent down, staring at his shoes as he always did, mumbled a reply.

'I'm going to speak to the Head of Surgery about this,' she said indignantly, unaware that she was already speaking to him. I watched Mr Butterworth, standing awkwardly, as Ruby continued to harangue him about the quality of post-graduate education. I wonder if he's regretting taking that job yet, I thought to myself.

* * *

I was staying late that day, trying to catch up on my outpatient letters and discharge summaries after the academic meeting, when I heard a woman on the ward calling out. I left my office and poked my head into one of the bays. A woman was sitting up in bed.

'Can I have a biscuit please?' asked Mrs McMahon.

This, you would think, was a fairly reasonable request. Not least because Mrs McMahon fell at home and lay there until a neighbour found her, so she hadn't eaten anything for nearly thirty-six hours. If I were her, I'd want more than just a biscuit.

'Or two, if that's possible.'

Ah, a woman after my own heart.

I relayed this request to the nursing staff.

'Don't fancy your chances of that,' replied one of them, sucking in her teeth and frowning. 'We've had some problems with biscuits, you see.'

In my naivety, I thought hospitals had problems with waiting lists or MRSA. Apparently in this particular hospital the problem was biscuits. Or indeed obtaining any foodstuffs past a certain time once the catering staff had gone home.

'A sandwich?' I ventured. The nurse just gave a hollow laugh.

The hospital where I worked had been one of the first large-scale PFI hospitals. I confess that the prospect of working somewhere like this was all rather exciting at first.

'The multi-faith room's got colour coordinated scatter cushions!' visitors would exclaim with glee. It was all bright and shiny and a blessed relief from the dire, grotty Victorian buildings we'd all been used to with their peeling paint and slight whiff of the workhouse.

In my first year of work, though, it soon became apparent that PFI – short for private finance initiative – wasn't quite what it purported to be. In fact, it was rubbish. Under this scheme, building projects and certain services are run by private companies, which the NHS then rents back off them. One such 'service' within this hospital was catering. The private company that was responsible for this, however, insisted on locking the pantries on the ward in an attempt to prevent 'unauthorised consumption'. Even the ward sister didn't have a key. For them, the food in the pantries represented profit margins. For the patients, of course, it just represented food.

Different hospitals have different arrangements and contracts, so perhaps another hospital might have twenty-four-hour access to biscuits, but no after-hours IT support, for example. Having experienced PFI at the sharp end, I have decided that the problem with PFI is that sick people are not very cost effective, and therefore the only way that companies can increase their profit margins is to cut corners and reduce provision of services to a minimum. They get away with this because the contracts that NHS hospitals are tied into can last for up to thirty years.

The nursing staff and I were mortified that we couldn't provide Mrs McMahon with anything to eat.

'I can see the tin just there,' said Mrs McMahon,

getting up out of her bed and pressing her nose against the glass to the pantry, like an orphaned child in a Dickens novel. It was, I decided as I stood, disbelieving that this was happen. A scandal. This was 'biscuit-gate'.

'I'm just so sorry. I know this is ridiculous,' I said to a ravenous Mrs McMahon. A&E had access to 'tuck boxes', which contained a sandwich, but when we telephoned down, they had run out. And anyway, this would come out of their budget and they were therefore disinclined to help, anyway.

Eventually, an enterprising nurse walked to the nearest twenty-four-hour petrol station while on her break and bought Mrs McMahon a packet of Hob-Nobs. Those who work in healthcare have learnt through bitter experiences like 'biscuit-gate' that PFI doesn't work for patients. PFI in the healthcare system has shown itself to be ultimately grossly inefficient, costly, restrictive and detrimental to patient welfare. I left the ward late and tired, but above all, embarrassed and ashamed. It wasn't my fault and it wasn't the nurses' fault that Mrs McMahon had been so spectacularly let down, but it was us who had to stand there next to a locked pantry full of food and explain to a patient that they were going to have to go hungry. This wasn't the NHS that I knew and loved. The final analysis shows that with PFI, all we end up doing is paying inflated prices for sub-standard services in order to provide healthy profit margins for private companies.

That really does take the biscuit.

* * *

I arrived back home and as I did, my phone rang. It was my mum. I put my bag and coat down in the kitchen and answered it.

'It's so cold,' my mum whispered down the telephone, 'I don't feel well.' Her voice faded in and out, barely audible at times.

'Have you been drinking?' I asked.

'Of course I haven't you odious child,' she replied.

Ah, there's my old mum back again.

But then silence.

'Are you still there?' I asked, and was met with violent chattering of teeth. 'Feel your forehead,' I said, still not giving the situation that was unfolding on the other end of the telephone my full attention. It was, after all, Friday night, and Terry, who was sitting in the kitchen, was beckoning me over with a glass of wine.

My mum had been having problems with her teeth for years. She had been nobly battling on with her NHS dentist because where she lives getting a place on the NHS dental register is like winning the lottery. Only not such good odds. But her dentist only worked two days a week and the appointment list was so long it would have been quicker for her to qualify as a dentist herself. Earlier that week my mum had had some work done because of an abscess. She'd been in excruciating pain since, she explained, but the earliest emergency appointment she could get was a week away. As I listened to her on the phone, she told me how she had starting vomiting earlier this evening because of the pain in her teeth and that she was now sweating profusely and yet felt cold. This was the first sign of septicaemia – blood poisoning. I began to get a creeping feeling that things had gone past the stage of tea and sympathy and I started to pay attention. She wasn't going to last the weekend like this.

'Don't worry, leave this with me,' I said, trying to keep her calm. I put the phone down and called my mum's dentist. An answer-phone. It was, after all, 9 pm. The message told me to call another number. I called it. I waited. I kept waiting. I gave up after twenty-five minutes of it just ringing.

Both Ruby and Flora were out, so I couldn't ask their advice. The only medicine Terry knew was from watching *Embarrassing Bodies*, and seeing that the problem was neither halitosis nor a funny-looking vagina, he would surely be no use. I wracked my brains over what I should do. Maybe I should jump on a train and go to see her. But then what would I do once I got there?

'Why not just call her GP?' Terry suggested. 'That's what they always say to do on TV if you're worried.'

Oh, good idea, I thought, and wondered why this hadn't occurred to me. I made a mental note to watch more TV medical programmes. I duly called directory enquiries, got the number for the out-of-hours GP covering my mum's area and left a message with the pager service for them. An hour later they called back. They were actually based twenty miles from where my mum lived and so told me to send her to A&E. This was technically their job, but I was too anxious about my mum to quibble by that stage.

My mum, with my aunt, then spent three hours sitting in A&E until she was told that there wasn't an on-site dental service and the junior doctor who saw her didn't know anything about teeth. He gave her antibiotics and painkillers. By 2 am she was back in her house, unable to sleep with the pain, describing puss flowing down the back of her throat. In desperation and despite usually being critical of private health care and the division and inequality it creates, I called a private dentist.

The phone rang. A dentist answered. A dentist. Not an answer-phone. Not a trained monkey. Not someone who just happened to be passing when the phone was ringing. An actual, qualified, drill-in-hand dentist.

'We'll see her tomorrow at 9 am,' she said. The following day my mum walked out of the dental clinic, pain and puss free, having had a second, expanding abscess drained and the old packing, which had been pressing on an exposed nerve, removed. Of course, it cost an arm and a leg (metaphorically speaking, otherwise sitting here typing this would be very difficult), but I just couldn't see what other option we had. But what if I hadn't had some savings to pay for her, what if my mum had been an old lady living on a pension? What would have happened then?

Since the start of the NHS, dental services have been neglected and resulted in the situation whereby people are faced with the prospect of either the exorbitant cost of private treatment or leaving their teeth to rot in their mouths, Elizabethan-style. Really, in a first-world country, you'd think we could come up with something a bit better. As far as NHS dentistry is concerned, the rot, it would appear, has well and truly set in.

15

Fandango in Paris

It has been said by psychologists that one of the most stressful experiences in life is moving house. I'd also like to add shopping in Ikea to the list. If hell were an object, it would be self-assembly and in unfinished pine. And almost certainly have a vital bolt missing. The stress of moving house isn't helped by estate agents. They know how ignorant you are and that, chances are, you've no idea whether or not 'up and coming area' actually just means the vice squad have raided the crack-house next door. Once they make a sale, they stop returning your calls and appear to vanish off the face of the earth. Lewis was being driven slightly mad while looking for a new flat for him and Dr Palache.

'Mark's away this weekend and I've got four view-ings booked. One of you has to come with me,' he implored us as we sat around the kitchen table.

Everyone suddenly found something incredibly interesting to look at on the floor.

'Max?' he asked, fluttering his eyelashes. 'I just keep on thinking, if only we could afford a few thousand more, we could have the ideal place. I think it would be good to get the advice of someone who's got lower standards than me when it comes to choosing where to live,' he said, looking around the kitchen.

Was there a compliment in there somewhere? No, I didn't think so.

'Oh come on, it will be fun,' he said imploringly.

Knowing how controlling and picky Lewis was, I doubted this and could think of better ways to spend my Saturday morning. Gouging out my own eyes with a spoon, for example.

'OK,' I sighed, and glared at the others.

That weekend, Lewis came round and collected me and we trundled off to view the properties. Lewis had drawn up a chart and handed it to me.

'You keep notes on what we think,' he said to my dismay. I want to be in bed, I wrote in neat handwriting at the top of the first sheet.

We were on the second property and Lewis was off inspecting the kitchen when the estate agent, Paul, turned to me.

'What do you do, then?' he asked after assuring me that I'd get used to the sound of the juggernauts passing directly below the bedroom window.

'Oh, I'm a doctor,' I replied as I ticked the 'damp' and 'noisy' box on the chart and added 'overpriced' and 'smelly' to the bottom. I was rather getting into this.

There was a silence. He sat down on the sofa with his head in his hands.

'You alright?' I asked, guessing that he too had become claustrophobic at the sight of the bathroom.

'I got diagnosed with multiple sclerosis last week,' he said quietly, and then began to cry.

I didn't know what to do and just stood, staring. It's a joke that at parties doctors are always collared for their opinions on some rash or lump, and inevitably the advice is to go to a GP and to pass the canapés. But that wasn't going to wash here. This was serious. I sat down next to him, looking around for some tissues. It felt bizarre to be consoling a man who wasn't my patient, who in fact I'd only met an hour ago and all this going on while sitting on someone else's sofa in someone else's home. Lewis came back in the room.

'Make sure you put down that it's got a granite work top,' he said, but then stopped in his tracks as he saw that Paul was crying. Lewis looked at me wide-eyed and mouthed at me asking what was going on.

'I don't know what to do. I'm not going to be able to keep this job up for much longer, my wife's not well and how are we going to pay the mortgage? What are the kids going to do?' he asked, looking directly at me while tears streamed down his face.

I didn't know what to say.

MS is a horrid disease. It has a variable course, with some people rapidly incapacitated and others remaining symptom-free for years with only the occasional flare-up. But this was of little consolation to him. His walking was becoming increasingly affected, and to make matters worse, he'd watched his sister die of the disease ten years ago. He explained that he didn't want to tell his wife how scared he was; that he didn't want to worry her. He'd make excuses not to go out so that she wouldn't see how bad his walking was. He'd drop and break things and hide the evidence from her.

There was nothing I could do, no wonderful solution I could offer him, but I guessed that he knew that and just wanted to talk to someone. Lewis had sat down on the other side of him. It was awkward but we couldn't just leave him there. Lewis promised to send him some information about the Multiple Sclerosis Society and encouraged him to tell his wife. I nodded in agreement. After half and hour, we left to meet the next estate agent. Lewis didn't buy the flat.

To our shame, it was weeks later before either Lewis or I remembered our promise to Paul. We sent him an email. It was sent back. The next day we called his office. He'd left his job two weeks ago. They couldn't tell us any more. We never found out what happened to him. There are, I reminded Lewis, more stressful things in life than moving house.

'We now consider this matter resolved,' said the email. I sat and reread it, convinced I was missing something. No, that was right, the trust had dropped the disciplinary action against me. So nothing was going down on my record, no official warning and no suggestion that I should resign. What on earth had happened to bring about this volte-face? It must have been Dr Webber. I'd always felt he'd defend me. I rushed over to Trudy to tell her the good news.

'You've heard then,' she said as I burst into her office. 'I bought some Battenberg to celebrate. I know it's your favourite.'

'I can't believe it, just out of the blue like that. It's incredible. Just wait till I see Dr Webber, I can't thank him enough for this.' Trudy stopped rooting through her bag for the cake and looked up.

'And what do you think he's got to do with this?' she asked.

'Well, he must have intervened. He gave me such a nice appraisal, that must have had something to do with it,' I explained. 'After all this agonising wait, why else would they suddenly change their mind?'

'Oh darling,' said Trudy, plonking the cake on her desk and searching in her drawer for a knife, 'you've still got so much to learn, haven't you.' I looked at her, puzzled. 'It's not Dr Webber you have to thank, it's me,' she said and with a flourish, cut the cake.

'You?' I said, puzzled, 'but you're . . .' I stopped myself.

'Just a secretary?' she said laughing. 'Ah, but we're the ones to watch,' she continued, with a wink. 'I've got more power in this hospital than you might think.' She smiled mischievously. 'Everyone has skeletons in their closet, you know. Unless, of course, you're the head of HR who, between you and me, has a wig and pantyhose in his, a little fact I'm sure his wife would be interested in.'

'You mean you threatened to tell his wife unless they dropped the disciplinary action?' I asked, appalled.

'Of course not!' she exclaimed. 'I wouldn't be so vulgar. I just gently reminded him of his past indiscretions and then how much I liked having you around.'

'I don't really know what to say,' I replied, amazed both at her lack of scruples and her willingness to help me.

'Thank you?' she replied.

'Erm, yes, thank you. Of course. Thank you Trudy.'

'And you know the MP has written to the trust asking for a full explanation? Someone has leaked the minutes of their confidential meetings to him so there's no denying what's been going on.' A thought suddenly occurred to me.

'You know, no one ever got to the bottom of who was behind all this. I mean, the trust assumed it was me, but we both know it wasn't. So who was it? Someone contacted the local press, leaked the minutes. It had to be someone with access to that sort of information.' I looked at Trudy intently.

'You don't think it was me?' said Trudy, laughing.

I shrugged.

'You're joking. Look, I don't agree with what they're planning, but it's not for me to stick my nose into that sort of thing. I'm not political like that, it's not my scene. If you bother me or one of my mates, then I'll be after you. But something like that, it's more than my job is worth.'

I wasn't convinced. She was shrewd and knew better

than to confess something so serious. But then, as lovely as she was, Trudy wasn't motivated by ideology, just personal allegiances.

'Anyway, thanks again Trudy, I really owe you one.'

'Oh, I know, don't you worry. When you're a consultant I'll be calling that favour in sometime, I'm sure.'

I laughed. Shrewd as ever, I thought to myself.

'Now, next time, the Battenberg is on you, alright?' and with that, she pushed a slice into her mouth.

Later that week I was on call. It had been particularly uneventful so I settled down in the doctor's mess to watch a late-night horror film. Unlike the main body of the hospital, which had been rebuilt, the doctor's mess was in what was originally the gatehouse and was old and creaky, standing alone on the far side of the hospital grounds. Despite being usually very sensible about this sort of thing, something about the Victorian Gothic architecture and the eerily silent building made the film all the more spine-chilling. At around 2 am I went outside to have a cigarette and found myself peering through the wrought iron fence surrounding the hospital and into the churchyard that was next door. I was looking up at the cloudless sky, listening to the leaves on the trees rustling in the breeze, when I noticed something moving between the gravestones in the far distance. I froze. I told myself that this was my overactive imagination and stood for a moment, marvelling at how suggestible the brain was.

I then told myself to run like hell when I saw, quite

clearly, a figure moving between the graves. I decided that there was a rational explanation for what I was seeing. I just couldn't think what on earth it was. If this was my mind playing tricks on me, then this was one damn impressive trick. I squinted further into the darkness. The figure, too far off to see properly, appeared to have a white face and was wearing a black cape. This is all in my mind, I told myself while trying not to let the sound of my knocking knees draw any unwanted attention. I hesitated for a moment. I prided myself on being a man of science and I didn't believe in ghosts. But I knew that if I went back to the doctor's mess without an explanation, I would forever wonder about what I had seen and question what I knew rationally to be true: there is no such thing as ghosts. There was only one thing to do. So, in the same way that victims in horror films enter the haunted house while the audience scream for them not to, I decided to go into the graveyard.

I went out of the hospital gates, walked down the path and entered the cemetery. I immediately saw something dart behind a headstone. I could feel my heart beating in my chest.

'This is Dr Pemberton. Please step out into the light,' I said with a ridiculous sergeant-major voice into the silence.

Nothing.

Then, slowly, from behind a headstone some way off, a figure rose. My heart beat faster. The figure moved forward. My mouth went dry. It had a white

face with black, sunken eyes and a black cape. I was
rapidly losing faith in rationalism. I was about to flee,
convinced I had seen an apparition, when it said with
a West-Coast American accent:

'Am I in trouble, sir?'

What's an American ghost doing here? I wondered.
And, come to think about it, do ghosts worry about
getting in trouble?

'Sorry, we weren't doing anything wrong,' said
another creature as it emerged from round the corner.
They stood in front of me. They were both in their
twenties, one male and one female. They actually
looked more scared of me than I was of them. It began
to occur to me that they weren't ghosts after all.

'Who are you?' I asked, tentatively.

'We're from St Martins,' the girl said. There was a
brief silence. 'The art college,' she added, helpfully, 'in
London.'

'We're doing an art project on death and the occult,'
explained the boy, showing me his camera. I couldn't
help smiling to myself, not least at my own stupidity
for actually thinking I might have seen a ghost.

Happy in the knowledge that there is indeed a
rational explanation for everything, I returned to my
room. I got into bed and turned off the light. And then
I promptly turned it back on again, and went to sleep.

After my night on call I decided to go into town to do
some shopping. I was sitting in the bus shelter when I
saw another unwanted apparition that struck fear into

me, and this time, there was no chance it was a figment of my imagination. To my horror I looked up and saw the matron who had been sacked from the nursing home standing just a few feet away at the bus stop. I panicked. Had she seen me? What was I going to do? This was the only bus that went into town. Right, think. How can I get away? Too late.

'Oh, hello,' she said coolly, noticing me and taking a few steps towards the bus shelter where I was cowering.

She knows, I thought to myself, she knows it was me that reported the home to social services and got her fired. My blood ran cold. There we were, no longer bound by professional courtesy, away from the hospital.

'How are you?' she asked, her lips thin and tight against her teeth. This could get very awkward, I thought to myself, my former bravado about what I had done quickly evaporating.

'Erm, fine thanks,' I said, still trying to think of what I was going to say when she confronted me. Should I be apologetic? Stand firm? I couldn't walk away now, it was obvious I was waiting for the bus. I hit upon the idea of saying I was waiting for someone so I wouldn't have to get on the bus with her when it arrived.

'I expect you've heard?' she said, looking at me directly.

'Heard what?' I asked, feigning innocence. This was excruciating.

'They fired me,' she said. 'Apparently someone put a complaint in about the nursing home to social services.' I watched her face intently to see if it gave away that she knew it was me.

'Who did that?' I asked, bracing myself.

'I think it was probably that Claire, the domestic. We never got on. She was angry because I wouldn't give her the annual leave she wanted. Vicious thing to do.'

'Hmm, yes,' I said, willing the bus to come and spirit her away. I kept watching her face and she turned away. She actually doesn't think it's me, I realised. Then, to my surprise and horror, I noticed she was crying. This was not what I was expecting.

'Why are you crying?' I asked, not knowing what else to say.

'It's so unfair. I loved that job. I gave everything to that place and look how I'm repaid. I can't be held responsible if sometimes things weren't perfect there. There was never enough staff, I always worked past my shift, came in on the weekends to see how things were going. I never complained. I never kicked up a fuss, I just got on with trying to run that place as best as I could.'

I stood silently listening, a gnawing sense of doubt eating away at me. Had things really been so bad that she deserved to lose her job? Was it all her fault? I began to see a different side to her. Here was someone who cared about her job; about the people she was looking after. My heart hardened, though, when I thought of Mrs Broadhurst. The matron had been in charge and was ultimately responsible for the welfare of those people. Of course all the blame couldn't be attributed to her. But she was complicit in neglect and that was wrong. I looked at her as she got a tissue out of her pocket. Even so, I thought, she was no ogre. I realised that she genuinely didn't think there was anything wrong with the way the home had been operating. That it was OK to sedate old ladies or not feed them enough. To ignore them when they called out and leave them sitting in their own urine until their clothes were sodden through up to their armpits. Perhaps she had become so used to working in an environment where human beings are reduced to a list of jobs and seen more as sources of revenue than people, that she had become immune to what was going on all around her. Was that the answer? The bus arrived and the matron wiped her face.

'I'm waiting for a friend,' I said, although part of me wanted to keep talking to her.

'See you around,' she said, and got on the bus.

As coincidence would have it, the matron wasn't the only person from that nursing home I met that week. A few days later I went on to the ward to find Mrs Lawrence sitting up in one of the beds. I barely recognised her, though, she was so thin.

'Oh hello,' she said as I walked over to her. 'Do you remember me?'

'Of course I do,' I replied, 'I spoke to you a few times when I visited your nursing home.'

'Yes, yes, we had a good chat,' she smiled.

'What's a lady like you doing in a place like this, then?' I joked.

'I'm dying,' she replied. The smile slid from my face. 'Oh, don't worry, I've known it was coming for a long time. Well, I suppose we know it's coming from the moment we're born.' She adjusted the pillows behind her so she could sit up properly.

'Why? What?' I stumbled, taken off guard.

'It's cancer, of my ovaries. It's been in remission for a while but now it's come back. Not much they can do now that it's spread. I was supposed to go up to the oncology ward but they didn't have any beds so they admitted me here. A bit of luck, eh?'

'Luck?' I asked.

'Well yes, that you're here. It's nice to see a familiar face.'

'Well, I won't be working on this ward much longer. I was only here for a year and it will be up soon, then I'll move onto another ward, I'm afraid,' I explained.

'Oh well, that gives me a bit of motivation to get it over and done with then. I'll try to pop my clogs before you leave,' she laughed. 'I'm just teasing with you. If my life were a film though, the ending is a bit boring, I'll tell you.' She leant over to her bedside table where she had a pile of books and patted them. 'Still, I've got these to keep me going.' I looked at the pile and was surprised to see they were mostly philosophy books, rather than the usual hospital literature fodder of *Mills and Boon*.

'I read philosophy at university. So long ago now. It was quite a thing then for a woman to go to university and certainly from my family. My father didn't want me to go, he didn't see the point, but my brother made him let me.'

'How'd he do that?' I asked.

'He was older than me by a few years but he had a bad heart and my father worshipped him. He was also so nervous of making my brother angry or upset in case it affected his heart, he used to let him do whatever he wanted. I'd been pleading with my father to let me go and he point blank refused. Then my brother came down the stairs – I remember it like it was yesterday – and just said, "let the lass go," and that was it, settled. He lived just long enough to see me graduate.' She picked up one of the books and ran her finger down the spine.

'So, what are they going to do for you in here?' I asked as I sat down on the bed.

'Oh, I think they're just going to try some stronger painkillers. They offered more chemotherapy but, at my age, I've had enough of all that.'

'Are you still in the same nursing home?' I asked.

'Yes, they've moved me to another room, it's quite nice. I can watch the squirrels outside playing.'

'Has the food improved?' I asked.

'Oh, I don't have much appetite these days. They bring it in and I try to eat a bit, just to be polite.'

I got up to leave. 'Make sure you have fun, won't you?' she said, looking at me intently.

'What do you mean?' I said, unnerved by her shift in tone.

'Just don't waste your life. Take every opportunity. I was always a worrier and looking back I wish I'd realised that most of the things we worry about don't matter, not really.'

'I try to have fun, don't worry,' I replied with a smile.

'Good' she said. 'I remember my sister was the opposite of me, always lived for the moment, so carefree. There was this time, when I was a girl, not much younger than you, probably, and there was a dance in the village. My sister bought a beautiful dress with canary yellow trim and went. I was always so sensible and saved all my money. I didn't have anything to wear and rather than spend money on a new dress, I didn't go. And looking back, I wish so much I had gone. I know it's silly, it was so long ago, but I remember looking down from my window when she came home. It was late and she got in so much trouble but she looked up at me from the driveway and laughed and giggled and I could see she'd had so much fun. And sitting here now, I wonder whatever happened to that money I saved by not buying a dress. There are times now when I think I'd give any amount of money to laugh and giggle like she did.' She put the book back on the pile and I went to make her a cup of tea.

* * *

One of the worst things a doctor can hear when off duty is the infamous phrase, 'somebody get a doctor'. What is worse than this, as I discovered, is hearing these same words but spoken in another language, when you're in the middle of the English Channel, miles from the nearest hospital and surrounded by German teenagers.

It was meant to be a nice relaxing weekend trip with the flatmates, Supriya and Lewis. But it descended into chaos before it had even begun when I realised the night before that I had forgotten to book the tickets for the Eurostar. A few frantic phone calls later, it was apparent that there were no seats left. So, ferry it was.

'It's an adventure,' I suggested as we made our way to the port in a coach full of people who, it appeared, had yet to discover deodorant. Everyone in my party scowled at me. It was not the moment to start a game of I-spy.

The cohorts of fellow passengers on the ferry fell into three categories: foreign students, drunk people or both. It was about fifteen minutes into the crossing when it happened. Ruby, Lewis, Supriya and Flora had gone up on deck, leaving Terry and I to look around the shop. Before we got there, though, we came across a young man in his late teens lying on the floor. Focused as I was on buying a king-size Toblerone, I assumed he was drunk and was about to step over him when I became aware that there were several people shouting.

'They're saying something about a doctor,' said

Terry, who had done GCSE German. My heart sank. I took a closer look at the boy lying on the floor. His friends were holding his legs up, assuming that he had fainted, not realising that he was actually in a coma.

'Do you speak English?' I shouted slowly, hoping that volume would be enough to penetrate any language barrier.

I was met with blank expressions. Could things get any worse, I wondered? A member of staff arrived and promptly informed me that it would take as long to turn back as it would to continue on to France. Ah, yes, apparently they can. I had to keep him alive for forty minutes.

'Can you ask his friends if he's on any medication?' I said to Terry, as I examined the boy who was totally unresponsive and whose tongue had obstructed his airway.

Terry was silent for a few moments.

'Erm, no,' he said with a frown, 'but I can ask them the way to the nearest tourist information centre,' he added, trying to be helpful.

I closed my eyes, hoping that I when I opened them again all this would be a dream.

I opened them.

The boy was still lying there and I was now surrounded by a group of people all shouting at me in German. You can shout as much as you like, I'm still not going to be able to understand you, I thought to myself. They could speak French but I'd given that up when I was twelve. I did do Latin at school, but unfortunately an emergency translation of Ovid was not really warranted. While Terry tried to find a German translator and tannoy for the others to come and help, I went into doctor-mode.

'You!' I said, pointing to a group of very large men wearing rugby shirts who were standing drinking. 'Come over here.'

They seemed shocked at being addressed in such a forthright manner but did as they were told. A stretcher had arrived at this point and on my count they lifted the boy onto the stretcher and carried him to the medical room below deck.

The term 'medical room' doesn't really do it justice. Cupboard would be more appropriate. It was so small, in fact, that we couldn't all fit in. The stretcher had to be pushed into the room from the door, with Terry guiding it from inside. The boy's legs had to dangle off the end of the bed and through the doorway, so Terry was obliged to stand, propping the heavy door open, so that it didn't swing shut onto the boy's ankles.

Just then, the boy started having a seizure. Until this point I had felt relatively confident. Suddenly, though, I was aware of how much I had come to rely on the comfort of a hospital setting. I frantically rummaged through the cupboards and eventually found some medication to terminate the seizure.

'I'll get a glass of water,' said Terry from the doorway.

'Erm, he's in a coma and having a seizure,' I said, 'it's not going in that end.' It suddenly dawned on

Terry what I was about to do and he let out a horrified gasp and averted his gaze. I gave the medication and the seizure stopped. I breathed a sigh of relief.

'OK, I think he's stable now,' I said. In the medical cupboard above the bed I'd found a plastic tube designed to keep his airway open and he was breathing unaided freely now.

'Can I ask you something?' said Terry. 'Does Flora ever talk about me?'

'What?' I asked distractedly.

'You know, talk about me. Like, do you think she's interested in me?'

'Terry, we have a comatose teenager afloat in the middle of the sea, who I've just had to give a suppository to without the luxury of gloves. This really is not the time or the place for me to be playing cupid.'

'Just wondered,' he said, undeterred, 'I really like her. Do you think she might go out with me?'

I was contemplating making Terry join the boy in a coma when I heard a strange noise. I looked at the boy and to my dismay he was having another seizure. It was at about this time I began wishing I'd become an accountant. I was sweating profusely as I tried to stabilise him once more while outside I could hear people talking in foreign languages.

Flora arrived, open-mouthed.

'Here you are. We've been looking everywhere for you.' She caught sight of the boy lying prostrate on the table. 'Oh God, so typical. Work follows us everywhere.'

'You've got to help. Get the others. I think he must have taken something but I don't know what,' I said in a fluster.

'This is all your fault,' she said, trying to negotiate her large pregnant stomach past Terry and into the tiny gangway between the bed and the wall. 'Stuff like this doesn't happen on the Eurostar, you know.'

The others had arrived and were all trying to peer into the room to see what was happening.

'I wonder where he got his trainers from,' said Lewis, as this was all he could really see of the action.

'Not helping!' I shouted back.

Finally, a member of staff came to say that we had docked and an ambulance crew were now boarding.

He hadn't died! I'd saved him! I emerged from the room expecting to be greeted with cheers and a slap on the back, but instead, a group of stony-faced French medics pushed passed me. I stopped the last one and explained who I was, the history and the medication I had given him. The doctor looked at me with a mixture of disgust and disinterest.

'You are in France now,' he said, in perfect English, 'you must speak French.'

I stood there blinking. Is this really the appropriate moment to be bringing up national animosities? The ambulance crew carried the boy past, totally ignoring me.

'But I can't . . .' I began.

The French doctor turned away.

I took a deep breath.

'Bonjour. Je m'appelle Max. J'ai douze ans,' I said with a shrug.

The French doctor shook his head and followed the stretcher into the ambulance.

Needless to say, we got the Eurostar home.

16

The Good, the Bad and the Pregnant

Two things happened that weekend while we were in Paris. The first was a cause for celebration, while the second made us all sad. Spurred on by the romantic ambience of the city – and several glasses of wine – Terry did declare his feelings for Flora. At first she didn't say anything but just laughed. On the Sunday, however, Lewis knocked on Flora's bedroom but there was no answer, and a little later, they both appeared at breakfast together, looking sheepish.

'Don't you mind that she's about to have a baby?' asked Lewis on the train home while Flora was in the toilet.

Ruby glared at him as though he might have given away a secret, although in reality it was impossible not to notice that she was pregnant and it seemed a reasonable question.

'Nah, not at all,' said Terry. 'Why would it? I think it's exciting. I'm from a big family – there're eight of us and I'm the eldest – so I'm used to babies.'

'Yes, but it's different if it isn't your own, though, isn't it?' said Lewis.

'Not really,' replied Terry breezily.

Supriya was reading but she looked up.

'Oh, leave him alone,' Supriya said to Lewis. 'Let them just enjoy themselves.'

'Well I think it's quite nice,' said Ruby, and I looked at her, surprised she had put aside her usual animosity towards Terry. 'This means I might not have to be her bloody birthing partner, thank God,' she whispered to me with a grin.

When we got home though, we discovered something else had happened while we'd been away. We piled out of the taxi and Ruby opened the front door. She picked up the mail and put it on the kitchen table and it wasn't until much later that, sitting, tired and contemplating bed, Flora absentmindedly picked up the mail and started sifting through it.

'There's a note here,' she said, brandishing a piece of paper. 'Someone must have pushed it through the door.' She opened it and her face fell. 'Oh. Oh no,' she said, bringing her hand to her mouth. 'He's died.'

'Who?' asked Ruby, moving forward.

'Geoff,' said Flora.

'No,' said Ruby, 'that can't be right. You must mean Anthony. It's Anthony who's got cancer, not Geoff.' Flora shook her head and handed the note to Ruby.

I got up and peered over her shoulder and sure enough, it was a note from Anthony, himself, apologising for letting us know in this way but he'd tried calling Flora's mobile and it had been off.

'I should have brought my phone with me to Paris,' she said, with her hand still over her mouth, 'I just didn't think I'd need it and didn't want the extra cost of making calls while abroad. Oh God, he's been all alone today, we should go and visit him.'

'It's past 11 o'clock,' I said, looking at the kitchen clock. We agreed we should go round and see if there was a light on, which there was. Flora knocked tentatively on the front door and we could hear shuffling and eventually, Anthony opened the door.

'We just heard. We've been away,' said Flora, hugging him.

We came in and sat down around him as he slowly eased himself back into his chair. Geoff, he explained, had died in his sleep sometime during Friday night. When Anthony had woken up on the Saturday, he'd found him lying dead in the bed next to him.

'Probably a heart attack,' he said quietly. 'It should have been me that went first. It sounds selfish but I wish it had been.'

We were all used to dealing with bereaved people but this was so utterly different. In hospitals we were safely cocooned from the raw grieving of relatives by the practicalities of death; the offering of tea, the small, bureaucratic necessities that crowded in and distracted everyone. Relatives were swept along, trying not to break down, stoically smiling and nodding at everything that was said. In this environment of clinical detachment, death and grieving was easy to deal with. But, with Anthony, there was none of this. It was the first time any of us had been faced with proper, untempered grief.

We stayed with him for an hour but we all had work the next day, so had to leave him.

'Shall we help you into bed?' said Flora as we stood up to leave.

'No, it's OK,' replied Anthony, 'I don't think I'll sleep much tonight. I'll just doze here in the chair.' He felt behind him and took a cardigan off the back of his chair and put it on his lap. 'I'll be alright,' he said, pulling the cardigan around him. 'This was Geoff's.'

We gently closed the door behind us and walked out into the darkness of the night.

'I'm sure he's not very well. He's often like this when he is developing a urinary tract infection,' said Mark as he showed me through to the lounge.

He knelt down by Mr Kelly and took his hand from his lap and held it gently.

'You can tell from his face,' said Mark. I looked at Mr Kelly and Mark watched me intently. 'See?' he said expectantly.

I wasn't sure I did. All I saw was an elderly man with his mouth wide open and dead, expressionless eyes.

'The doctor's come to see you,' said Mark.

Nothing.

I looked through Mr Kelly's notes while Mark sat him up so I could examine him. Mr Kelly had dementia. Specifically, he had both Alzheimer's disease and vascular dementia. I'd been asked to review him at one of the nursing homes the hospital covered after the nursing staff had become concerned.

'There!' said Mark triumphantly. 'Did you see that?'

I looked at Mr Kelly. Still nothing.

'He curled his lip slightly. He always does that when there's something the matter. Usually it's because he's hungry or thirsty, but he's been doing it for a few days now.'

I stared at Mr Kelly. In all honesty, I could barely see any change in him and it seemed incredible that someone who was totally shut off from the world, utterly incapable of any form of communication, could still interact with people. But what was most striking was that Mark knew his patient so well he could detect these minute, idiosyncratic changes in facial expression and deduce from them what was wrong. Even after examining Mr Kelly I could find nothing wrong. But Mark was so insistent that something was the matter, I arranged for Mr Kelly to be transferred to hospital for a full investigation, just to appease him. Dr Webber is going to kill me for admitting him when there's nothing wrong, I thought to myself.

However, on the ward it was discovered that not only did he have a urinary tract infection but that it had spread to his kidneys. It was sobering to think that this must have been acutely uncomfortable for Mr Kelly, but thanks to the relationship that Mark had with him, he did not have to sit there and suffer.

Mr Kelly lived in a specialist dementia care home and its residents ranged from those severely disabled by the condition to those who were mildly confused. It was clear the minute you walked through the doors that the patients were treated with dignity and respect and their welfare was paramount. Unfortunately, as I had learnt while working in this job, the standard of care that people with dementia experience varies widely. Why was the level of skill in caring for such a vulnerable group of individuals allowed to vary so much? Listening to Mark talking about Mr Kelly it was obvious that providing excellent care for those with dementia was about more than just sending staff on a course. A degree of compassion and respect, combined with empathy and reflexivity was also needed and it was this, it seemed, that eluded so many care staff and was a difficult thing to teach.

I was more grateful to Mark than he could possibly know. Not just for his insight into Mr Kelly's infection, but also for showing me how things can be, when the people caring for those with dementia actually care.

Tony was vomiting. From behind the curtains I could hear a nurse comforting him and the sound of him being sick made me wretch as I tried to write up my notes.

At the reception in A&E I could hear a woman crying before being escorted by a nurse to the cubicle. She rushed forward, flung back the curtain and embraced Tony as she sobbed. He started crying as well.

The nurse looked at me and mouthed the word 'mum' to me by way of explanation.

'Why?' his mum said again and again as she cradled him.

I looked away. Tony was fourteen and had taken sixty paracetamol. Suicide attempts are a common presentation in A&E departments. There remains, however, something about children who have tried to kill themselves that is particularly chilling. What could provoke a child into doing something so extreme and destructive, and incomprehensible to most people? Yet it happens. Children kill themselves.

Tony took an overdose because he was being bullied at school after he told a friend he thought he might be gay. This friend told another friend and before long the whole school knew. People began sending him text messages calling him names and gradually it escalated. For the past three months he had experienced a catalogue of horrendous physical and verbal abuse from other pupils. He told a teacher but they did nothing to stop it.

That afternoon, after being set upon by a group after school, he decided life wasn't worth living. He stopped off at several shops on the way home from school to buy the paracetamol and, after writing a note to his mum, sat in his bedroom and swallowed the tablets with orange juice. His sister found him lying on his bed crying and called an ambulance.

I'd like to think this was an isolated incident, but in fact it was the second case of a young person trying to kill themselves as a result of homophobic bullying we'd seen in A&E in just two weeks. I thought back to the time I'd visited Geoff and Anthony and they'd been so scared about how people would react to their civil partnership. I'd stood there, reassuring them that times had changed and blithely saying how no one cared any more. This, I thought as I listened to Tony's mother sobbing while the paediatricians tried to explain that he would have to be admitted to assess the damage he had done to his liver, had not been entirely true. While things have certainly changed for the better, they are far from perfect. One of the frustrations of being a doctor is that we are confronted with the fall-out of social problems we are powerless to do anything about. From the young girl living on the streets who's been beaten up by her pimp to the lonely pensioner who's fallen over and broken her hip, all we can do is patch people up and send them back out.

Similarly, no tablet or drip that a doctor could prescribe would take away the bullying that Tony experienced. That was beyond our capabilities.

Earlier I had sat in the cubicle with Tony as I'd assessed him. He looked at me with desperate, lost eyes. He couldn't cope with the torment he experienced each day, not just from the bullies but from the overwhelming sense that he would never be accepted. Tears streamed down his face and I opened my mouth slightly to tell him that things would be OK. I wanted to tell him that I was gay and I remembered being his age. I remembered coming home each day after school and going into the bathroom and locking the door and crying quietly to myself because I couldn't bear the feelings I was having or the idea of being different. I'd allow myself to cry for half an hour and then I'd dry my eyes and wash my face and go downstairs as though nothing was wrong. I did that every day for over a year. And then one day I stopped. I remember thinking that crying hadn't solved the problem and that it clearly wasn't going away, so I should focus on my studies and try and make something of my life. So in part, being gay made me a doctor.

But now all that is a distant memory. Of course, things haven't always been easy. But I look at my life and it's fantastic and I wouldn't change a thing about it, including my sexuality. For my family and friends and colleagues, it's just not something that's an issue. I wanted Tony to know that this was how it could be. I checked myself. It would be unprofessional to say that to him; to disclose so much about myself, particularly something so intimate and personal. I hesitated and the moment passed. Tony asked for some water. I got up and left him.

While 'gay' remained an acceptable playground slur and teachers shied away from talking about sexuality openly in the classroom, all we could do was treat the medical problem and hope that things changed. The time to tackle homophobic bullying was in the class-room, not when the child was sitting in A&E.

Lewis had also been on the receiving end of homo-phobia, although he never discussed it with us directly. Ruby and I had been out for a cigarette at our usual spot by the bins at the back of A&E, when Dr Palache joined us. This was great news, as both Ruby and I had some urgent scans we wanted to book and this saved a trip to see the radiology secretaries and having to bribe them with Quality Street.

'Do you mind just squeezing in my patient this afternoon?' pleaded Ruby. This was a game we often played with Dr Palache and was made all the more fun by his initial resistance, which was worn down by our persistence during the course of one cigarette. While he pretended to be irritated by it, I was sure that deep down, he enjoyed it. Probably. But this time, he wasn't playing.

'Sure, whatever,' he said in a distracted tone.

'Oh, that was too easy. You're no fun today,' said Ruby, handing him the ultrasound request and rolling her eyes at me.

'I've just got some stuff on my mind,' said Dr Palache, taking a drag on his cigarette. 'I'm quite worried about Lewis.'

'Why?' asked Ruby.

'Well, he got it into his head that he should tell his parents about us. I told him not to, just to let it lie, but he wouldn't.'

'Oh yeah, he said he was going to tell them. Why's that a bad thing? I think he just wanted to be honest with them. Stop living two lives, you know?'

Dr Palache looked at us both. 'You've got to promise not to tell him I've told you. He doesn't want to talk about it, not even to me. But I think you should know, so you can keep an eye on him.'

'Didn't his parents take it well?' asked Ruby.

'You could say that. They've sent him a letter, saying that as far as they are concerned he's no longer their son. The whole family have cut him out. Apparently his Gran in Ghana has photographs of all her grandchildren lining her hallway and when she found out, she took his picture off the wall and went into the garden and burnt it. His parents hang up every time he tries to call. I've told him to stop torturing himself about it, but it must be so difficult, he totally idolises them both.'

'When did all this happen?' I asked.

'Oh, a few months ago. He's just had to accept that he might never see them again.'

I thought back to all the times we'd seen Lewis and he'd never said anything to us. It was all too dreadful.

'I found him looking at a photo album the other day and crying. I just think you should know, as his friends.' We nodded and finished our cigarettes in silence.

Later that day I saw Lewis in the canteen and went up to him. 'You OK?' I asked.

'Yeah, fine thanks. Absolutely run off my feet today with work though.'

'You sure you're OK? Everything alright?' I said, watching him closely.

'Yes,' he said, looking at me and smiling quizzically. 'Why shouldn't I be?' and he turned and walked off towards the wards. In fact, Lewis never told us about his parents and never mentioned them again except once, when his father died a year or so later. He mentioned it in passing, then checked himself and looked at us.

'I didn't go to the funeral,' he said, quickly but slightly faltering, 'I was on call and couldn't get out of it. We weren't close.'

We all knew this was a lie, but none of us said anything.

The birth of a baby is a miracle.

Not so much that life has been created, but rather that something so big has come out of somewhere so small. My spatial awareness is not great at the best of times, but I clearly remember studying obstetrics and gynaecology at medical school and being convinced that there had been a serious design error somewhere along the way.

'Surely,' I said to my professor, 'that' – pointing at the plastic baby lying in front of me – 'isn't supposed to fit through that' – pointing at the plastic vagina peering up at me from the table. Sure enough, with a bit of pushing and pulling and the occasional whack on the edge of the table, I demonstrated that the baby did indeed fit through. Hooray, I've just delivered a cabbage patch doll, I thought, getting all emotional.

The birth of Flora's baby was a miracle for another reason as well: that it happened in hospital and not in the back of a cab.

Looking back on Flora's pregnancy, it was obvious to even the casual observer that she had not given it the thought and attention that most women do. Some might have considered this was because, being a doctor and having worked in obstetrics in the past, she already knew what to do and what to expect.

Ruby and I, however, were of the opinion that her apparent relaxed attitude to the ever-growing protrusion of her abdomen was because she was actually in denial. She had claimed to be too busy to go to antenatal classes and although she'd attended a few outpatient appointments in the hospital, it was only because the midwives had collared her in the canteen and made her attend. She was also expecting to work right up until the due date, just a week before we finished our jobs. This turned out to be wishful thinking.

Flora loved her bed and in many ways, having her water break during the middle of the night while in it, was appropriate. She woke up, realised what was happening but then figured she wasn't going to let a little thing like labour interrupt her sleep. So, she woke up Terry, told him the bed was wet and assured him the baby was a long way off coming and they decamped from her bed to his, where she stayed until the morning. By then, the pain was quite bad.

Ruby and I left for work, totally unaware of what was going on. Flora phoned the hospital and they insisted she come in, despite her protestations that she wasn't dilated enough.

Her and Terry trundled into the hospital where a midwife examined her and, to Flora's great annoyance, told her what she'd been saying all along: she wasn't dilated enough and to come back later. Flora, for reasons that eluded both Ruby and I when she told us all this later, decided she would go for a pizza.

'The waitress did look at me strangely when a contraction came as I was ordering and I just had to sit there, gripping on to the table until it passed.' After that, she and Terry decided to go back to the flat, where she stayed, listening to a programme on Radio 4 about otters. As you do. Poor Terry just assumed this chaotic approach to childbirth was normal procedure. The contractions were getting closer and closer together until, suddenly, Flora felt something between her legs.

'It's coming!' she screamed while Terry ran around, flapping. She stood up, but could feel the baby's head coming out. 'Quick, open the door for me,' she shouted at Terry while she used both hands to keep the baby in.

'I thought the idea was that the baby came out?' asked Terry in a panic.

'Yes, but not on the pavement,' said Flora through clenched teeth.

In the cab, Flora had to sit leaning back, with her legs up against the partition. Thankfully the taxi driver didn't turn round to look what was happening. She raced up to the maternity ward and called out for someone to help just as a final wave of contraction came and the baby shot out. A midwife, who had not even had time to change into scrubs, caught the baby while Flora crouched in the corridor.

'Sorry about the mess,' said Flora as she was ushered into a side room.

Ruby and I were both finishing work when we got a text message from her. 'It's out! A girl. In the maternity ward. Come and visit.'

Ruby and I rushed to the maternity ward and went into the side room. There was a curtain immediately inside the room and as we pulled it back, Flora was sitting on a chair and looked up furtively, quickly moving something out of view. 'Oh, it's you two,' she said, bringing out a bottle of beer from by her side.

'Are you supposed to be drinking?' I asked, hastily pulling the curtain behind us.

'Oh, it's only one and it's been nine months, give me a break.' Terry had also bought pizza, which was lying in a box on the bed. And there, in the corner of the room, was a cot.

'Meet Rose,' said Flora, standing up and walking over to the cot. She scooped the baby up in her arms. 'Look,' she said to Rose, whose eyes were clamped shut, 'meet your new flatmates.'

17
Doctor to Be

Flora had been keen to leave the hospital with us that evening, but the midwives tried to persuade her to wait until the morning.

It was Ruby who pointed out to Flora that she was so wonderfully underprepared she hadn't even bought any baby clothes or a cot, so what was she going to dress Rose in and where was she going to sleep? Faced with practical issues like this, Flora caved in and agreed to stay until the morning when she and Terry could pay a long overdue trip to John Lewis.

Flora's attitude towards motherhood turned out, thankfully, to be very different from her attitude towards pregnancy. She embraced it and, to our relief, seemed a natural. She still had no clear plan about what she was going to do with regard to her career, but at the moment, she was trying not to dwell on that too much. She was still keen to pursue a career in surgery and there was the possibility, in theory at least, of flexible training, although the issue around the long, unsociable hours, the weeks on call and the prospect of many more years in training on a junior doctor's salary, meant it would not be easy. There was the option of training to be a GP, which would be easier for her to juggle with the demands of a baby. Thankfully, Housewives' Favourite had promised that, should she decide to come back to surgery, he would keep a job open for her. All she had to do was let him know. She would have to decide, but for the time being, she was just enjoying being a mother. It was clear that while Abdul wanted little to do with the baby, Terry was very willing to get involved. In fact, we all chipped in, even Ruby who, to our collective amazement, was seen changing a nappy.

Only once, mind you.

My job was now coming to an end. Things ticked along on the ward. In A&E, the pressure continued to mount on management to reverse the decision to close the department and now that the local MP was involved, it looked likely that it would remain open. For the time being, at least.

On the morning of my last day, I dropped in my last outpatient dictation tape to Craig.

'I'll be on the same email address, so you can just send them over for checking, there's no rush to get them done before I change jobs,' I said, knowing that he'd have them done by that afternoon regardless. He nodded and continued with his typing.

'Oh,' he called out as I was walking out of the door, 'nearly forgot to tell you. I got in to medical school, so I'll be leaving, myself, in a few weeks. Gonna have a bit of a break before I start.'

'What? Why didn't you tell us earlier? That's amazing news,' I said. I'd completely forgotten about his interview and part of me was hurt that he hadn't taken me up on my offer of help and the other part, immensely proud of him that he hadn't needed it. Mary 1 looked up from painting her nails.

'What did you say you little tyke? Oh my God, why didn't you tell us?'

'He's going to be a doctor,' said Mary 2, as though she were a proud mother. 'The boy's going to be a doctor.'

'I told you I should have asked him out on a date,' Mary 3 said under her breath to Mary 2.

'Yeah yeah, it's no big deal,' said Craig, trying to play it cool, but I could tell he was pleased to have all this attention and deep down, he knew that it was an achievement he should be proud of.

'What did your parents say?' I asked.

'Oh, they were alright about it in the end. I've saved up some money and I've said I'll get a part time job while I study, so it's not like it's gonna cost 'em anything,' he said with a shrug.

Between them, the three Marys decided that they should have a celebratory lunch for Craig, and they scurried off to get supplies. Sure enough, a few hours later I was back in their office sitting on one of the Marys' desks while they fussed over Craig and plied him with sandwiches. I brought Ruby with me and Trudy popped in too. She brought some cake, naturally.

'You've got to become a plastic surgeon,' said Mary 1 to Craig.

'Yeah, she's gonna be your first patient,' said Mary 2.

'Oi, that was my punch line,' retorted Mary 1, sulkily.

I looked at Craig and wondered how he'd put up with this for a whole year without resorting to medication or homicide. Housewives' Favourite poked his head round the door and, seeing Ruby, made a beeline for her while I talked to Craig.

'You enjoyed working 'ere, then?' asked Craig.

'Yes, it's been a good job, although I could have done without that whole business with the managers trying to sack me.'

Craig looked at me slyly.

'They never worked out who'd leaked that stuff to the press, did they?' he said quietly and smirked knowingly.

Suddenly it dawned on me. Of course.

'You?' I whispered. Craig shrugged but his smile gave it away.

'It weren't right what they were doing though, was it?' he said.

I thought back to when I had first met Craig and how I'd woefully underestimated him.

Back on the ward I said goodbye to Marsha. I also went to see Mrs Lawrence. Although she had gotten progressively frailer, she was still very much alive. At least I thought she was. As I approached her bed, I noticed she was slumped to her side, her hand hanging lifelessly over the side. I started and moved closer.

'Bye then!' she said, springing into life and laughing. 'Sorry, I couldn't help myself. Not dead yet. That means I'm going to have to go through all the hassle of making friends with the next doctor.'

I said goodbye.

'Don't forget to have fun,' she said, calling after me.

I collected my things from the office and walked out into the corridor.

'Where's my money?' asked Mr Berridge, wandering out of the television room and making his way up to me.

'Ask Marsha,' I said, as she was trying to usher him back to his bed, and blew her a kiss.

Ruby was finishing up and then met me at the back of A&E and we walked to the bus stop together.

'You know, Housewives' Favourite isn't actually that bad,' she said wistfully.

'Yeah, I saw you talking to him at lunch, you seemed to be getting on pretty well.'

'I know. He's redeemed himself a little by the way he's been towards Flora. I've been quite surprised. He was assuring me he's a changed man and, do you know, there was actually a moment when I found myself seriously wondering if we could rekindle our relationship.'

'Ruby,' I exclaimed 'are you mad?'

'Oh, don't worry, I saw him eyeing up Mary 3 and I came to my senses.'

We arrived home and Ruby and I plonked ourselves down at the kitchen table. Flora came in.

'Right, I'm off. I'm meeting Terry down at the pub. I'll only be an hour or so,' she said, putting her coat on.

'What about the baby?' asked Ruby with horror.

'Oh, Terry's done a babysitting rota. It's on the fridge. It's you and Max tonight. Hope you don't mind. I'll be back in time for the next feed,' and before we could protest, she was out of the door.

Ruby and I looked at each other for a few moments. Then the baby started screaming. And screaming.

'I never thought I'd say this,' said Ruby covering her ears, 'but I think I actually prefer the sound of my pager.'

I was inclined to agree.

Acknowledgements

I am very grateful to a number of people who helped and supported me while I wrote this book:

The staff at the *Daily Telegraph*, both past and present: Liz Hunt, Maureen O'Donnell, Richard Preston, Maria Trkulja, Damian Thompson, Genevieve Fox, Paul Clements, Joyce Smith, Robert Colvile, Sarah Oliver, Fiona Hardcastle and Tony Gallagher. Barney Calman and Sarah Hartley at the *Mail on Sunday* and Sarah Sands at *Evening Standard*. All the staff at *Reader's Digest*, in particular Gill Hudson, Catherine Haughney and Bobbie Mitchell. Sincere thanks to those at Hodder for their ongoing support and encouragement: Lisa Highton, Valerie Appleby, Jaime Frost and Jo Cantello. Special thanks must go to Heather Rainbow, whose commitment to this book was so strong even relocating to another continent didn't put her off. And warm thanks to Heather Holden-Brown and Elly James, without whom I don't know what I'd do.

Special thanks also to friends and colleagues: Tasha Coccia, Rhiannon Doyle, Sarah McMahon, Anna

Berridge, Nick Deakin, Ben, Becky and Harry Fisher, Ruth-Ellen Davies, Toby Commerford, Andrew Solomon and John Habich-Solomon, Sue McCartney-Snape, Marios Pierides, Dr Katz, Dr Ellis, Dr Hassiotis, Dr Rands, Dr Farnham, Dr James, Professor Bhugra, Jacob Freeman, Fernando Alves, Jill Leslie, Nadine Banna, the Gardiners, Katharine Lynch, Neil Kirsch, Dean Thorpe, Christine Webber and David Delvin. Andrew Almond-Smith, Ben Beska, Scott McKenzie, Jeni Barnett, Sue Gibbs, Anne Hughes, Gill Hughes, Jeannie and Tod Jones, Joanna Maggs, Sister Mary Stephen, Katharine Patrick, Rob Dinsdale. Thanks also to Sue and Andrew from Simply Books in Bramhall and all the other independent bookshops that have supported my books. And of course, not forgetting, Professor Mary Robertson.

I remain indebted to Jan Moir for all her advice and kindness and a great big rainbow-flag-waving thank you to Simon Millward for painstakingly reading through the drafts and making suggestions, as well as being a great friend.

And then there is, of course, my sister Ellie and my mum, who have both been wonderful and who I'm very lucky to have (and they never let me forget it).

Author's Note

While everything that happens in this book is based on real events, key details have been changed and the characters are composite characters and should be considered the inventions of the author.

About the Author

Max Pemberton is a practising doctor, working full time in the NHS. He is also a columnist for the *Daily Telegraph* and *Reader's Digest*. He has won several awards for his writing, including the Mind Journalist of the Year award and the Royal College of Psychiatrists' 2010 award for Public Educator of the Year.

We hope you enjoyed *The Doctor Will See You Now*. If you weren't already aware, Max has written two other books:

TRUST ME, I'M A
JUNIOR DOCTOR

WHERE DOES
IT HURT?

If you'd like to find out more about these books or other Max-related news and events, visit his website, www.maxpemberton.com, or follow him on twitter, @maxpemberton.

We'd also recommend a visit to Hodder's website, www.hodder.co.uk, or twitter feed, @hodderbooks, to find out what else is happening in our world of books. We have a huge community of readers you may well like to be part of.

We'd love to hear from you, and welcome you to sign up for our newsletter or just drop by and let us know what you think.